family
handyman
WHOLE HOUSE
PRO TIPS

A NOTE TO OUR READERS: All do-it-yourself activities involve a degree of risk. Skills, materials, tools and site conditions vary widely. Although the editors have made every effort to ensure accuracy, the reader remains responsible for the selection and use of tools, materials and methods. Always obey local codes and laws, follow manufacturer's operating instructions, and observe safety precautions.

Image Credits

14, 43, 76, 200, 224-227, 243-245 (tech art) Frank Rohrbach III; **14** (blue sky) Pakhnyushchy/Shutterstock; **14** (stormy sky) STILLFX/Shutterstock; **40-41, 42** Courtesy of CLOSETMAID; **44** izzet ugutmen/Shutterstock; **45** PeopleImages.com - Yuri A/Shutterstock; **46** Ladanifer/Shutterstock; **47** Shyntartanya/Shutterstock; **51-52** (tech art) Mario Ferro; **55** Lars Hallstrom/Shutterstock; **56** arosoft/Shutterstock; **57** (t) Andrey_Popov/Shutterstock; **57** (b) Sergiy Kuzmin/Shutterstock; **58** New Africa/Shutterstock; **59** Kwangmoozaa/Shutterstock; **60** Pixel-Shot/Shutterstock; **61** Filmbildfabrik/Shutterstock; **62** Fecundap stock/Shutterstock; **63** Wiiin/Shutterstock; **66-67** Strejman/Shutterstock; **109** (m) Ellen Thomson; **110** (b) Mike Haberman; **111** (m) Jeff Gillman; **114** Energyscapes; **115** (dirt x 2) Sue Blackburn; **115** (tr) Bob Rogers; **116** (tl) Eric Lucas; **116** (br) Nora Spencer; **117** Carolyn Rogers; **123** traveler1116/Getty Images; **135** (br) Thompson; **137, 138** (bl inset), **139** (6, 7) Larry Roepke; **174-177** (tech art) Nat Harris; **201** (bl) irina88w/Getty Images; **205-206** (illos) Steve Bjorkman; **212** (br) Whirlpool brand; **220** (moving straps) Pixel-Shot/Shutterstock

All other photographs by Tom Fenenga, Mike Krivit, Paul Nelson and Bill Zuehlke.

Electrical consultant: John Williamson
Plumbing consultant: Bret Hepola, All City Plumbing, Minnetrista, Minnesota

SAFETY FIRST–ALWAYS!

Tackling home improvement projects and repairs can be endlessly rewarding. But as most of us know, with the rewards come risks. DIYers use chain saws, climb ladders and tear into walls that can contain big, hazardous surprises.

The good news is that armed with the right knowledge, tools and procedures, homeowners can minimize risk. As you go about your projects and repairs, stay alert for these hazards:

Aluminum wiring

Aluminum wiring, installed in millions of homes between 1965 and 1973, requires special techniques and materials to make safe connections. This wiring is dull gray, not the dull orange characteristic of copper. Hire a licensed electrician certified to work with it. For more information, go to *cpsc.gov* and search for "aluminum wiring."

Spontaneous combustion

Rags saturated with oil finishes, such as Danish oil and linseed oil, as well as oil-based paints and stains, can spontaneously combust if left bunched up. Always dry them outdoors, spread out loosely. When the oil has thoroughly dried, you can safely throw the rags in the trash.

Vision and hearing protection

Safety glasses or goggles should be worn whenever you're working on DIY projects that involve chemicals, dust or anything that could shatter or chip off and hit your eye. Also, sounds louder than 80 decibels (dB) are considered potentially dangerous. For instance, sound levels from a lawn mower can be 90 dB and from shop tools and chain saws can be 90 to 100 dB.

Lead paint

If your home was built before 1979, it may contain lead paint, which is a serious health hazard, especially for children 6 years old or under. Take precautions when you scrape or remove it. Contact your public health department for detailed safety information or call (800) 424-LEAD (5323) to receive an information pamphlet. Or visit *epa.gov/lead*.

Buried utilities

A few days before you dig in your yard, have your underground water, gas and electrical lines marked. Just call 811 or go to *call811.com*.

Smoke and carbon monoxide (CO) alarms

The risk of dying in a reported home-structure fire is cut in half in homes with working smoke alarms. Test your smoke alarms every month, replace batteries as necessary and replace units that are more than 10 years old. As you make your home more energy efficient and airtight, existing ducts and chimneys can't always successfully vent combustion gases, including potentially deadly carbon monoxide (CO). Install a UL-listed CO detector, and test your CO and smoke alarms at the same time.

Five-gallon buckets and window-covering cords

Anywhere from 10 to 40 children a year drown in 5-gallon buckets, according to the U.S. Consumer Products Safety Commission. Always store empty buckets upside down and ones containing liquid with the covers securely snapped.

According to Parents for Window Blind Safety, hundreds of children in the United States are injured every year after becoming entangled in looped window-treatment cords. Visit *pfwbs.org* for more information.

Working up high

If you have to get up on your roof to do a repair or installation, always install roof brackets and wear a roof harness.

Asbestos

Texture sprayed on ceilings before 1978, adhesives and tiles for vinyl and asphalt floors before 1980, and vermiculite insulation (with gray granules) all may contain asbestos. Other building materials made between 1940 and 1980 could also contain asbestos. If you suspect that materials you're removing or working around contain asbestos, contact your health department or visit *epa.gov/asbestos* for information.

CONTENTS

Chapter one
KITCHEN & BATHROOM

Chapter two
LAUNDRY ROOM, CLOSETS & CLOTHES

Chapter **three**
GARAGE & WORKSHOP

Chapter **four**
LAWN, GARDEN & OUTDOORS

Chapter **five**
FLOORS, CEILINGS, WALLS & TRIM

Chapter **six**
AROUND THE HOUSE

Special Section
REMODELING

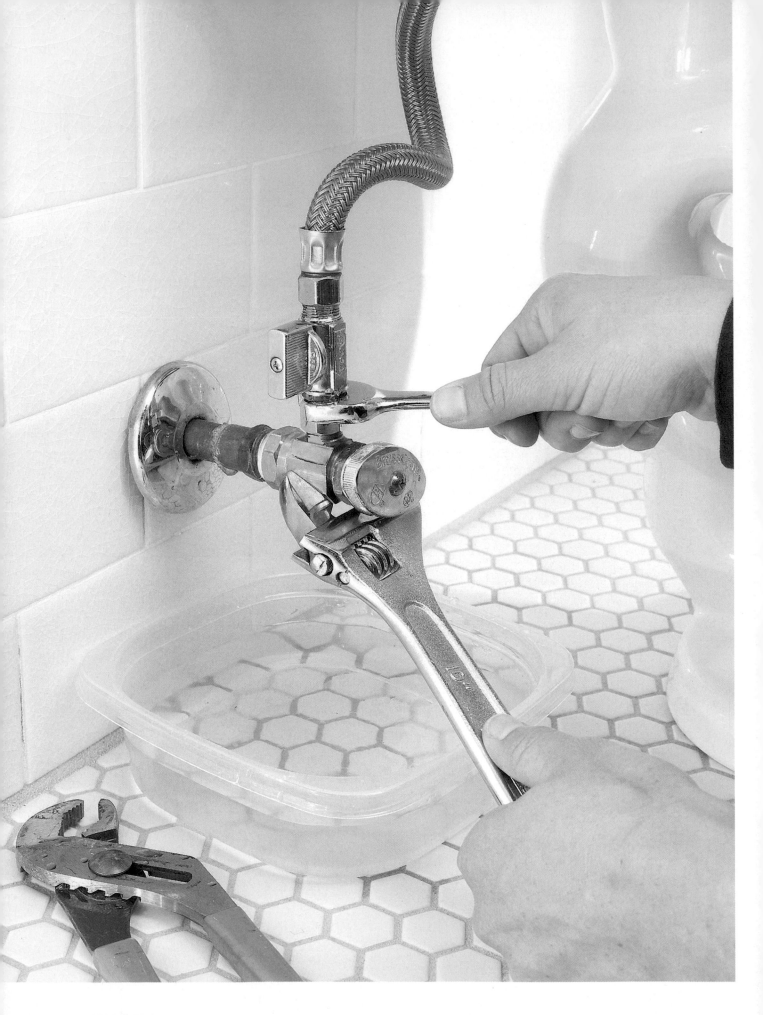

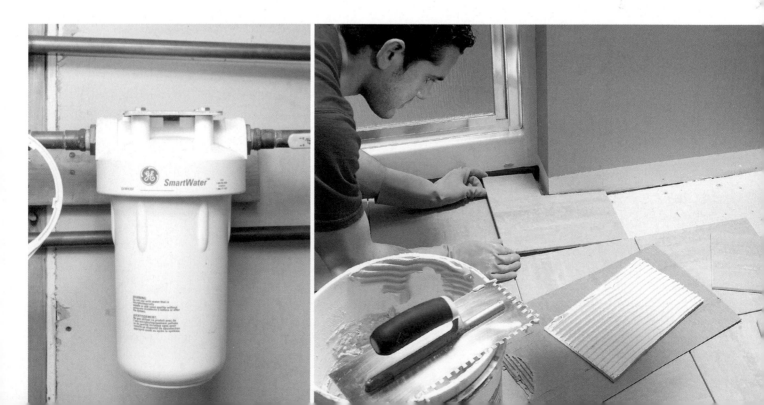

CHAPTER ONE

KITCHEN & BATHROOM

Tile Without Trouble

Go for easier installation with less frustration.

In theory, setting tile is easy. You just stick tiles to the wall or floor and fill the gaps with grout. But in the real world, tile jobs are full of concerns. This collection of tips—collected from pros and DIYers—may not eliminate all your tile troubles, but it will help you avoid the most common headaches.

A. MIX IT SMOOTH

After all the prep and layout work, you're finally ready to set tile and see some results. The last thing you want to do is stop and wait. But giving the thin-set time to "slake" (absorb water) is the key to a smooth, chunk-free mix. A chunky mix will drive you crazy when you try to comb the thin-set onto the wall or floor. After slaking, remix and add a smidgen of water if needed. Play the same waiting game when you mix up the grout later.

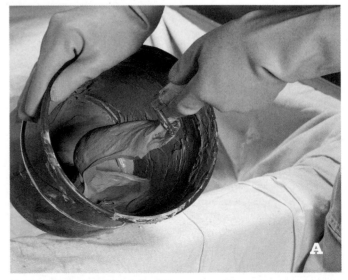

For a smooth mix, wait. Mix up the thin-set or grout, then let it stand for about 10 minutes. That allows dry chunks time to absorb water before you do the final mixing.

B. START WITH A FLAT FLOOR

Tiling a wavy floor is a nightmare. You push and pry to get each tile flush with its neighbors and you still end up with "lippage" (edges that protrude above adjoining tiles, usually at corners). So before you tile, check the floor with a 4-ft. straightedge. If you find low spots more than 1/4 in. deep, screed thin-set over them to create a flat surface.

For really bad floors, self-leveling compound (also called "self-leveling underlayment") is a lifesaver. You just mix the powder with water and pour to create a flat, smooth surface. A perfect tile base doesn't come cheap, though—expect to pay about $2 per sq. ft. Some products require metal or plastic lath; some don't.

Self-leveling compound is almost goof-proof, but there are two big pitfalls. First, it will slowly seep into the tiniest crack or hole, leaving a crater in the surface. So before you put down the lath, grab a caulk gun and fill every little gap—even small nail holes. Second, you have to work fast. Most compounds begin to harden in about 30 minutes. To get the whole floor poured in that time frame, you need at least one helper to mix the compound while you pour. And even with help, you'll have to move quickly.

C. REMOVE THE BASEBOARD

You could leave base trim in place, lay tile along it and caulk the gap. But that "shortcut" will look second rate and cost you hours of fussy measuring and cutting. With baseboards gone, your cuts don't have to be precise or perfect; the baseboard will hide chipped edges and small mistakes. If you're just dead set against pulling off baseboards, consider adding base shoe molding along the bottom of the baseboard after you set the tile.

D. SET AGAINST GUIDE BOARDS

The usual way to position the first rows of tile is to snap chalk lines. But there are two problems with that method: First, chalk lines are hard to see if you've slopped thin-set over them. Second, the first row of tile can move as you set the next row. Guide boards solve both problems. Position the boards the same way you would position layout lines and screw them to the floor. Be sure to choose perfectly straight boards or cut strips of plywood. Also, wrap the edge of the guide with duct tape so the thin-set won't stick to it.

Pour a perfect floor. Self-leveling compound gives you a flat, smooth base for tile. It's also a fast way to embed in-floor heating mats or cables.

PLASTIC LATH

SELF-LEVELING COMPOUND

HEATING CABLE

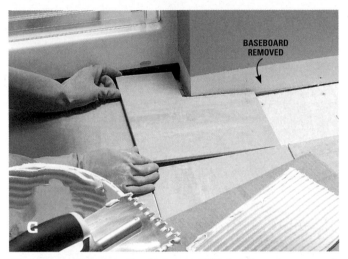

BASEBOARD REMOVED

Give yourself some wiggle room. With baseboards removed, measurements and cuts don't have to be precise. That means faster work and fewer miscut tiles on the scrap pile.

GUIDE BOARD

Boards are better than lines. Unlike chalk lines, guide boards don't get lost under thin-set or allow tiles to shift as you set other tiles.

E. GET A STRAIGHT START ON WALLS

The obvious way to tile a wall is to start at the bottom and work your way up. And that works fine if the base of the wall (usually the floor or bathtub) is perfectly flat and level. If not, the tile will simply amplify the imperfections; you'll end up with misaligned tiles and grout lines that vary in width.

To get a straight, level start, position a ledger on the wall, leaving a gap below—about 1/2 in. less than a full tile. The ledger shown here is a length of steel angle held in place by wood blocks screwed to the wall. A strip of plywood or a perfectly straight board will do the job too.

F. TACKLE TOUGH CUTS WITH A GRINDER

A grinder isn't the best tool for cutting tile. It whips up a nasty dust storm and often leaves jagged or chipped edges. Plus, it's just plain slower than a tile cutter or wet saw. But equipped with a diamond blade, a grinder will cut curves and make enclosed cuts that those other tools can't. Choose a "dry-cut" blade and do the cutting outdoors.

G. CLEAN UP RIGHT AWAY!

When you're done setting the tile, stand back for a minute to admire it. Then get back to work. First, drop your mucky tools in a bucket of cold water. That will slow—but not stop—the hardening of the thin-set. Next, inspect all the joints for thin-set that has squeezed out between tiles and clean it out before it hardens. Also look for thin-set smudges on the face of the tile. If a smudge has hardened and won't wipe off easily, wet it and scrub with a synthetic abrasive pad (the kind you use to scour cookware). Use minimal elbow grease; if you rub really hard, it's possible to dull polished stone or even glazed tile. Now go clean up those tools.

SLOW DOWN THE DRYING

Pros like to finish the job fast and will sometimes use fast-setting thin-set. For the rest of us mortals, slower is better, and even the standard products sometimes harden or dry out too fast. Here are two ways to give yourself extra working time: First dampen the backer board or concrete with a sponge before you spread the thin-set. A damp surface won't immediately suck moisture out of the thin-set. Second, mix the thin-set with latex additive rather than water ($25 for 2 gallons). Latex additive dries more slowly than water and boosts adhesion in both thin-set and grout. It also makes grout more stain-resistant. (A few latex additives are designed to speed the hardening process; check the label.) If thin-set or grout begins to harden before you can use it, just toss it. Don't add water and remix. That's a recipe for weak bonding and trouble later.

LEDGER

E

Set tiles on a ledger. Fasten a straight ledger to the wall to support the tiles. Remove the ledger later and trim tiles to fill the gap below.

BACK OF TILE

EXTEND CUTS PAST CORNERS

F

Cut outlet holes. Outline the light switch or outlet box on the face of the tile. Cut as much as you can, then finish the cut from the back, where you can overcut the corners slightly.

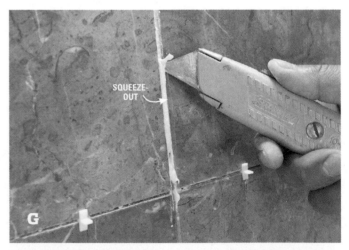

SQUEEZE-OUT

G

Clean out the squeeze-out. Plow excess thin-set out of joints with a utility knife, a pencil or a tile spacer. Whatever you use, do it now, not later.

1 **Remove the middle section.** Drill a 3/4-in. hole in each corner of the traced cutout line. Then run your jigsaw along the line. Remove the old swollen floor.

2 **Drop in the new floor and screw it into place.** Predrill holes around the perimeter using a countersink bit. Then install brass-colored drywall screws.

Got a Swollen Sink Base Bottom?

Let's face it—it's easy to get water on the floor of your sink base cabinet. We'll never understand why cabinetmakers use particleboard for the base, but they do. And once it starts swelling, your only option is to replace it. But you don't have to cut out the entire bottom. Here's an easier way to install a new sink base bottom.

Remove the drain lines (and garbage disposal, if there is one) to get maneuvering room. Then trace a cutting line about 3 in. in from all four edges. Then cut out the middle section of the swollen sink base with a jigsaw **(Photo 1)**. Next, cut a piece of 1/2-in. plywood to the interior size of the sink base. Cut slots for the water supply tubes. Then seal the edges and face of the plywood with urethane varnish. Then install the new plywood floor and fasten it to the old floor **(Photo 2)**. Caulk around the edges and pipes to prevent water from seeping under the new floor. Then reattach the P-trap and garbage disposal.

Leaky Bath Fan

Water stains on the ceiling around your bath fan may indicate a leak coming from the vent cap on your roof, but condensation is the more likely culprit. If bath fan ducting isn't properly insulated, the moist air from your house will condense inside the duct.

The first step is to head to the attic. You may find that the insulation simply needs to be refastened. If you see that your duct isn't insulated at all, pick up duct insulation (less than $20) at a home center. Use zip ties or aluminum tape to fasten the insulation.

If your ducts are properly insulated, another potential cause of condensation is lack of use. Bath fans have a damper designed to keep the outside air from entering through the fan, but that valve doesn't stop warm air from escaping. Whether you use your bath fan or not, some warm air will still escape into the ducting. On very cold days, that warm air is likely to condense inside the ducting, especially if the fan is never run to dry it out. Guest baths are particularly prone to this problem.

The bottom line: Before climbing on the roof to look for leaks, make sure your bath fan duct is insulated, and run the fan more often and for longer periods. Switches with built-in timers are available.

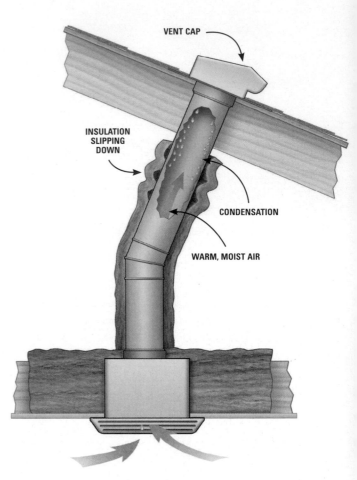

Moist indoor air condenses inside a cold, uninsulated duct and water runs down into the fan.

Beware of "Color Shifting"

Be careful when selecting tile for a bathroom floor and vanity top on a sunny afternoon. The two can complement each other beautifully—but maybe only on sunny afternoons. On cloudy days or evenings, the vanity may take on a blue tone and the floor a green one. It could end up looking awful. Always examine color combinations in different light conditions, natural and artificial, and in fair weather and foul.

Installing Cabinets

Kitchen cabinets aren't cheap, and while you shouldn't be afraid to install them, you don't want to screw them up, either.

We asked Jerome Worm, an experienced installer, to show what it takes to install basic box cabinets successfully. His tips can save you time and help you avoid costly mistakes on your next installation.

A. MARK UP THE WALL FIRST

Every good cabinet installation starts with a good layout. Jerome calls it "blueprinting" the wall. Here's how to do it: Measure from the highest point in the floor, and draw a level line marking the top of the base cabinets. Measure up 19-1/2 in. from that line and draw another line for the bottom of the upper cabinets. Label the location of the cabinets and appliances on the wall. Draw a vertical line to line up the edge of the first cabinet to be installed. Finally, mark the stud locations.

B. REMOVE DOORS AND DRAWERS

Removing shelves, doors and drawers makes installation easier and prevents damage. Mark the location of the doors on painter's tape, and make a pencil mark at the top of the hinges so you have a good starting point when you reinstall them. Remember that many upper cabinets have no designated top or bottom. They can be hung either direction depending on which way you want the doors to swing. So decide that before you mark the hinges.

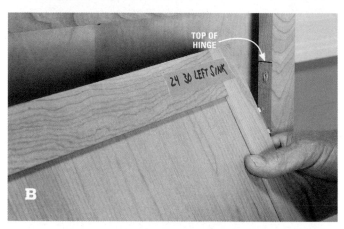

C. SHIM EXTREME BOWS

Most of the time you can shim the cabinets as you go, but if there's an extreme bow in the wall (more than 3/8 in.), shim it out before you hang the cabinet. If you don't, you may accidentally pull the back off the cabinet while fastening it into place. Hold a level across the wall, and slide a shim up from the bottom (go in from the top when you're doing the top side) until it's snug. Then pin or tape it into place.

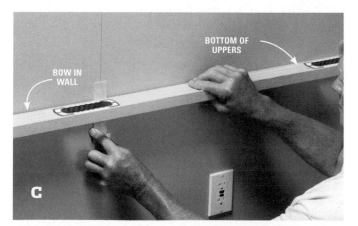

D. START WITH THE UPPER CABINETS

It's easier to hang the uppers when you're not leaning way over the base cabinets. Rest the uppers on a ledger board—it'll ensure a nice straight alignment and eliminate the frustration of holding the cabinets in place while screwing them to the wall.

E. CLAMP, DRILL AND FASTEN

When connecting two cabinets to each other, line up the face frames and clamp them together. Both cabinets should be fastened to the wall at this point, but you may have to loosen one cabinet or the other to get the frames to line up perfectly. Jerome prefers hand-screw clamps because they don't flex, and less flex means a tighter grip. Predrill a 1/8-in. hole before screwing the cabinets together with a 2-1/2-in. screw. Choose the less noticeable cabinet of the two for drilling and placing the screw head.

F. USE A BLOCK OF WOOD FOR SCRIBING

Find the largest distance between the outside of the cabinet and the wall. Take that measurement and make a pencil mark on your filler strip (measure over right to left in this case). Clamp the filler onto the cabinet flush with the inside of the vertical rail. Measure over from the wall to your pencil mark, and make a scribing block that size. Use your block to trace a pencil line down the filler strip. Masking tape on the filler strip helps the pencil line show up better and protects the finish from the saw table.

MARK THE STUD LOCATIONS ON UPPER CABINETS

Jerome prefers to predrill the screw holes from the inside of the cabinet so the drill bit doesn't "blow out" the wood on the inside where it can be seen. Do this by marking the stud locations on the inside of the cabinet and drilling pilot holes. Start by finding the distance from the wall or adjacent cabinet to the center of the next stud. For 1/2-in.-thick cabinet walls, subtract 7/8 in. from that measurement, and measure over that distance from the inside of the cabinet. Make a pencil mark on both the top and the bottom nailing strips. The outside of the cabinet walls are not flush with the rest of the cabinet; that 7/8 in. represents the thickness of the cabinet wall and the distance the walls are recessed.

G. USE GOOD SCREWS

Jerome prefers GRK's R4 self-countersinking screw, which he calls "the Cadillac of screws." You'll pay accordingly, but why scrimp on screws when you're spending thousands of dollars on cabinets? Whatever you do, don't use drywall screws—they'll just snap off and you'll end up with an extra hole.

LEDGER BOARD

D

E

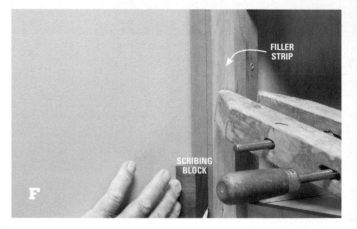

FILLER STRIP

SCRIBING BLOCK

F

SELF-DRILLING

SELF-COUNTER-SINKING

G

H. FASTEN THE BACK, THEN SHIM

Line up the base cabinets with the level line on the wall. Fasten the backs of the cabinets to that line. Once the backs of the cabinets are level, use shims to level the sides. Take your time on this step—nobody likes to have eggs roll off a slanted countertop.

I. USE 2x2S TO SECURE CABINETS TO THE FLOOR

Cabinets that make up islands and peninsulas need to be secured to the floor. Join the island cabinets and set them in place. Trace an outline of the cabinets on the floor. Screw 2x2s to the floor 1/2 in. on the inside of the line to account for the thickness of the cabinets. Anchor the island cabinets to the 2x2s with screws. If needed, place flooring blocks under the 2x2s (**J**).

J. RAISE THE CABINETS FOR FLOORING

If the kitchen flooring is going to be hardwood or tile, and you're installing it after the cabinets, you'll have to raise the cabinets off the floor or the dishwasher won't fit under the countertop. Use blocks to represent the finished floor height, and add those distances to the guide line for the base cabinet tops. Hold the blocks back a bit from the front so the flooring can tuck underneath. Your flooring guys will love you for this.

K. CUT OVERSIZE HOLES

Cutting exact size holes for water lines and drainpipes might impress your wife or customer, but such precision is likely to result in unnecessary headaches for you. Cutting larger holes makes it easier to slide the cabinet into place and provides wiggle room for minor adjustments. No one's going to notice the oversize holes once the cabinet is filled with dish soaps, scrubbers and recycling bins.

H

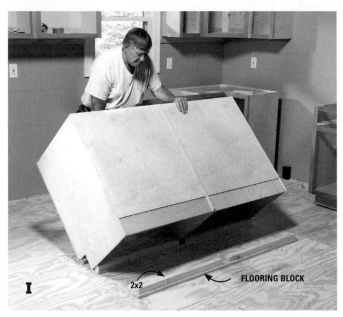

I   2x2   FLOORING BLOCK

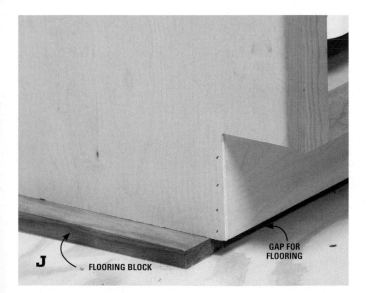

J   FLOORING BLOCK   GAP FOR FLOORING

K

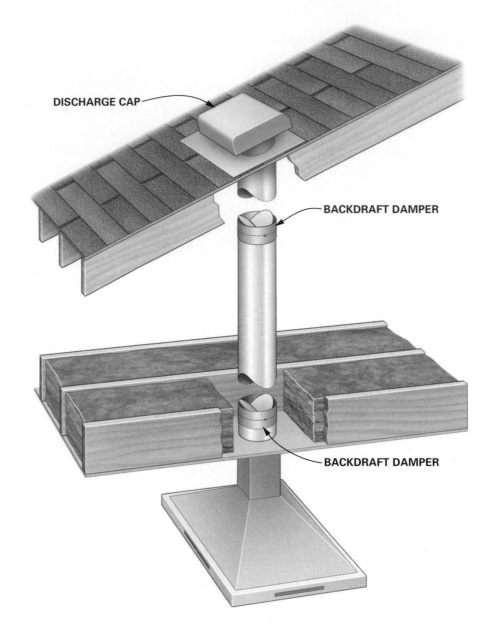

DISCHARGE CAP

BACKDRAFT DAMPER

BACKDRAFT DAMPER

Clanging Vent Hood Damper

Q: Every time the wind kicks up, it opens the damper on my kitchen vent hood. When the wind dies down, the damper slams shut, making a metallic *clang*. The noise drives me crazy. What's the fix?

A: New spring-loaded backdraft dampers ($9 to $30, depending on the size) should solve the problem. Measure the diameter of the vent pipe and order the dampers from a duct supply company (*hvacquick.com* is one source). Start by

replacing the backdraft damper directly above the vent hood. If that doesn't solve the problem, install a second damper near the wall or roof discharge cap. The second damper will greatly reduce the clanging problem.

Rid the Bathroom of Pink Slime

Ever notice red or pink slime forming inside your toilet or on your shower walls?

It's a bacterium called *Serratia marcescens*, and it can grow in wet areas. Chlorine in city water helps prevent it. But if you have an activated charcoal filter, you're removing the chlorine, according to the North Dakota State University Extension Service. Water from a private well has no chlorine either.

This bacterium has been known to cause pneumonia, wound infections and urinary tract infections in hospital settings, so it's important to get rid of it. Stains are easy to remove with a general-purpose cleaner containing chlorine bleach. You can also add 1/4 cup of bleach to your toilet tank, let it sit for 20 minutes, and then flush the toilet a few times to remove all the bleach. Don't leave it in your tank—it can damage rubber valves and seals.

Touch Up a Stainless Steel Appliance

Stainless steel is a great look until you scratch it. Then it looks awful. But you can "sand" out the scratches with sandpaper (400 to 600 grit) and a sanding block, with an abrasive pad or with rubbing compound. Or buy a stainless steel repair kit and get everything you need. (The Scratch-B-Gone kit is available at *amazon.com*, home centers and appliance parts stores.)

The sanding technique only works on plain (uncoated) stainless steel panels. Never try this procedure on simulated stainless steel or stainless panels with a fingerprint-resistant clear coat. Hint: If your appliance fingerprints easily, chances are it's plain stainless steel.

The key to removing the scratch is to start with the finest-grit paper or pad and zigzag a stream of sanding fluid on it. Then sand the scratched area. If the scratch won't come out after sanding for a few minutes, move up to the next coarsest grit. When the scratch disappears, sand the rest of the panel until it blends in.

You'll have to develop a feel for the technique, so start on an inconspicuous area of the appliance panel. Finish by applying a stainless steel cleaner/polish (Sprayway is one brand; about $5 at home centers and appliance parts stores).

Start with the scratch and then blend in. Determine the direction of the "grain" and start sanding in one direction only, following the brushed pattern. Don't sand back and forth and never sand against the grain.

Swap Door Handles on a Fridge

Switch an opening in no time with these tips.

You moved the old fridge into the Men's Crisis Center (aka the garage) and now the doors open the wrong way, making for inconvenient beverage access. It's an easy DIY project, but you do have to pay attention to the disassembly and reassembly steps and keep track of the plastic parts. If you put them back in the wrong place or leave them out, the doors won't close properly. The entire job takes less than an hour and requires just screwdrivers, pliers and a socket set.

Start by removing all the food from door shelves. Then pry off the upper hinge trim piece (if equipped) with a flat-blade screwdriver. Hold the door in place while you remove the upper hinge screws. Then remove the upper door **(Photo 1)**.

Next, remove the middle hinge screws and the bottom door. Check for plastic parts at both hinges and label them. Then remove the bottom hinge and mount it on the opposite side of the fridge. Swap the door handles and the door stops to the opposite sides of the door **(Photo 2)**.

This next part makes most people crazy, but it makes sense when you think it through. When you flip the middle hinge to the opposite side of the fridge, the upper and lower hinge pins will be facing the wrong direction. Don't panic! Just reverse the hinge pin **(Photo 3)**.

With the middle hinge pin reversed, go ahead and reassemble the doors and hinges and reload your fridge.

2 **Swap the handles.** Unsnap the plastic "vanity" plugs that cover the door handle screws. Then remove the door handle screws and swap the door handles.

REVERSIBLE MIDDLE HINGE PIN

3 **Reverse the hinge pin.** Grab the hinge pin with pliers and unscrew it. Flip the pin upside down and screw it back into the hinge.

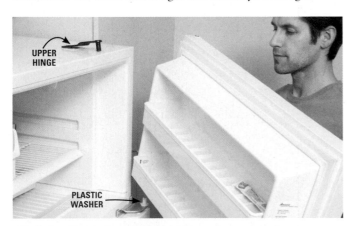

UPPER HINGE

PLASTIC WASHER

1 **Lift off the door.** Tilt the upper door away from the fridge and lift it up and off the middle hinge pin. Immediately check for a plastic washer or guide that fits into the bottom of the upper door. Locate those parts and put them in a safe place.

4 **Mount the middle hinge.** Hold the bottom door in place and insert the middle hinge. Then install the screws and tighten.

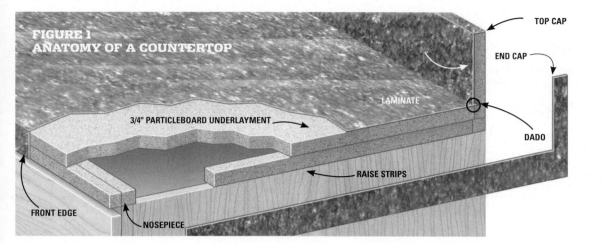

**FIGURE 1
ANATOMY OF A COUNTERTOP**

TOP CAP

END CAP

LAMINATE

3/4" PARTICLEBOARD UNDERLAYMENT

DADO

RAISE STRIPS

FRONT EDGE

NOSEPIECE

Build a Seam-Free Laminate Countertop

Get a new look in your kitchen for less.

Laminate is a budget-friendly alternative to granite, quartz and other solid-surface countertops. And building custom countertops in place is a great way to deal with unique shapes and sizes. There are hundreds of colors to choose from, and you can order 5 x 12-ft. sheets of laminate at most home centers. With a sheet that size, you can avoid cutting difficult miters and usually eliminate long, crumb-catching seams.

If you've never tackled custom countertops, don't be intimidated—let us walk you through the process. You'll need a couple of specialty tools, including a compound router with an offset base, a laminate slitter and a laminate file, but the several hundred dollars you'll save by installing your countertops yourself will be more than enough to pay for these tools. And just think of the bragging rights!

CUT A DADO IN THE BACKSPLASH

Before you assemble the underlayment, plow a 1/4-in.-deep, 1/4-in.-wide dado into the backsplash **(Figure 1)**. The laminate slips into the groove to give you a little wiggle room when you install it. We cut the dado by making a few passes on a table saw.

A. ASSEMBLE THE UNDERLAYMENT IN PLACE

If you're working with factory-built cabinets, you'll have to install "raise strips" made of 3/4-in. particleboard on top of the cabinets **(Figure 1)** to make room for the top drawers to clear the front edge of the countertop. Install a board instead

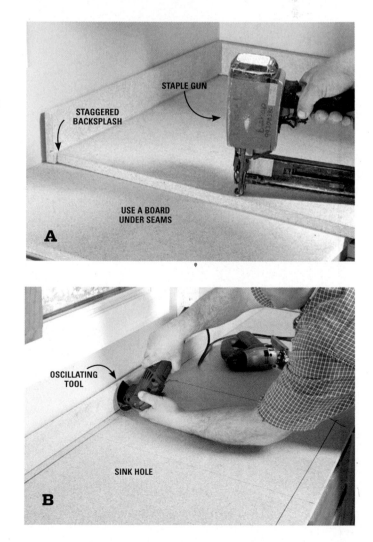

STAGGERED BACKSPLASH

STAPLE GUN

USE A BOARD UNDER SEAMS

A

OSCILLATING TOOL

SINK HOLE

B

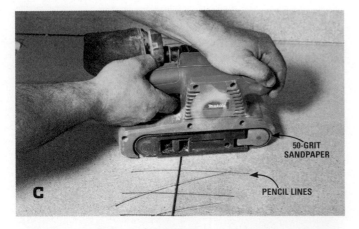

C

50-GRIT SANDPAPER

PENCIL LINES

of a raise strip where the underlayment corner seam will be. Cut the underlayment so it sticks out 1 in. past the finished end of the cabinet (or make it flush if the cabinet abuts an appliance). Stagger the top, backsplash and nosepiece seams at least 1/2 in. Fasten it all together with 1/4-in. crown staples that are 1-1/4 in. long and spaced about 5 in. apart—no glue required.

B. CUT THE SINK HOLE

Cut the hole for the sink after the underlayment is installed but before you install the laminate. Most sinks require a 21-1/4-in. x 32-1/4-in. hole, but make sure you have your sink on hand so you'll know what size hole to cut. Cut the back side of the hole with an oscillating tool, and then cut the sides and front with a jigsaw.

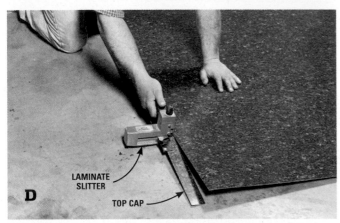

D

LAMINATE SLITTER

TOP CAP

C. SAND THE SEAMS

There can be a small gap between the underlayment boards, but the seam has to be absolutely flat. Mark the seam with a pencil, then sand with 50-grit paper until the lines disappear.

D. USE A "SLITTER" FOR NARROW STRIPS

A laminate slitter is almost a must for cutting thin laminate strips. It has an adjustable guide, so you can cut strips ranging in width from 1/2 in. up to 4-1/4 in. Cut any narrow strips first, before rough-cutting the large countertop pieces. All the pieces will be cut a bit long and trimmed down after they're installed. Make sure you have enough of the sheet left over to cut the large L-shaped section.

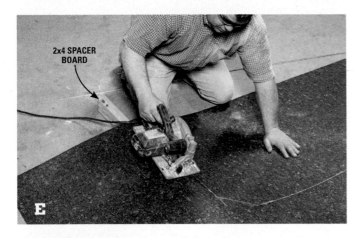

E

2x4 SPACER BOARD

E. CUT THE TOP WITH A CIRCULAR SAW

Cut the main top piece of the laminate with a circular saw. Use a board to create a space so the saw blade doesn't grind into the floor. Avoid scratches by sticking a few strips of masking tape to the underside of your saw base. The front side of the laminate will hang over the edge and be trimmed off, so your cuts don't need to be perfect.

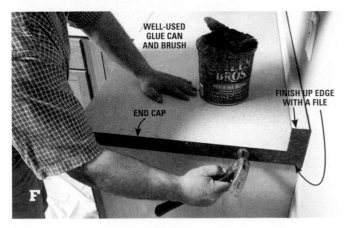

F

WELL-USED GLUE CAN AND BRUSH

END CAP

FINISH UP EDGE WITH A FILE

F. GLUE THE END CAPS FIRST

Cut the end cap so the bottom portion and the very top are close enough to be cleaned up with a file. The rest will be trimmed with a router. Cut the end cap to size with snips, then paint a thin layer of glue on both surfaces. Let the glue dry just until it's no longer wet to the touch, then carefully line up the top and ends and tip the piece into place. Embed the end cap by lightly tapping the whole surface with a smooth, burr-free hammer, and then it's ready for the router.

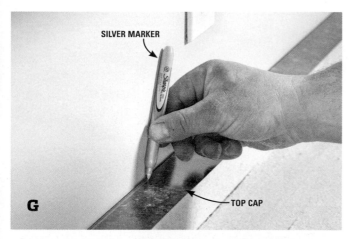

SILVER MARKER

TOP CAP

G

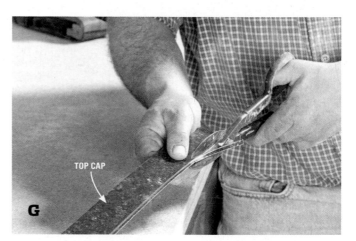

TOP CAP

G

OFFSET
BASE

COMPACT ROUTER

H

FLUSH-
CUTTING BIT

I

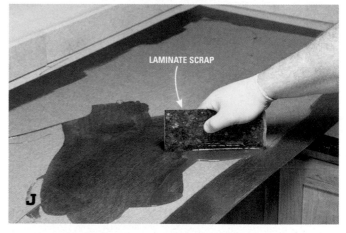

LAMINATE SCRAP

J

G. SCRIBE AND CUT THE TOP CAP

Before you get your first whiff of glue, make sure every piece fits. The top of the backsplash will need to be scribed and trimmed down. A silver marker works to scribe the top, and then carefully cut it with tin snips. To avoid cracking the laminate, don't cut more than 1/4 in. at a time. Clean up the edge with a belt sander.

H. INSTALL THE FRONT EDGE

Install the front edge flush with the bottom of the underlayment, and set it with a hammer. Then trim off the excess with your router. A compact router with an offset base is a must-have when you're building countertops in place.

I. ROUTING TIP

When you trim the main countertop and the top of the backsplash, the guide of your router bit will be running along finished laminate, so keep the router moving. If you stop for any length of time, the bit will grind into the surface of the laminate. Rub a little petroleum jelly along the edge where the bit rides to prevent marring.

J. APPLY THE ADHESIVE WITH A SCRAP

Clean all surfaces with compressed air before gluing up the top surface. Cover the perimeter with a brush and then grab a scrap piece of laminate to spread on the rest. Apply the glue on the underlayment the same way. It gets messy trying to glue the backsplash after the top is installed, so cover the backsplash with glue at the same time. And this stuff is a potent chemical, so always use an organic vapor respirator, open a window and turn on the exhaust fan.

K. USE SPACERS TO INSTALL THE TOP

Laminate adhesive is sometimes referred to as "contact cement" because it sets as soon as the two coated surfaces come into contact. That's not necessarily a good thing when you're trying to maneuver a large, floppy sheet into place. Cut strips of leftover laminate and use them as spacers. Because the adhesive won't stick to the strips, you'll be able to slide the sheet around. Start pulling out the spacers once the top sheet is in position. Make sure the spacers are clean so they don't leave debris behind.

L. SMOOTH IT WITH A BOARD

Instead of using a roller to smooth out the surface, use a board wrapped in a towel. If a piece of debris does get in between the two surfaces, the soft rubber on a roller can indent around the lump and actually crack the laminate that surrounds it. Start on the back side and work out to edges.

M. TRIM DOWN THE BACKSPLASH WITH SNIPS

A router won't be able to reach the inside corner of the backsplash, so use tin snips to trim it down before you install it (make small cuts). That way you won't have as much material to remove with your file. Press the section on with a board the same way you did the top. Set the top cap piece into place with a hammer.

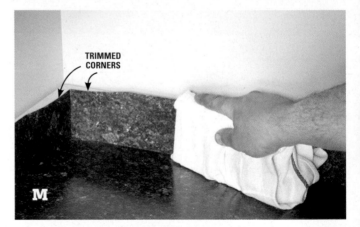

N. TRIM OUT THE SINK HOLE

Use your router to trim the hole for the sink. Just poke through the material with a spinning bit and work your way to the edge. Right before you finish the cut, support the scrap material so it doesn't fall down and tear out the last section.

O. FILE DOWNWARD

Once all pieces are in place, file all the edges, including the bottom. You can buy a file designed for plastic laminate for less than $20. Always file in a downward direction, never back and forth. Clean off excess glue with lacquer thinner or a solvent that your adhesive manufacturer recommends.

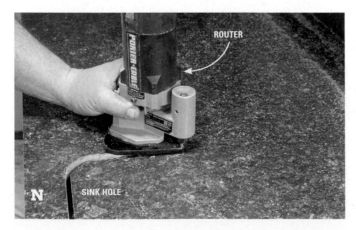

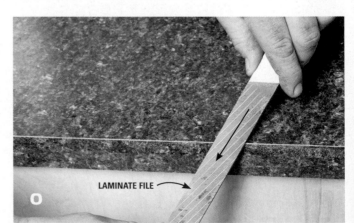

Better Kitchen Outlets

To add outlets without interrupting a beautiful backsplash, install under-cabinet outlet strips. They also make life easier for the tile setter and (sometimes) the electrician. A 5-ft. prewired raceway costs about $100. To browse the options, search online for "20 amp raceway."

OUTLET STRIP

Fresh, Clean Dishwasher

Once a month or so, add a cup of vinegar to your empty dishwasher and let it run a full cycle. Your kitchen may smell a bit like a pickle jar for a few hours, but hard-water lime buildup will be rinsed away, freeing up the spray arm and other dishwasher parts.

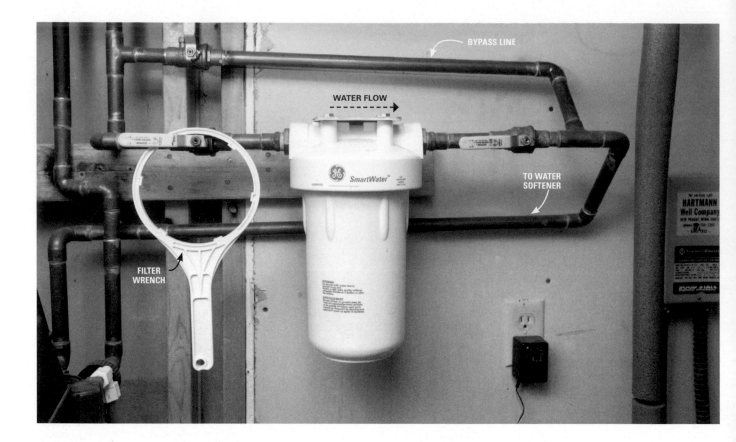

WATER FLOW

BYPASS LINE

TO WATER
SOFTENER

FILTER
WRENCH

SmartWater

Remove Sediment from Your Water

Do you get a little grit in your glass of tap water? Well-water and older public water systems sometimes contain sand, iron, silt and other forms of sediment. An inexpensive whole-house filter may be the ticket. It's worth trying before investing in a full-blown water filtration system, which can cost thousands. If you can sweat a pipe, installation is easy enough.

Install the filter on the water supply line just before it enters your water softener. You may want to install yours with a bypass line so you can change the filter while the water is being used in another part of the house.

You can buy this fairly standard model for about $100 at home centers. It can be used with two different types of filters. The carbon paper–style filter removes much smaller particles than the pleated-style filter, which generally costs a bit less. If your water is particularly "chunky" and you use the carbon paper–style filter, you may find yourself changing the filter every week, which could get expensive. The manufacturer recommends that the filters be changed every three months. If you go too long without changing it, you may notice a drop in your water pressure.

CARBON
PAPER FILTER

PLEATED
FILTER

A big filter for small grit. A sediment filter keeps the crud out of your water. It's easy to install on your main water supply line and will filter the water for your entire home. Carbon paper filters catch smaller particles, but pleated filters cost less and last longer.

Don't Ignore a Rocking Toilet

If your toilet isn't solidly fastened to the floor, there may be trouble in your future. Any movement of the toilet damages the wax seal. That leads to leaks and major repairs. To steady a rocking toilet, cut plastic shims to fit and slip them underneath (you may have to remove caulk before adding the shims). Then caulk around the toilet and snug down the nuts on the bolts. But don't crank them down super tight; that can crack the toilet.

Lube a Sticking Shower Valve

WATERPROOF PLUMBER'S GREASE

Lube the contact points. A thin film of grease makes sticking valves operate easily. Use plumber's grease; other lubricants may harm the valve.

Does your shower valve require two hands and considerable upper body strength to operate? The culprit is probably hard water. Over the years, it can cause the cartridge inside a shower valve to stick. You can avoid a lot of elbow grease by simply applying a little plumber's grease. Get a small container for less than $5 at home centers.

Most cartridges are held in with just one screw; however, with some models it may be necessary to remove the trim ring. After removing the retainer screw, just pull the cartridge straight out and lube all the contact points. It should work like new.

If you're unsure how to remove your cartridge, check the manufacturer's website. Many companies have detailed diagrams on their sites. And of course, don't forget to turn off the water supply to the valve before you pull the cartridge.

Tips for Weekend Plumbers

Every little bit of advice helps when it comes to plumbing know-how.

More than any other type of home improvement job, plumbing can drive a DIYer crazy. Problems arise, projects grow, frustrations multiply. Even pros are not immune. But one way to manage the frustrations and achieve a successful plumbing project is to allow plenty of time—at least twice as much time as you think the project should take. Another smart step is to learn some tricks of the trade. Here are a few of our favorites.

A. "UN-SOLDER" CONNECTIONS— BUT ONLY WHEN YOU HAVE TO

The best way to disconnect a soldered pipe is to cut it. But sometimes you can't—either because you can't get a cutting tool into the space or because cutting would leave the pipe too short to make a new connection. The solution is to heat the joint and pull off the fitting as the solder melts.

Have a wet rag handy and immediately wipe away the molten solder before it hardens. (Wear gloves to prevent

burning your fingers!) Sometimes a quick wipe will leave the pipe ready for a new fitting. More likely, you'll have to scour off some excess solder with sandpaper or emery cloth before you can slip on a new fitting.

A

B. CHOOSE CAULK, NOT PUTTY

Despite the name, lots of plumbers never use plumber's putty. It damages some types of plastic and stains surfaces such as natural stone. Plus, it tends to dry out, crack and allow leaks. Silicone caulk is a safer, longer-lasting sealant in most areas where you might use plumber's putty.

C. DON'T FIGHT WITH METAL DRAIN LINES

Metal drain lines under sinks look a lot more reliable than plastic. But plastic is better in almost every way. It's cheaper, easier to install, and easier to adjust or tighten if a leak develops. And unlike metal, plastic won't corrode. So when a metal drain leaks, often the smartest move is to replace the entire assembly with plastic.

D. DOPE EVERYTHING

Thread sealant (aka "pipe dope") is formulated to seal threads. But it's great for almost any connection, even if the threads don't form the seal. Use it on compression fittings, ground fittings and rubber seals. Because it's slippery, it allows connections to slide together correctly for a good seal. And, if you use a type that doesn't harden, disassembly and repair will be easier years later. Some types of dope harm plastic parts, so check the label.

E. FIX A CLOG IN SECONDS

Before you run a drain snake into a clogged pipe or disassemble the trap, there are a few other tricks worth trying: Often, you can yank out a clog with a flexible-shaft pick-up tool (shown below) or a Zip-It (about $3 at home centers). Likewise, a wet/dry shop vacuum just might suck out the clog.

B — SILICONE CAULK

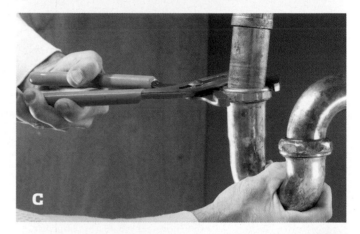

C

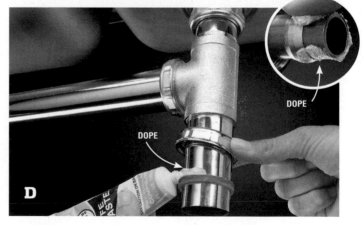

DOPE

DOPE

D

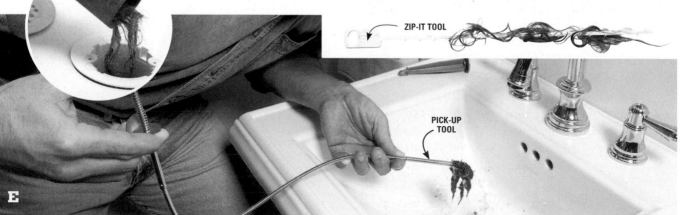

WET/DRY SHOP VAC

ZIP-IT TOOL

PICK-UP TOOL

E

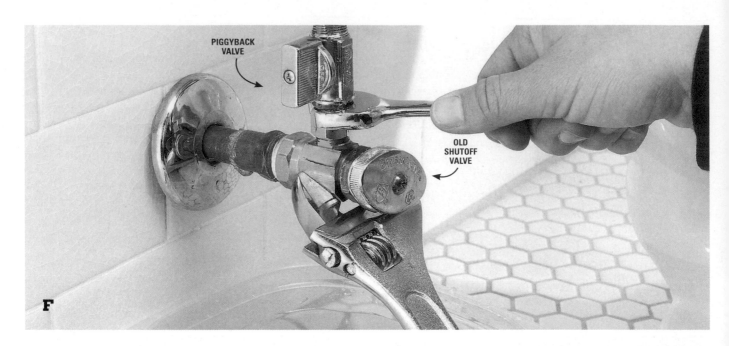

F

F. PIGGYBACK STUBBORN SHUTOFFS

Shutoff valves under sinks and toilets have a rotten reliability record. Sometimes they won't close completely; sometimes they won't close at all. In either case, there's an alternative to replacing the shutoff. Most home centers carry "piggyback" shutoff valves (about $10) that connect to existing shutoffs. Just disconnect the supply line and install the new valve (a new supply line is a good idea, too). If the old shutoff closes most of the way, you won't even have to turn off the main water valve; just set a container under the valve to catch the trickle while you work.

G. LOOSEN STUCK PIPES WITH HEAT

When a threaded connection won't budge, heat sometimes does the trick, especially on ancient connections that were sealed with pipe dope that hardened over time. Be patient. Getting the metal hot enough can take a couple of minutes. Protect nearby surfaces with a flame-resistant cloth (about $10 at home centers). This method is for water and waste pipes only, never for gas or fuel lines.

H. DON'T OVERTIGHTEN SUPPLY LINES

It's tempting to crank supply lines on tight, just to be safe. But overtightening supply lines is actually riskier than undertightening. A loose connection that leaks is easy to tighten, but overtightening can wreck rubber seals and crack the threaded nuts. So get into this habit: Make the connections at both ends of the supply line finger-tight, then give them another one-eighth to one-quarter turn with pliers. If they leak, snug them up a little more.

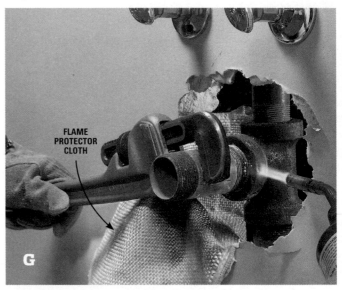

G

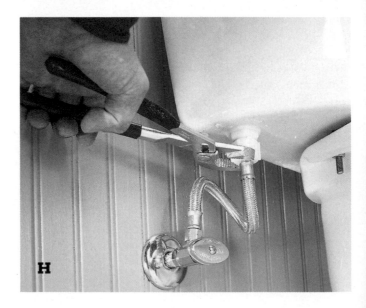

H

BUY MORE STUFF!

Weekend plumbers often spend more time driving back and forth to the home center than actually working on the project. So before you go shopping, think through each step and try to anticipate problems. Make a list of everything you might need and buy it all. One trip to the return counter is better than three trips back to the store (while your family waits for you to turn the water back on).

I. DON'T REUSE SUPPLY LINES

When you're replacing a toilet or a faucet, you can save 10 bucks by reusing the old flexible supply lines. But don't. Plastic degrades over time, and even a small leak can lead to catastrophic water damage. It's a small risk, but not one worth taking. Buy new lines that are encased in braided stainless steel; they're much less likely to burst. But even if you already have braided lines that are several years old, replace them.

J. TIPS FOR USING THREAD TAPE

Tape and dope are equally reliable for sealing pipe threads. The main advantage of tape is that it won't smear onto your hands or tools and end up on the carpet. Here are some tips for tape:

- Cheap tape works fine, but the thicker stuff (often pink for water, yellow for gas) is easier to handle and tears more neatly.
- Unlike dope, tape is for pipe threads only. Don't use it on compression or other connections.
- How many times should you wrap around the pipe? There are no rules, but the most common answer we got from pro plumbers was three.
- Always wrap the tape clockwise around the threads. Otherwise, the tape will unwrap as you screw the joint together.

K. CUT STUBBORN PARTS

Corrosion and mineral deposits have an amazing power to lock parts together, making them almost impossible to disconnect. Often, the best solution is to cut the stubborn part. Either slice it off or cut kerfs in the part so you can break it off. A hacksaw blade works well. Oscillating or rotary tools work even better.

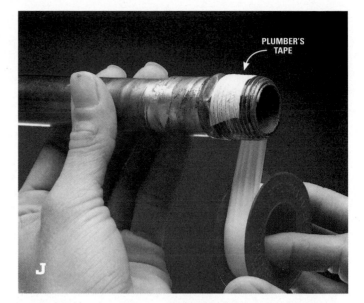

PLUMBER'S TAPE

J

ROTARY TOOL

K

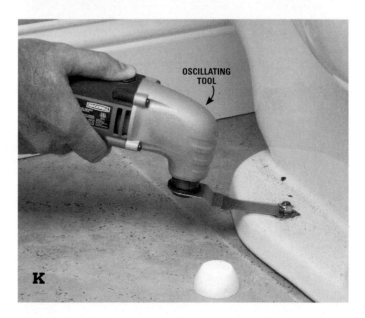

OSCILLATING TOOL

K

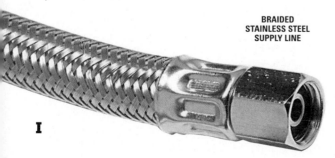

BRAIDED STAINLESS STEEL SUPPLY LINE

I

GREASE
AND FOOD

SPLASH
GUARD

Brush off the crud and rinse. Dip an old toothbrush in antibacterial grease-cutting kitchen cleaner (Clorox Antibacterial Degreaser is one choice) and lift up one corner of the splash guard. Scrub off the crud and rinse with cold water. Repeat with each flap until it's totally clean and rinsed. Then submit your resignation to the stink patrol.

Clean a Stinky Garbage Disposal

Even if you run your garbage disposal until the last shred of food is gone, and you let the water run the recommended time, you can still wind up with an out-of-control science experiment that stinks up your kitchen. Face it; some food is going to stick to the inside of the grinding chamber, and it's going to decay. You can clean the chamber by grinding ice and lemon rinds, adding baking soda or rinsing with vinegar and water. Or you can add commercial cleaners like Disposer Care, which is available at discount stores and most home centers.

However, if you don't clean the underside of the splash guard, you haven't finished the job and may still wind up with a stinker. Cleaning the splash guard is easier than you think. You don't even have to remove it. Just clean it with a toothbrush and cleaner as shown above.

Fix a Broken Water Dispenser Switch in the Fridge

So the kids were really thirsty and jammed their glass into the water dispenser on the refrigerator door. Now the paddle is hanging by a wire, and you're seeing a $300 repair bill. No way! You can do this repair yourself with ordinary hand tools in about an hour. A replacement paddle/switch costs about $75. We made the repair on a Whirlpool refrigerator. Repairs on other makes are similar.

Open the fridge door and write down the model and serial number of the fridge. Then contact a local appliance parts dealer or use the internet (*repairclinic.com* is one online source for discounted parts) to buy a new switch and paddle.

Start by unplugging the refrigerator. Then remove the drip tray to expose the trim panel screws. If you don't see any screws, unsnap the panel using a plastic putty knife and paint can opener (**Photo 1**). Lift the trim panel off the door. Next, remove the microswitch (**Photo 2**). The switch retaining pegs are usually broken, so replace them with screws (**Photo 3**). If the paddle is broken, first disconnect the water tube. Then remove the metal paddle retainer plate and swap in a new paddle (**Photo 4**).

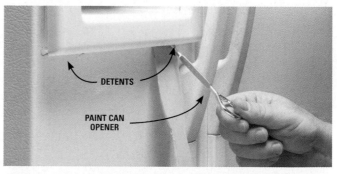

1 Remove the trim panel. Locate the detents in the trim panel. Slip a plastic putty knife up against the trim and wedge off the trim with a screwdriver or paint can opener.

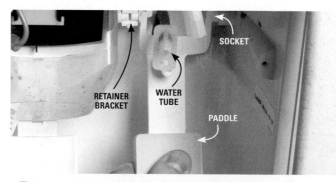

2 Remove the microswitch. Pull the snap retainers away from the switch and slide it off the pegs.

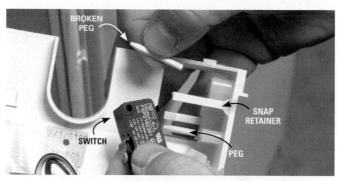

3 Replace the pegs. Drill out the pegs and replace them with two No. 4 x 1-1/4-in. machine screws. Slide the new switch onto the screws and tighten the nuts.

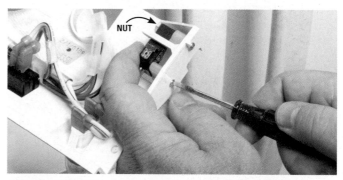

4 Install a new paddle. Remove the metal retainer plate (not shown). Replace the broken paddle with a new one. Reattach the water tube.

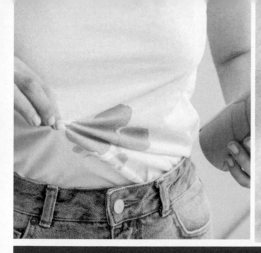

CHAPTER **TWO**

LAUNDRY ROOM, CLOSETS & CLOTHES

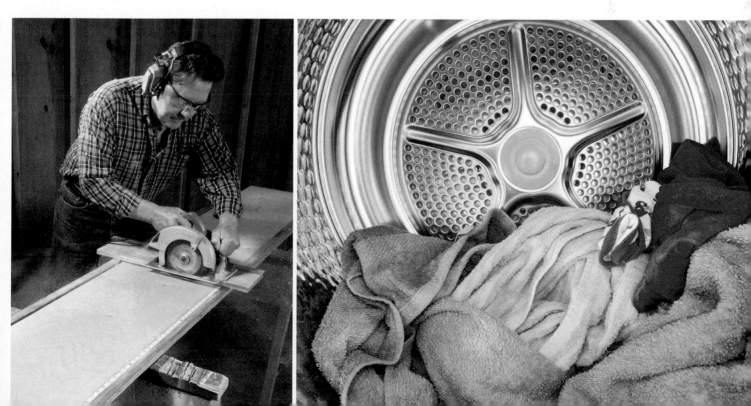

Wire Shelving Made Easier

Make hanging a new closet a lot more doable with these simple tips from one of our pros.

Wire shelving is popular because of its price, flexibility and ease of installation. Wire shelving can be designed to meet almost any need at a fraction of the cost of a custom built-in system. And while installing wire shelving isn't quite a no-brainer, you don't need to be a master carpenter or own a fully equipped cabinet shop to get it done. We picked the brain of a pro for this advice to help you on your next installation.

A

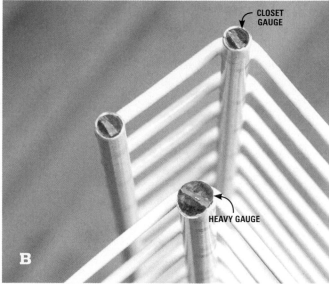

CLOSET GAUGE

HEAVY GAUGE

B

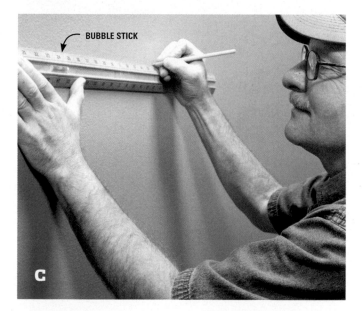

BUBBLE STICK

C

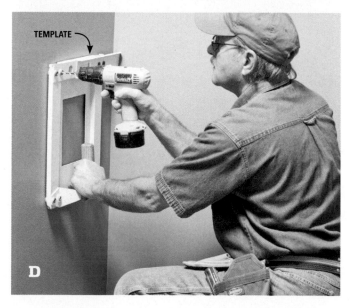

TEMPLATE

D

A. BUY EXTRA PIECES

Even if you're just planning to build one closet shelf, have extra parts on hand. It takes a lot less time to return a few wall clips than it does to stop working to make a special trip to the store for just one. And plans change, so if you or your customers decide to add a section of shelving, you'll be prepared.

B. LEAVE THE HEAVY STUFF FOR THE GARAGE

We worked with ClosetMaid's standard wire shelving, sold at home centers. Most manufacturers make a heavier-duty product for garage storage, but the regular stuff is plenty strong for the average bedroom or hall closet. However, if your customer's closet is going to store a bowling ball collection, you may want to consider upgrading. The materials for the closet shown here (approximately 22 ft. of shelving and rod) cost about $150.

C. LAY IT OUT WITH A BUBBLE STICK

We used a bubble stick rather than a level. A bubble stick is like a ruler and a level rolled into one. Holding a level against the wall with one hand can be frustrating. Levels are rigid, and they pivot out of place when resting on a stud that's bowed out a bit. A bubble stick has a little flex, so it can ride the imperfections of the wall yet still deliver a straight line.

D. USE A TEMPLATE ON THE END BRACKETS

Our first template was nothing more than a 1x3 with a couple of holes drilled in it. We rested a torpedo level on top of the board and marked the end bracket locations with a pencil. The template used here has a built-in level and allows you to drill the holes without marking them first. At $190, this is for those who do lots of closet shelving. If that's you, it's a great investment. You can order one from your local ClosetMaid dealer.

E. AVOID UPHEAVAL

Back wall clips are designed to support the shelf, but if there are a bunch of clothes hanging on the front of the shelf with nothing on top to weigh them down, the back of the shelf can lift. To keep the shelf in place, install a retaining clip in a stud near the middle of the shelf. One clip toward the middle of an 8-ft. shelf is plenty.

F. A BOLT CUTTER WORKS BEST

Cut your shelving with a bolt cutter. It's quick and easy, and it makes a clean cut. To make room for the cutter, use your feet to hold the shelving off the ground.

G. SPACE THE ANGLE BRACKETS EVENLY

Consider aesthetics when installing angle brackets. If a shelf needs only one bracket, find the stud closest to the center. If two or three brackets are required, try to space them evenly, making sure that at least one bracket toward the center is hitting a stud.

H. MEASURE AN INCH SHORT

When cutting the shelf, measure wall to wall, then subtract an inch. This allows for the thickness of the end brackets plus a little wiggle room. It's the top, thinner wire that actually supports the shelf, and one wire per end is enough. Cutting exact lengths will just earn you wall scratches and a trip back to the cutting station.

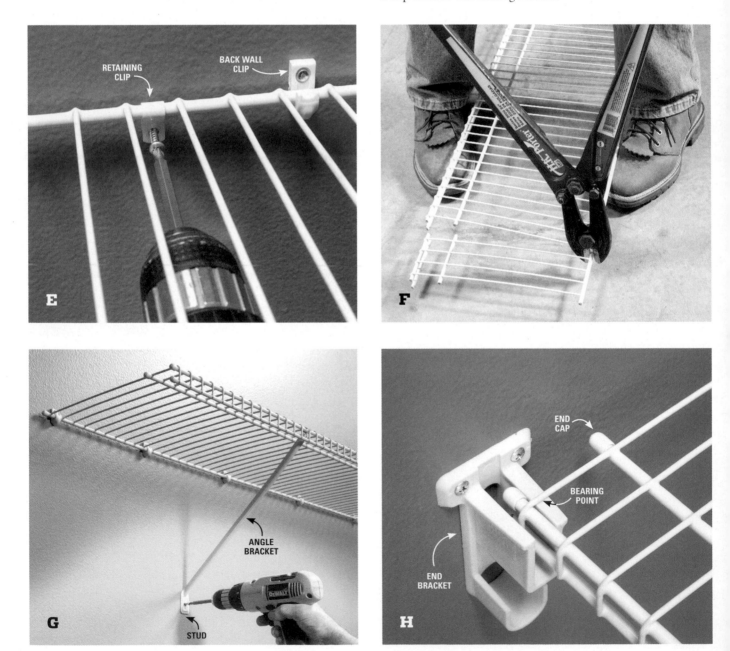

E RETAINING CLIP — BACK WALL CLIP

F

G ANGLE BRACKET — STUD

H END CAP — BEARING POINT — END BRACKET

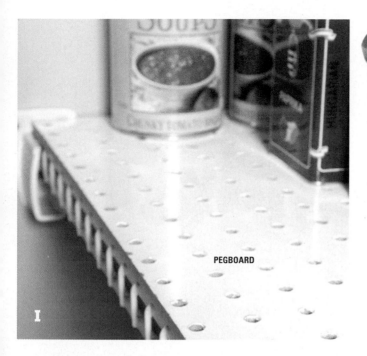

PEGBOARD

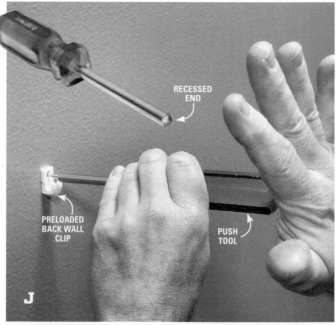

RECESSED END

PRELOADED BACK WALL CLIP

PUSH TOOL

I

J

I. PEGBOARD PREVENTS TIPPING

When installing wire shelving in pantries, cap the top of the shelves with white 1/4-in. pegboard. This stops the skinnier items from tipping over. Use white zip ties to hold the pegboard in place. A 4 x 8-ft. sheet costs around $20 at most home centers, which makes it an inexpensive option.

J. BACK WALL CLIPS DON'T NEED TO HIT STUDS

It may go against your every instinct, but hitting a stud when you're installing the back wall clips slows the process down and isn't necessary. After marking their locations, drill a 1/4-in. hole and pop the preloaded pushpin in with a push tool, which has a little indentation in the tip that won't slip off the pin when it's being set in the drywall. The occasional wall clips that do land on studs need to be fastened with a screw instead of a pin. You can order a push tool from your local ClosetMaid dealer. It should cost around $25. Visit *closetmaid.com* and use the dealer locator.

K. HANGER SLIDING FREEDOM

One common complaint about wire shelving is that it restricts the movement of the hangers because the hangers are stuck between the wires. That's why you may want to upgrade to a hanger rod. Most manufacturers make some version of one. A hanger rod allows clothes to be slid from one end of the closet to the other, even past an inside corner. This upgrade will add about 30% to the cost of the materials on a standard shelf design. Make sure the type of shelving you buy will work with the hanging rod hardware you plan to use.

CORNER HANGING BAR

BAR HANGER SUPPORT

K

Closet Smarts

Follow advice from organizational and design experts to stretch your closet's storage capacity.

A closet is a contradiction: the smallest space in the house, but the biggest repository of our stuff. It's the first place we look for a lost jacket or missing shoe but the last place we clean or organize. Eliminate excess, add organizational gear and use a few tried-and-true tricks to make your closets more personal and practical. We guarantee you'll never waste time hunting for that long-lost pair of jeans again.

BE SPACE SAVVY

The trick to optimizing storage is having the equipment to accommodate the things you own and the ability to look beyond the expected to find solutions. Organization experts share their favorite stowaway strategies and simple ways to extend storage.

Annex a Door The back of your closet door is vastly underused. "You can install hooks there for jackets, ties, belts, whatever," says Scott Roewer of Solutions by Scott. He also suggests hooking on an inexpensive over-the-door shoe rack with pockets. "They work great for storing brushes, hair ribbons, gloves, scarves, belts, socks, flashlights, even car keys," he says. Pegboard is another back-of-door option. Its hooks come in shapes and lengths to hang everything from purses and makeup mirrors to robes and pajamas.

Look Out Below Look for low-lying voids awaiting filling. Arrange shoes in clear, stackable containers beneath hanging clothes. Tuck pretty bins for holding sweaters or boxes for holding hats under a console table or long-legged chair. Fill under-the-bed storage containers or canvas storage bags with out-of-season clothing or bulky blankets and stow them under your bed.

Free Up Shelf Space Hang compartmentalized or shelved storage bags (generally made with canvas sides) on a closet rod to hold in-season sweaters, linens, casual clothing, shoes or hats. This will leave a closet's upper shelves open for storing out-of-season garments.

Corral Sweaters Think boxes, not loose stacks. Stacked sweaters can slide to take over a shelf. Instead, place them in boxes or bins designed to fit on 12- or 16-inch-deep shelves.

Finely Furnish Amplify your storage capacity with freestanding wardrobes or antique armoires. Move in sideboards and china cabinets to store jewelry or sweaters. Place bookcases with shelves deep enough for boxes of shoes and clothing near your closet, dressing area or bathroom.

MEASURE TWICE, INSTALL ONCE

Before purchasing a closet system, take accurate measurements and sketch out a plan. The folks at ClosetMaid, a supplier of closet and shelving systems, share a few considerations and tips.

First, use a measuring tape to measure the length of the walls and the closet's ceiling height. Measure the width of walk-in closets and the depth of reach-in closets. These dimensions will affect the depth of shelving you can use, the amount of shelving and hardware you will need and the options you can add to a basic configuration.

Ceiling height also affects shelving's vertical placement. Typical shelf or rod heights are 70 in. from the floor for long hanging space and 84 in. and 42 in. from the floor for double or short hanging space. Low ceilings will affect shelf or rod placement. (An easy way to determine shelf or rod height is to use an assembled closet-system support pole as a guide.)

You can also determine the amount of long and double hanging storage you'll need by measuring the space you're currently using to store long and short garments.

Unlike dresser drawers, shelves keep things in plain sight, which eliminates digging through neatly folded clothing.

MAKE OVER A CLOSET

Consider installing a closet system that can be customized to meet your storage needs. You can configure and install a basic closet system in a weekend. Wire systems are less expensive and more easily customized than solid-wood systems. You can buy a complete wire closet setup with an array of shelves, drawers and hanging bars for around $150.

Easy installation and virtually unlimited accessories make wire setups a popular option, but these utilitarian systems aren't as aesthetically pleasing as their wooden counterparts. Wooden closet systems look sophisticated and substantial, but can cost 10 times as much as wire. Wood systems are heavy, which makes them more challenging to install and more difficult to change. Consider installing a simple wooden closet setup and supplementing it with wire closet accessories and/or stacked boxes, bins or hanging bags.

DIG IN!

Follow our three-step plan—in a weekend or over several weeks—to minimize clutter while maximizing utility.

1. Empty It You can't organize your closet when it's filled to the brim. So empty it—completely or by clearing out one section or wall at a time. This allows you to look at available space and gives you a chance to clean your closet and its fittings. Most important, once your stuff is spread on the floor or bed, it's easier to tackle the next two steps.

2. Prune Possessions Once or twice a year, do a little weeding and pruning, suggests organizing expert Harriet Schechter, author of *Let Go of Clutter*. If you can't remember the last time you wore or used an item, store it or give it away. Do likewise with "someday" items, such as clothes that you hope you'll fit into, accessories that might be fashionable again, and items in need of repair or alterations.

3. Organize Precisely "Closets are like puzzles: If you want to solve the puzzle, find a place for every piece," says Roewer. Divide your closet however you like, but designate spaces for specific items.

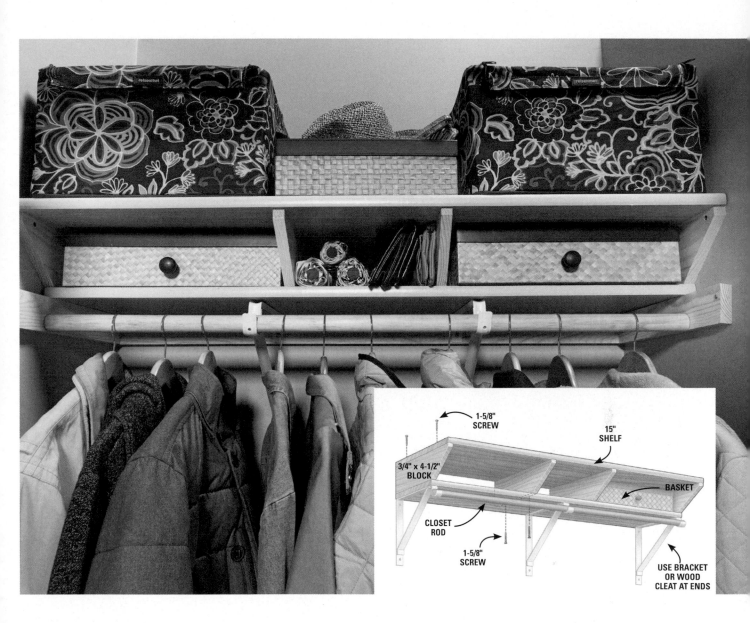

Diagram labels:
- 1-5/8" SCREW
- 15" SHELF
- 3/4" x 4-1/2" BLOCK
- BASKET
- CLOSET ROD
- 1-5/8" SCREW
- USE BRACKET OR WOOD CLEAT AT ENDS

Twin Closet Shelves

If one closet shelf is good, two must be better.

Tossing a hat onto the closet shelf, you might realize there's actually a whole lot of unused real estate up there. It made our experts think that if one shelf is good, two would be better. And the upper shelf could be 15 in. deep instead of 12 in. because there's no closet rod hanging out below. The deep baskets (we bought these at Michaels; *michaels.com*) help with the organization; cabinet knobs make for easier access. We show a two-tier shelf; you can install three if your closets (and you) are tall enough.

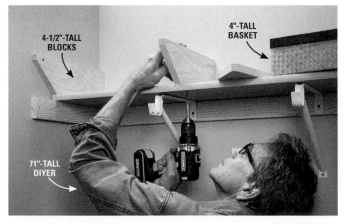

Labels:
- 4-1/2"-TALL BLOCKS
- 4"-TALL BASKET
- 71"-TALL DIYER

Secure blocking to the existing shelf. Buy your baskets, then cut spacer blocks 1/2 in. wider than the baskets are tall. Cut the ends of the blocks at an angle to accommodate the wider top shelf. Screw blocks to the bottom shelf, spacing them 1/2 in. farther apart than the baskets are wide. Then install and secure the top shelf.

Transform a Closet on Your Own

Cancel that appointment with the custom closet company. For better results that cost a whole lot less, follow these expert-approved steps.

Do you have closet envy? Turn on any home makeover show or glance at an advertisement for a fancy closet company, and you likely will. Everything is just so neat and perfect and, well, organized.

Of course, enlisting a custom closet company to remodel your space can cost big bucks (or at least bigger bucks than

you may have right now). But creating the closet of your dreams doesn't have to be out of reach—not if you know a few pro tips and pick up a few essential organizing items.

As a professional organizer and the author of *Keep This, Toss That*, Jamie Novak can give you the inside track to closet-organizing bliss. The good news? It won't cost you a bundle. The even better news? This expert-assisted DIY project is a lot easier than you think.

Here's exactly what Novak would do to your closet to maximize your space, store your items in a way that makes sense, and keep everything clean and organized for the long haul. So let's get the closet transformation underway! When you're done, you can try these organizing tips for the rest of your home.

GET YOUR SHOES OFF THE FLOOR

Shoes are practically impossible to identify when they're heaped on top of one another on the closet floor. Plus, it's dusty down there and not well lit, and it's all too easy for shoes to get scratched.

Add cubbies as convenient places to stick everyday athletic sneakers and other frequently worn shoes. Store pairs that you don't wear as often in clear, stackable, drop-front boxes, which allow you to reach the pair you want without unstacking the boxes. They make life easier and keep your closet so much neater.

Save even more space by storing shoes as the experts do—heel to toe, instead of side by side.

DESIGNATE A TREASURE BOX

From a concert T-shirt to your favorite worn-out hat, some clothing evokes fond memories. Although you likely won't wear these pieces again, you're not ready to say goodbye. That's where a treasure box comes in.

Instead of letting mementos get in the way when you're trying to get dressed every day, tuck them into a box specially set aside for this purpose. Then you can take a walk down memory lane any time you like.

SWITCH TO SLIM HANGERS

Mismatched hangers make your closet look messy. Stop using the random hangers you've collected over the years and instead swap in a set of slim hangers to give your closet a boutique look. And because slim hangers are thinner than typical hangers, you'll also save space.

Hang the clothes you reach for most often in the front and center. Infrequently used clothing, like out-of-season and occasion-specific items, can go farther back. And here's another pro tip: If you run out of hangers, don't buy more—free up a few by giving away clothes that no longer fit or that you no longer love.

DIVIDE THE ROD

Keeping your hanging clothes categorized by season, style and color is a whole lot easier with rod dividers. Just like the ones you find in boutiques that divide clothes by their size, these write-on dividers allow you to label your different sections.

Follow this method for organizing bliss: First, hang tops from the shortest to the longest sleeve length, and bottoms from the shortest to the longest hem length. Then, within each category, arrange clothes by the color of the rainbow. Start with dark shades followed by purples, blues and greens. Then go into yellows, oranges, reds and whites. You'll feel happy seeing your clothes all neatly lined up.

SHELVE SOME OF THOSE CLOTHES

Not all clothes are meant to be hung up. In fact, most sweaters are best folded; otherwise, they can get stretched out. Adding in a hanging shelf with drawers gives you space for folded sweaters and more.

It's also a smart spot to stash loungewear and workout clothes. By grouping all workout gear in one spot, it's easy to grab and go when you're in the mood to exercise.

INCLUDE SHELF DIVIDERS FOR EASE

Slipping on shelf dividers allows you to stack higher on a shelf without the risk of the pile toppling over. Slim dividers create barriers, sectioning off one large space into several smaller and more functional ones.

In addition to using shelf dividers for sweaters and linens, you can also line up bulky accessories, such as handbags, between the dividers. Before stacking and storing sweaters, check to see if they need to be refreshed.

ADD A CATCHALL FOR LITTLE STUFF

Without a place to drop those packets with an extra button that come with new clothes, you can end up with them littering the floor of the closet. Keep small stuff together

in a catchall bag. It's perfect for those button packets and a small sewing kit with tiny scissors for clipping off loose threads and tags. You can even toss in a few safety pins for last-minute fashion emergencies and some fashion tape to avoid a mishap. One more thing you can put in there? A lint roller.

USE A DOUBLE-HANG CLOSET ROD

Rethink that single rod. Adding a second closet rod instantly doubles your available hanging space. While you could install a traditional rod, a much easier solution is hanging a bar doubler—no hardware necessary! It attaches to your existing rod and you can hang clothes on it immediately. Use the upper bar for tops and the lower one for skirts and pants.

You can ruin your clothes without realizing it by jamming too many of them into a closet.

LABEL EVERYTHING

Labels make it clear what belongs where, and they also inspire you to take the extra (often ignored) step of putting things away in the right place. Plus, they let you easily know what you've stored in containers. You think you'll remember a season from now, but you most likely won't.

Apply labels to bins, even clear ones, as well as on the edges of shelves, so all it takes is a glance to know what goes where.

ADD HOOKS

Stick-up hooks are one of the easiest ways to transform your clothes closet. They make the perfect storage spot for tote bags and statement necklaces. Plus, a hook can hold worn-once jeans that are too dirty to put away but too clean to launder. But the best use of a hook may be to hold empty clothes hangers so they don't get lost between clothes.

STICK LIGHTS ONTO THE CLOSET WALLS

Illuminating dark spaces, such as the floor or the far back of the closet, makes it much easier to see what's stored there. This simple addition brightens the whole closet and means you'll no longer struggle to tell navy and black clothing apart.

Skip the expensive electrician visit to run wiring and instead opt for battery-operated LED lights. If you go with the motion-activated design, you'll never even have to remember to turn them off. Now that you can see all your clothes, you can better organize your closet.

USE THE BACK OF THE CLOSET DOOR

Take advantage of all the usable storage space you have—including the spot behind the door. Adding a

behind-the-door organizer gives you a convenient place to stick clutches, scarves, hats and other accessories.

If your door lacks the clearance to hang the organizer from hooks over the door, hang it from peel-and-stick hooks directly on the door.

GET CLOTHES YOU NO LONGER WANT OUT OF THE CLOSET

Remove the items that don't belong in your closet. Clothes and shoes that need to go somewhere else—like to the dry cleaner, back to the store or to a donation location—belong in your car. Organize these items in a set of foldable, reusable bags, dedicating one for each category.

Fill the bags and get them to the car. When you're done, simply roll the bags into a tiny pouch (many reusable bags have one attached).

SLIDE IN A STEP STOOL

No more tossing stuff up to that top shelf and hoping it doesn't fall back down. Give yourself quick access to the whole closet by adding a step stool. That extra lift makes it easier to reach those less accessible spots. To save space, pick a stool with a slim profile. And make sure to choose a bold color that stands out so you can spot it quickly.

STICK TO A FEW IMPORTANT RULES TO MAINTAIN A TIDY CLOSET

Now that you've transformed your basic closet into the closet of your dreams, keep it mess-free by giving it a daily tidy. Pull out any items you won't need until next season and store them in convenient see-through bins.

Also make sure to schedule a time to sort through things at the end of every season. That's when you can reconsider if you should keep the clothing you didn't wear and the shoes that never left their boxes. Remember: Fashions fade fast, so periodically donate super trendy items that won't stand the test of time.

TWO-PART EPOXY

REPLACEMENT HARDWARE

Bi-Folding Door
Replacement Hardware

Bi-fold door
top pivot and guide
Puertas de dos dobladuras:
Punto del eje y guía superiores
Pivot and guide supérieurs
de porte pliante à deux
battants

N-7266

QTY / PZ / QTE: 2

MASKING TAPE

PIVOT SLEEVE

TWO-PART EPOXY

LOCTITE EPOXY QUICKSET

Glue in the new pivot. If the hole that holds the pivot is stripped out, fill it with epoxy. A strip of masking tape keeps the epoxy out of the end of the pivot sleeve.

Worn Out Bifold Door?

One common problem with bifold doors is the hardware—it wears out. This is simple and inexpensive to fix. You can buy new pivots and rollers for $5 to $10, and installing the new hardware is straightforward enough. Sometimes the particleboard that the hardware fits into gets stripped out from years of use. If this is the case, simply fill the hole with a quick-set, two-part epoxy before installing the new hardware. Let the epoxy set up for a minute or two. If you try to apply it when it's too runny, the epoxy will run right down through the hole or make a big mess on the floor.

Here's one important caveat: When you push the new hardware into the hole, the epoxy may gum up the works, preventing the new roller or pivot from compressing, which is necessary to reinstall the door. Wrap the bottom side of the new hardware with masking tape to prevent this.

Bifold Doorknob Fix

You're supposed to mount hollow-core bifold doorknobs along the edge closest to the hinge, because that area is reinforced with solid wood. But that's also a "pinch zone," so many people mount the knobs in the middle of the hollow section. Eventually the screw head pulls through the thin veneer and the knob dangles out the front side. The fix is easy. Just buy a 3/16 x 1-in. fender washer (about 15¢) at any hardware store. Remove the screw. Slide the washer down to the screw head and reinstall.

GOUGED-OUT HOLE

FENDER WASHER

Endless combinations! Here's the key to this whole system: The large box is twice as tall as the small box, and the height of each box is equal to twice its width. That means you can combine them in dozens of configurations. For more versatility, you can drill holes and add adjustable shelf supports to any of the boxes.

An Organized Closet

Make easy-to-build boxes that can suit any situation.

Are you getting the bug to organize your closets? Don't get dizzy wading through websites and visiting stores. (There's a shelf for this, a rack for that…) We put pencil to paper and devised a simpler system that is easy to build, easy to customize and a money-saver besides. You'll be so happy with it that you may want to used the same system in your home office, too.

MATERIALS AND TOOLS

We used 3/4-in. birch plywood because it's strong and thick enough to accept screws. It also finishes well, and the simple grain and warm color look good with just about any decor.

Get a 4 x 8-ft. sheet. Here's a rule of thumb for estimating the plywood you'll need: One sheet will get you two large boxes or four small boxes, plus some leftover parts. If you don't have a pickup truck, have the plywood ripped into roughly 16-in.-wide pieces at the home center and then rip the pieces to 15 in. at home.

Before you start cutting up box parts, check the thickness of your plywood. Most 3/4-in. plywood is actually 23/32 in. thick, and the measurements given in the Cutting Lists (p. 52) are based on that. If your plywood is thicker or thinner, you'll have to adjust your box part sizes. The measurements given also account for the typical thickness of iron-on edge band.

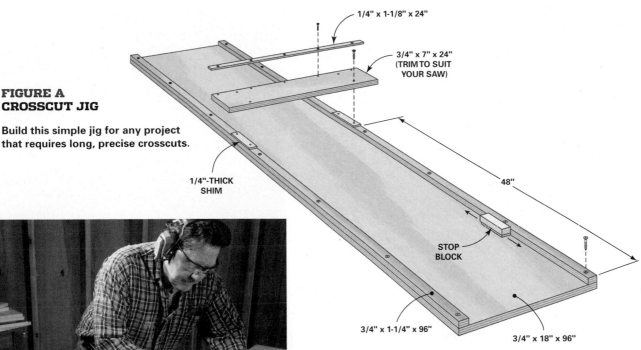

1/4" x 1-1/8" x 24"

3/4" x 7" x 24"
(TRIM TO SUIT
YOUR SAW)

**FIGURE A
CROSSCUT JIG**

Build this simple jig for any project
that requires long, precise crosscuts.

1/4"-THICK
SHIM

48"

STOP
BLOCK

3/4" x 1-1/4" x 96"

3/4" x 18" x 96"

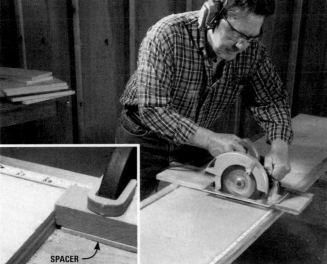

SPACER

1 Cut a bunch of box parts. This simple jig lets you
churn out precise, identical box parts fast. Raise the
stop block on a 1/4-in. spacer so dust buildup doesn't
throw off the accuracy.

IRON-ON
EDGE
BANDING

2 Edge-band the parts. Cover the visible edges with
iron-on edge band. Band only the front edges of the
short parts (B, E). On the long parts (A, D), band three edges.

A SIMPLE JIG FOR
PERFECT CROSSCUTS

To make this closet system work, you need to cut lots of box
parts to exact, identical lengths. This plywood jig makes that
foolproof. Build the jig and you'll find lots of other uses for
it, such as building bookcases, cabinets or shelves.

If your saw is out of whack, you won't get accurate cuts.
So do a quick inspection: Measure from the front and back
of the blade to the edge of the saw's shoe to make sure the
blade runs parallel to the shoe. Then grab a square and
make sure the blade is set at 90 degrees to the shoe. Install
a 40-tooth carbide blade for clean cuts.

Take your time when you build and install the carriage
assembly. First, screw the guide to the carriage. Then run
your saw along the guide—that will trim the carriage to
suit your saw. When you mount the carriage on the rails,
use a framing square to make sure the carriage is perfectly
perpendicular to the rails. We added a stick-on measuring
tape to our jig. One last note: Be sure to set the saw depth
so it just grazes the jig's base. If you set the saw too deep,
you'll cut your new jig in half.

BAND, BISCUIT AND ASSEMBLE

If you haven't edge-banded plywood before **(Photo 2)**,
don't be intimidated; it's a skill you can master in a few
minutes. For a crash course, go to *familyhandyman.com* and
search for "edge band." You could glue and screw the boxes
together, but we used biscuits to avoid exposed screw heads
(Photo 3). For information on using a biscuit joiner, go to
familyhandyman.com and search for "biscuit." Glue and clamp

FIGURE B
LARGE CLOSET BOX

Overall dimensions:
19-1/2" x 39" x 15"

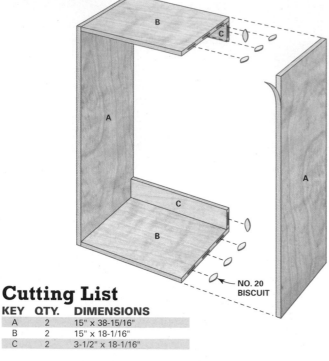

NO. 20
BISCUIT

Cutting List

KEY	QTY.	DIMENSIONS
A	2	15" x 38-15/16"
B	2	15" x 18-1/16"
C	2	3-1/2" x 18-1/16"

FIGURE C
SMALL CLOSET BOX

Overall dimensions:
9-3/4" x 19-1/2" x 15"

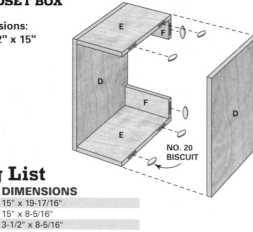

NO. 20
BISCUIT

Cutting List

KEY	QTY.	DIMENSIONS
D	2	15" x 19-17/16"
E	2	15" x 8-5/16"
F	2	3-1/2" x 8-5/16"

SUPPORT
BOARD

3 Cut the biscuit slots. Clamp a support board flush with the edge to keep the biscuit joiner from rocking as you cut.

each box together **(Photo 4)** with a clamp at each corner and check the box with a framing square. It should automatically square itself if you've made accurate square cuts. Let the glue set for at least an hour before removing the clamps.

FINISH AND INSTALL

Finishing the boxes could be frustrating: Birch tends to get blotchy when stained, and brushing on a clear finish inside boxes is slow, fussy work. We sidestepped both problems by applying two coats of Watco Golden Oak finish. It's a

Materials List

ITEM
3/4" plywood
No. 20 biscuits
Iron-on edge band
M4 x 35mm Female Connecting Sleeve 1-3/8"
M4 x 15mm Male Connecting Screws

SLEEVE CONNECTORS

4 **Assemble boxes.** A cheap disposable paintbrush makes a good spreader. Keep a damp rag handy to wipe off excess glue.

5 **Join the boxes.** Gang the boxes together with screws or special sleeve connectors at the front and back.

penetrating oil that leaves only a light film on the surface, so you don't have to worry about brush marks. And the light color minimizes blotching. Minwax Wipe-On Poly would work well too. Use a brush to apply either finish and then wipe it with a lint-free cloth.

Once the finish is dry, join the boxes together **(Photo 5)**. We used sleeve connectors (see the Materials List) because they look a lot better than exposed screws. Just remember to use a Pozidriv screw tip to tighten the connectors. It may look like a Phillips, but it's slightly different. Pozidriv screw tips are available at home centers and hardware stores. You'll also need a 3/16-in. or 5 mm drill bit.

To simplify mounting the boxes to the closet wall, install a cleat **(Photo 6)** on the wall studs about 8 in. from the floor. The 8-in. elevation keeps the boxes off the floor and provides usable space below. Make the support from long plywood scraps. The elevated ledge will support the assemblies while you get them placed and then screwed to the wall studs. Drive 2-1/2-in. screws through the box backs and the studs. If a box doesn't land on studs, use drywall anchors such as those from E-Z Ancors.

Once you have all the boxes secured to the wall, you can add closet rods (centered about 11-1/2 in. from the back wall) and other organizers, like tie racks and belt hangers, and screw them directly into the 3/4-in. plywood construction.

6 **Support the units with a cleat.** A level cleat screwed to studs makes aligning and installing the box units a lot easier. Assemble the cleat from leftover plywood scraps.

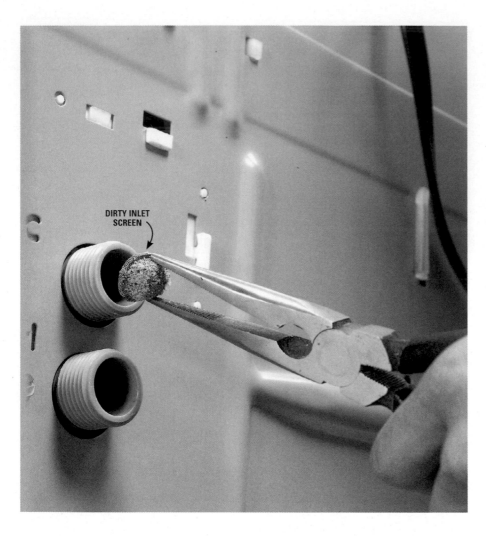

DIRTY INLET
SCREEN

Slow-Filling Washer

The inlet screens inside the washing machine supply connections can become clogged. First, turn off the water to the machine, then disconnect the supply hoses and gently remove the inlet screens from the machine with needle-nose pliers. Either clean them or replace with new screens. Also check the inlet screens in your supply hoses.

Dryer Won't Start

When people slam the dryer door, it can bend the plunger. Open the door and inspect the plunger. If it's bent, adjust it until it's straight and the door will close properly.

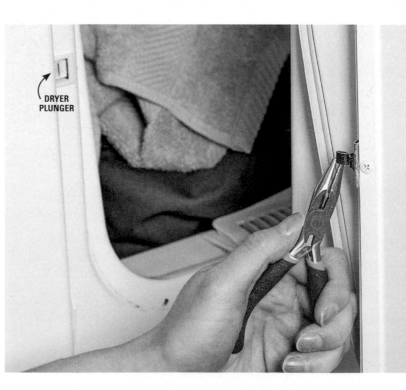

DRYER PLUNGER

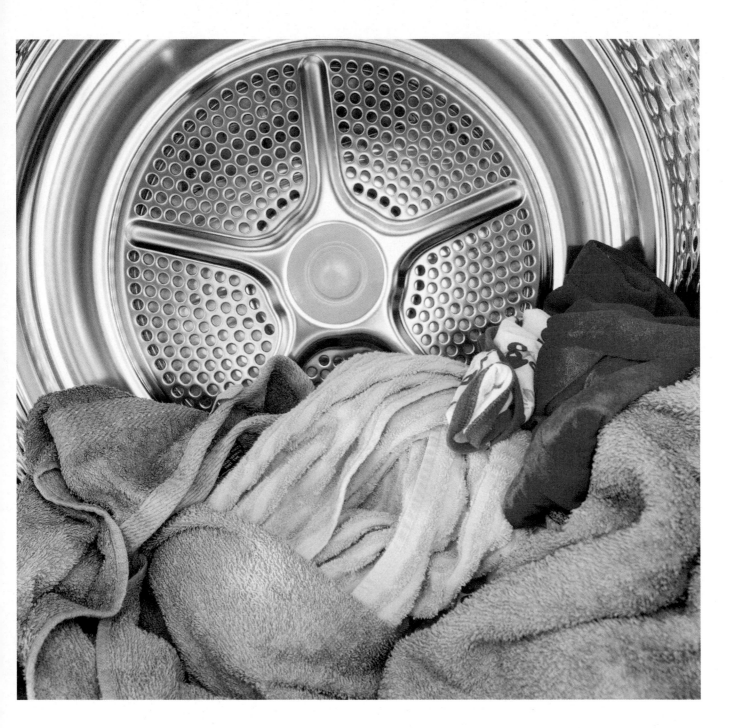

Expert Tips for Washing Your Clothes

Gain some super know-how to execute this common household task.

The dirty laundry basket never seems to be empty. You wash, you dry, you iron or fold, and then you do it all over again. But are you washing your clothes the right way?

Here are 13 laundry tips you might not know for the best way to wash clothes.

1. USE ALUMINUM FOIL

If you're out of dryer sheets, throw a ball of aluminum foil in your dyer. The aluminum will fight static buildup and help keep your clothing separated.

2. FREEZE YOUR JEANS

If you like to wear your jeans more than once between washings, stick them in the freezer between wears. The frigid air will kill bacteria that can cause odor.

3. CHECK THE TEMPERATURE

Use cold water for dark colors that tend to bleed and for delicate fabrics that are prone to shrinking. Cold water is also an eco-friendly choice that will save you money on your energy bill. Warm water is best for synthetic fibers and for jeans. Use hot water for whites, cloth diapers, bedding and towels.

4. UNSHRINK CLOTHES

Did your favorite T-shirt shrink? Soak the shrunken clothing item in lukewarm water with a splash of baby shampoo. This will allow the fibers to relax, allowing you to stretch it back out.

5. USE LESS DETERGENT

Using too much detergent can cause your clothes to remain dirty—since too much detergent causes an abundance of suds that can trap soil on your clothing. Instead, try using half the recommended amount of detergent and adjust from there.

6. USE A SALAD SPINNER

If you have some articles of clothing you don't want to put in the dryer, use a salad spinner to remove excess water. Then hang them on a rack to dry.

7. CHOOSE DETERGENTS WISELY

There are several recipes online for making your own laundry detergent, which can save you money. Store-bought detergents should be chosen carefully. If you have kids and need to fight tough stains, choose a detergent with a strong cleaning and stain-fighting ingredient such as OxiClean or bleach. For those with sensitive skin or sensitivities to fragrance, look for a formula that's unscented and free of dyes.

8. WASH BRIGHT COLORS WITH SALT

You can use salt to prevent colors from fading. Just toss a teaspoon of salt in with your dark clothes to help make the color last longer. Washing colored clothing inside out can also help maintain color.

9. SWEATERS SHOULD SKIP THE DRYER

Skip the dryer when laundering winter sweaters. Instead, dry them flat to help them maintain their shape.

10. SAVE DRYING TIME

When you're running short on drying time, throw a dry towel in with the load. The towel will absorb some of the moisture and help your clothes dry quicker.

11. REDUCE WRINKLES

To reduce wrinkles and the need to iron, use a dryer sheet and set your dyer to the lowest setting possible. As soon as the clothes are dry, remove them from the dryer and fold or hang them to keep them crisp.

12. TOP-LOADING OR FRONT-LOADING?

If you're in the market for a new washing machine, the options can be overwhelming. A top-loading machine with an agitator often costs less and has a faster cycle than a top-loading machine without an agitator (known as a high-efficiency machine). High-efficiency machines are better at cleaning and use less water than agitator models. Front-loading machines are more expensive, but they do a better job at cleaning than top-loaders and are gentler on clothing. However, front-loaders can take longer to complete a cycle than top-loaders. Do some research to find which model will work best for your needs.

13. DO CLEAN YOUR MACHINE

Your washing machine does need to be cleaned regularly. Every couple of months, set your washer to the largest load setting and hottest water temperature. Add a quart of white vinegar and a cup of baking soda and let the washer agitate for a minute. Then open the lid or pause the cycle and let the mixture sit for an hour. Scrub any parts, such as the lid, with a toothbrush to remove buildup. After an hour, let the cycle complete and run a second cycle on hot to remove any residue left behind.

Laundry Myths that Are Ruining Your Clothes

If you remember this advice, your clothes and appliances will thank you!

Doing laundry is always a learning experience. Should you wash your clothes in warm water? Do all-purpose cleaners work for all stains? Read on to hear from laundry experts on what you should (and shouldn't) be doing to your clothes.

1. MORE DETERGENT MEANS CLEANER CLOTHES

One popular myth you've probably heard is that using more detergent means cleaner clothes. The truth? It doesn't. "Using more detergent doesn't make it work extra hard. Instead, it can leave residue on your clothes," says Brian Sansoni, senior vice president for communications at the American Cleaning Institute. "You'll probably just need to wash them again, and over time these extra washings can make them wear out faster. Check the detergent label for how much detergent to use for your size load and washer, especially since many detergents these days are concentrated."

2. THE HOTTER THE WATER, THE BETTER THE CLEANING POWER

Surely, the temperature of the water has a profound effect. But hot water may not have as much of an impact as you might think. "Hot water won't necessarily get clothes

cleaner," Sansoni says. "In fact, it can damage some fabrics or cause some stains to become permanent instead of being removed. This is the case of a myth that may have been true in the past, but detergents these days have been designed to work just as well, if not better, in cold water. Always follow the fabric care label."

3. THE MORE DRYER SHEETS, THE BETTER

Sometimes too much of a good thing can actually be, well, a bad thing. "There is such a thing as too many dryer sheets," says Laura Johnson, a research and development rep at LG Electronics. "Overuse of dryer sheets can reduce the efficiency of your machine by leaving behind a sweet-smelling residue and congesting your lint screen."

4. WASH CLOTHES AFTER EVERY WEAR

Sometimes, you may not need to wash your clothes every single time you wear them. "If you throw clothes in the hamper to be washed after every wear, you may be overwashing some items and causing them to wear out prematurely," Sansoni says. "Unless there's a stain, it may not need to be washed."

5. OVERLOADING YOUR WASHER WITH BULKY ITEMS CAN DAMAGE YOUR MACHINE

"Any larger items must be placed in the washer in a balanced manner to prevent laundry casualties," explains Johnson.

6. YOU CAN IGNORE THE FABRIC CARE LABEL

As with everything, always read the instructions—and that includes the fabric care label. "There are times when it's tempting to throw all the clothes in the washer and be done with it," Sansoni says. "However, every piece of commercial clothing has a tag with care instructions from the manufacturer designed to keep the item looking its best. Learn what the symbols mean and follow those instructions to extend the life of your favorite clothes." (For a guide to washing symbols, see pages 66 and 67.)

7. ALL STAINS ARE CREATED EQUAL

If you think you can use the same laundry detergent for coffee stains as baby formula, you might need to rethink that plan. The stain's type actually determines how you can remove it, according to the laundry experts at Carbona, who take stain removal seriously. Carbona has a collection of nine stain removers called Stain Devils that are specially formulated to remove tough stains every time.

8. YOU CAN USE HAND SOAP TO THOROUGHLY WASH CLOTHES

It's happened to the best of us. You put in a load of laundry and then realize that you're out of laundry detergent. As a last resort, would hand soap do the job? "While hand soap will, to some extent, clean your clothes, it will not do an effective job, since soap for the body has more gentle chemicals," says Leanne Stapf, chief operating officer of The Cleaning Authority. "It is best to use items that have the right amount of stronger chemicals to provide a deep clean."

9. YOU CAN ONLY HAND-WASH YOUR BRAS

Who has hand-washed their bras and then found out there's an easier way to wash them? "There is a myth that you can only hand-wash your bras, which is not true," says Jené Luciani Sena, an intimate apparel and lifestyle influencer. "You can put them in a mesh garment bag, zip it up and put on a cool-water gentle cycle with a gentle detergent in the washing machine."

10. USING HAIRSPRAY TO REMOVE CLOTH STAINS

"This is untrue of course," says Robert Johnson, founder of Sawinery. "Hairspray worsens stains, especially the ink ones by spreading them out more. Instead, blot some water to the stain. And to make it more effective, use a versatile stain remover powder."

11. FILLING THE MACHINE CONSERVES WATER AND ENERGY

What is a full machine, anyway? "Your definition of a full machine may be different from the manufacturer's definition," says *USInsuranceAgents.com* insurance expert Melanie Musson. "Washing machines are designed to work optimally at two-thirds full, maximum. If you pack the machine to the top, the detergent won't be able to spread around and clean all the clothes and you'll have to wash them again, saving neither water nor energy."

12. VISIBLE STAINS ARE THE ONLY ONES TO WORRY ABOUT ON CLOTHES

You might think that a shirt is dirty when you see a stain, but there's a lot more than meets the eye. "Your clothes might be dirtier than you think," says Jennifer Ahoni, a senior scientist for Tide. "In fact, only 30% of the soils in your laundry are visible—things like food, dirt and grass stains. The other 70% include invisible 'body soils' like sweat and body oils, which if not removed by a deep-cleaning laundry detergent will build up over time and cause odors, dinginess and dullness. A deep clean provides removal of both visible and invisible dirt."

13. YOU NEED TO SORT LAUNDRY ONLY BY COLORS

While sorting by colors is always a good idea, you also need to consider sorting by fabric type. "Heavier fabrics such as denim can damage finer and more delicate fabrics," says Ahoni. "Make sure to always check the care label for the best guidance on washing and for recommendations on washing with other fabrics."

14. YOU SHOULD FASTEN BUTTONS BEFORE WASHING

How many times have you buttoned up your shirt before placing it in the washer? In fact, you may not need to do this at all. "Fastening buttons before washing can lead to the buttons falling off due to the stress the washing machine puts on the clothes," Musson says. "It can also lead to the article of clothing getting stretched out because of the uneven pressure on the cloth."

14 Things that Should Never End Up in the Dryer

You'll be thankful for these expert "words to the wise" to prevent problems.

If you're short on time and in a rush, it's easy to just throw everything from the washer into the dryer and call it a day—but there can be major consequences for some of your clothing if you do that. So, we reached out to dryer experts to find out exactly what should never, ever end up in a dryer. And trust us, it's worth taking an extra minute to make sure your machine is free of these 14 things.

1. FLAMMABLE STAINS

According to the National Fire Protection Association, between 2010 and 2014, U.S. municipal fire departments responded to almost 16,000 fires that involved dryers and washing machines. And dryers were the culprit of 92% of them. While it might seem obvious to never put anything that could catch on fire in your dryer, it's easy to just toss those pants you spilled gas on in the dryer without thinking. "Washing clothes will not completely remove oil residues," says Tim Adkisson, Director of Product Engineering at Sears Home Services. "Failure to obey this warning can result in fire, explosion or death."

2. ACTIVEWEAR

While tossing your activewear into the dryer won't damage the machine itself, it could ruin your clothing. Since most activewear is sweat-wicking or even coated to protect from the sun's rays, it's definitely not dryer-friendly. "Drying your activewear in the dryer and exposing it to all that high heat and friction can be damaging to the functional components that these technical fabrics are developed for," says Brit Turner, cofounder of Fit Atelier. "The heat can also wear away any elastic properties that your garments may contain and can weaken the material—leading to tears, holes, picks and runs." Instead, Turner suggests hanging or laying your activewear flat to dry after washing it in a cold or delicate washing cycle.

3. DRYER SHEETS

Yes, you read that right. While dryer sheets might be intended to be used, well, in the dryer, that doesn't mean they're good for your health. "They are bad for your respiratory system, your skin and, moreover, the environment," says Elizabeth Trattner A.P. DOM, a doctor of Chinese and integrative medicine. "They are toxic and cause long-term health hazards. It is worth throwing them out and trading them in for a healthier option, like wool dryer balls scented with essential oils."

4. LINGERIE

As anyone who has tossed lingerie in the dryer might know, this greatly reduces its lifespan. "Do not put a good investment in the dryer. Heat will shorten the lifespan of a bra and wear down the latex, lace and other fabric in it," according to Dr. Trattner. "Treat your undergarments with respect. Wash bras in special lingerie bags, then remove them from the washing machine and hang them up to dry. Or better yet, hand-wash them."

5. SANDY TOWELS AND BEACHWEAR

Warm sand might be nice to sit down and relax in when you're at the beach, but it can be a pretty pesky nuisance if it ends up in your dryer. "Sand can get trapped between gaps in the drum," says James Peters, Kenmore Laundry Product Manager. "This adds an irritating sound when drying and can damage the dryer over time."

6. PET HAIR

Anyone who has a furry friend at home knows just how messy things can get—the hair ends up everywhere. But one place where it should never, ever end up is in the dryer. If the hair builds up over time, it could begin combining with lint and debris around it, especially if the lint screen isn't emptied before every load. "Excess dryer lint is a major fire hazard, can cause your dryer to become damaged and also reduces the efficiency of your dryer," says Dave Lavalle, founder of Dryer Vent Wizard and a specialist in dryer vent repair, cleaning and maintenance. "To avoid a possible fire sparking, make sure to keep the areas around your dryer, including underneath and behind it, free of extra pet hair, lint and debris that might build up."

7. CHEWING GUM

While you're probably not actively trying to dry your chewing gum, it does occasionally get thrown in there by accident. And unfortunately, by the time you notice, the damage has probably already been done. "Gum can have lasting damage if left in the pockets of your clothes," says Josh Matteson, a writer for Lula, a company offering on-demand home services. "It can either permanently stick itself to clothes or fall out of the pocket and stretch all over the wall of your dryer."

8. SPANDEX

If you've ever bought spandex leggings or yoga pants, you probably know that they can be pretty expensive. With that being said, if you toss them in the dryer, they probably won't ruin your machine itself—but there's a good chance they'll shrink a bit, which could be costly to replace. "[They should] be hung to dry to avoid shrinking," says Peters. "Although many people will also dry them with an air-dry cycle with good results."

9. FAUX LEATHER

According to *jsonline.com*, while some faux leather is actually washable, it should never be put in the dryer. "Heat melts plastic, ruining your garment and possibly your dryer. This obviously rules out ironing as well."

The same goes for dry-cleaning. Ultimately, air-drying your faux leather garments is definitely your best bet.

10. TIGHTS OR PANTYHOSE

If you've ever worn tights, you probably know how easy it is for them to rip and tear. And after a trip in the dryer, that little hole that wasn't noticeable before is probably running down the entire leg. The material your tights are made of might also cause them to shrink when exposed to high heat. "The best thing you can do is to air-dry them, but do NOT hang them! Hang-drying tights will stretch out the material and even potentially ruin them," says Caleb Backe, a health and wellness expert for Maple Holistics. "As an alternative, try rolling your freshly laundered tights into a dry towel and letting them dry overnight."

11. LACE

Lace is another delicate fabric that should never meet your dryer. In fact, according to *thelaundress.com*, you should really be avoiding machines altogether. Instead, lay your lace garment flat to dry so it doesn't lose its natural shape or damage the fabric.

12. ANYTHING EMBELLISHED

Unfortunately, you should probably find another way to dry your favorite sequined top. Sequins, gems, stones or whatever other items that embellish your garments can hook onto other items in the dryer, or even the dryer itself. This can potentially damage the garment and its surroundings. According to *goodhousekeeping.com*, "It's way easier to hang-dry [embellished garments] or—if the material is thin or delicate—lay them on a towel to air-dry."

13. SILK

According to *tide.com*, you should avoid both the washer and dryer when it comes to your silk garments. Instead of adding your delicate silk clothing to your dryer load, the website suggests laying it flat on a towel and rolling it up inside the towel to squeeze out excess moisture. Then hang up the garment or lay it flat to dry.

14. RUBBER-BACKED BATH MATS

Putting a rubber-backed bath mat in the dryer can end up being pretty messy. According to Peters, "The rubber can crumble and get caught in the dryer, which can cause a fire hazard."

8 Ways to Use Baking Soda in the Laundry Room

Want a cheap ingredient for whitening and brightening laundry, and eliminating odors and stains? Turn to good old reliable baking soda.

There's a secret weapon for your laundry room that you may have never thought about using. Baking soda, or sodium bicarbonate, has a multitude of uses beyond baking, such as personal health and hygiene and household chores.

When used as part of your laundry routine, it can help whiten and brighten clothes, eliminate stubborn odors and stamp out stains. Plus, it's one of the cheapest ingredients you can find to up your laundry game.

1. AS AN ODOR FIGHTER

Baking soda is alkaline, so it neutralizes acids—and many of the nastiest odors, such as sweat, urine and vomit, are acidic. If you're wondering how to get cat urine out of clothes, try baking soda. Leslie Reichert, who runs the Green Cleaning Coach website, suggests adding a few tablespoons of baking soda to your regular laundry soap to help remove odors. For really tough odors, soak the smelly item overnight in a solution of baking soda and water.

2. AS A STAIN REMOVER

According to baking soda manufacturer Arm & Hammer, baking soda and water are a potent duo for stain removal. Make a paste with 6 tablespoons of baking soda and 1/3 cup of warm water, rub it into the stain and let it do its thing. The baking soda will lift the stain out of the fibers. Discard the baking soda before you put the item in the washer. For oily stains, Reichert recommends sprinkling baking soda directly on the stain and letting it sit overnight before washing.

3. FOR EXTRA-CLEAN CLOTHES

A half-cup of baking soda added to a load of laundry will create a cleaning boost. "It will help lift dirt and grime from clothing," says Reichert. Don't put baking soda in your washer's detergent dispenser, however. Instead, sprinkle it into the empty drum of your washer, then add clothes and whatever detergent and fabric softeners you'd normally use.

4. AS AN ALTERNATIVE TO BLEACH

For whites and colors, baking soda does double duty. When added to the washer, it makes whites whiter and brightens colored items. It's a good substitute if you prefer not to use bleach. Or, for loads of white clothing, give bleach a boost by adding a half-cup of baking soda. It helps the bleach work better, cuts some of the "bleachy" smell and whitens whites.

5. TO SANITIZE NEW BABY CLOTHES

Plenty of parents are concerned about chemical finishes, such as starches and sizing, with which baby clothes might be treated. They don't want to take the chance that these will come into contact with their baby's skin.

Remove these components from new baby clothes by washing them by hand or in the washer with a solution of a half-cup baking soda and a mild detergent, like Ecos Hypoallergenic Laundry Detergent. If you wash by hand, be sure to thoroughly rinse the items so that no traces of detergent or baking soda remain.

6. AS AN UNSCENTED FABRIC SOFTENER

If you have a top-loading washer, you can use baking soda in place of fabric softener. It has the same softening effects without heavy perfumes or chemicals that might trigger allergies.

During the rinse cycle, when the washer is full of water, sprinkle a half-cup of baking soda into the water. It's not recommended that you put baking soda in the detergent dispensers of front- or top-loading washers. The baking soda can clump up and block the dispensers.

7. TO SAVE ON DETERGENT

Because baking soda gives detergent a boost, you can get by with using less detergent. Or you can forgo detergent altogether by adding a full cup of baking soda in its place. Not convinced? Try it on a load or two and see if you're satisfied with the results. If it works well enough for you, you've found a simple, eco-minded alternative to conventional laundry detergent!

8. TO CLEAN UP A LAUNDRY "OOPS"

If you've had a laundry mishap, such as a stray red sock getting mixed in with your load of white underwear, or a crayon or other waxy item getting left in a pocket, baking soda just might be able to come to the rescue.

For a crayon or other item that has colored all the clothes and possibly left marks on the inside of the drum, rewash everything in hot water with a cup of baking soda added. To get that pink tinge out of underwear, try soaking the clothing in a bath of warm water, baking soda and salt before washing.

What Do Those Washing Symbols on Clothes Mean?

You know those hieroglyphics-like symbols on clothing labels? They're intended to give consumers important cleaning information. But can anyone really decipher them? We sure can. Here are a few of the most common ones, explained.

Hand Wash Only If you see this symbol on an article of clothing, it means that it must be washed by hand. Any item with this tag should never end up in your washing machine.

Do Not Wring Sadly, this symbol is not a reminder to make sure there are no wrapped candies in your pockets when you throw your clothes in the washing machine. (Though that is great advice.) Instead, it means that you shouldn't wring out that particular article of clothing.

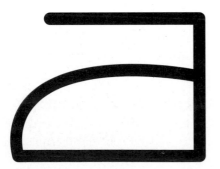

Iron or Steam This symbol, depicting an old-fashioned iron, means that you can (you guessed it) iron that article of clothing. Take a closer look at this laundry symbol on your clothes, too. Often the iron has one, two or three dots inside it, representing the appropriate level of heat.

Hang to Dry This one's a little less self-explanatory than the others! But it means you should hang that article of clothing to dry, rather than throwing it in the dryer.

Do Not Dry-Clean What a plain, generic circle means could be anyone's guess. But we'll help clear it up. When it comes to laundry symbols, the circle indicates dry cleaning. And if you see a circle with an X through it? It means you shouldn't dry-clean that item.

No Steam Finishing The dry cleaning circle returns! The positioning of the little line around the circle can be confusing, because the specific position indicates different things. If it's in the upper right like this, it means that you should dry-clean the item, but with no steam.

Machine Wash Though this one looks as if it could also mean "Hand Wash," since it does look like water in a regular old bucket, it actually means "Machine Wash." Nothing complicated here—just toss it in the machine! (Check first for other laundry symbols with more specific instructions.)

Wash at 104 Degrees This symbol advises the temperature at which the item of clothing should be washed. What can be frustrating for the American crowd, though, is that this is in degrees Celsius, not Fahrenheit. So this laundry symbol means you should wash at 40 degrees C, or 104 degrees F.

Machine Wash, Permanent Press The little line under the regular "Machine Wash" symbol means that you should wash that article with the permanent press setting. A double-line underneath the Machine Wash symbol means to use the delicate or gentle cycle.

Do Not Wash Don't put anything with this symbol on it in the washing machine—or in that bucket of water to wash by hand, either. If something has the "Do Not Wash" symbol on it, have it dry-cleaned.

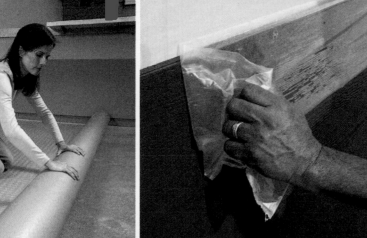

CHAPTER THREE

GARAGE & WORKSHOP

1 **Remove the chain.** Unscrew the outer nut on the chain tensioning rod. If necessary, use pliers to prevent the chain from turning. Then slip on a pair of gloves and remove the greasy chain from the sprocket at the top of the opener.

CHAIN TENSION ADJUSTING ROD AND NUT

Rebuild a Garage Door Opener

Replacement gears can help a finicky door operate smoothly.

If you press the garage door opener button and hear either a humming or a grinding sound but the door won't open, you may think you need a new opener—and you might. But before you give up on the old unit, pop off the cover and check for stripped gears. It's a common problem, and one that you can fix yourself.

You'll have to get a replacement gear kit (two new gears, grease and washers), which may take some running around. But once you have the kit in hand, you can do the repair in about two hours. You'll need a 2x4, a small drift punch, a standard 1/4-in. drive socket set, hex wrenches, a circular saw, a drill and a hammer. With the steps laid out here, you can remove and replace the gears without damaging the shafts.

Start by unplugging the opener, and then remove the retaining screws for the metal cover and put the cover

aside. Shine a flashlight directly at the gear set. If you see chewed-up teeth, you've nailed the problem. If the gears are in good shape, you've got a more serious problem and your best bet may be to replace the entire unit. To find a replacement unit kit, write down the make, model and serial number of your opener (you'll find this information on a label on the back of the opener). Then call a garage door opener repair company. It'll probably charge a bit more than an internet site, but at least you'll have the parts right away and be up and running the same day.

GET OUT THE GEAR SHAFTS

Use a combination wrench to loosen and remove the chain (**Photo 1**). Next, use a 1/4-in. drive socket, extension and ratchet to remove the helical gear assembly retaining screws

2 Remove the helical gear assembly. Unscrew the hex-head screws that hold the helical gear assembly in place. Save the screws for reassembly. Then lift the entire assembly (sprocket, plate, shaft and helical gear) up and out of the top of the unit.

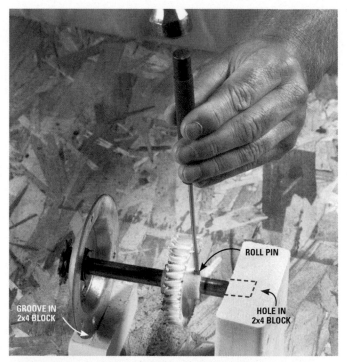

3 Remove the helical gear from the shaft. Support both ends of the helical gear assembly with the two jigs. Hold a small drift punch over the roll pin and tap the pin out of the shaft with a small hammer.

(**Photo 2**). Take a photo of the wiring connections from the motor or label them with masking tape. Then, disconnect the motor wires and remove the entire motor assembly. Move the helical gear assembly and the motor assembly to your workbench.

REMOVE THE HELICAL AND WORM GEARS

Cut a shallow groove into a 2x4 with a circular saw. Then slice off about a 3-in. section to make a jig to hold the helical gear assembly circular plate (**Photo 3**). Place the plate in the groove, hold the gear assembly level and mark the end of the shaft on another 2x4. Drill a hole in the wood and insert the end of the shaft. Then remove the roll pin (**Photo 3**). Slide the old gear off the shaft and replace it with the new gear. Reinstall the roll pin using the same jigs.

Next, remove the retaining collar and thrust washers on the end of the motor shaft (**Photo 4**). Pull the motor out of the chassis and slide the worm gear off the shaft (the roll pin stays in place on this shaft). Slide on the new worm gear with the notched end facing the roll pin.

Reassemble the motor assembly and place it back in the opener. Then install the helical gear assembly. Coat the gear teeth with new grease. Reattach the chain and tighten it to the proper tension (see your owner's manual). Test your repair with the door disconnected from the opener trolley.

4 Remove the worm gear. Loosen the collar setscrews with a hex wrench and slide the worm gear off the shaft. Then remove the motor retaining screws.

SPRAY-PAINTED
FOUL LINE

Lock Up the Overhead

Some people "lock" the door when they go on vacation by unplugging the opener. That's a good idea, but physically locking the door is even better. An unplugged opener won't prevent fishing and—if you have an attached garage—won't stop a burglar who has entered through the house from opening the garage door from inside, backing in a van and using the garage as a loading dock for his plunder. Make a burglar's job more difficult and time-consuming by locking the door itself.

Lock the track. If your door doesn't have a lockable latch, drill a hole in the track just above one of the rollers and slip in a padlock.

Don't Cross the Foul Line

Here's the straight solution for keeping bikes, trikes, garden tools and car bumpers from being squashed by a descending garage door or triggering the electric eye. Close the garage door and press down a strip of 2-in.-wide masking tape along the inside edge. Open the garage door, then lay another strip of tape 1-1/2 in. from the outside of the first. Spray-paint the line, pull up the tape and let the paint dry. Now when you close the door, glance at the line to be sure the door will seal on concrete, not on a tool or the tail of your sleeping cat.

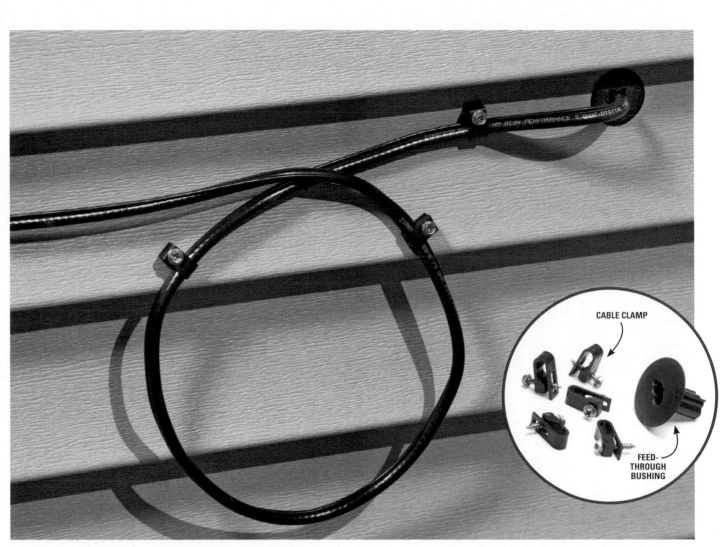

CABLE CLAMP

FEED-THROUGH BUSHING

Loop the cable. A loop provides extra length for minor repairs or rerouting later. It also forces water to drip off the cable rather than follow the cable into the wall. A bushing seals around the cable and protects it from the sharp edges of the siding. Fasten the cable with clamps.

Watertight Cable

A few key tips can prevent coaxial cables from bringing unwanted moisture into your home.

TV and internet signals are the only things coaxial cables should be bringing into your house, but improperly installed cables can let in water, which can lead to rot and mold. So the next time you're trimming the bushes, take a quick look where the cable enters the house. A quick fix might save you a lot of hassle down the line.

Cable should never run downward and directly into your house. Rainwater will adhere to the cable and follow it right into your home. Ideally, the cable should run upward and then in. If your cable was installed incorrectly, contact your service provider and voice your concerns. If the provider

refuses to fix the problem, see if you can reroute the cable in order to gain a couple of feet. Try to avoid splices if you can. They can weaken your signal.

If you're installing new cable, loop the cable before it enters the building. The loop will not only help shed water but also provide extra cable in case a mistake is made inside the house.

A properly sized feed-through bushing will allow you to drill a slightly larger hole so that you can fish the cable in without damaging it. Dab silicone caulk behind the bushing before pushing it into its final resting place.

Create a Good Seal

If you want to keep the heat in your garage this winter or retain the cooled air next summer, you'll have to do more than just install an insulated door. Most of the air escapes around and through all the cracks. Here are four simple ways to seal that door as much as possible. You can do the whole job in an afternoon, depending on the size of the door.

MEASURE THE GARAGE DOOR

Start by measuring the width, height and thickness of your garage door. You'll need those measurements to buy a doorstop with a built-in sealing lip and a new bottom seal. While you're at the home center, buy V-seal weather stripping, a tube of exterior caulk and a small can of wood sealer (if you have a wooden door). And for extra sealing power, buy a rubber threshold (one choice is the Storm Shield Garage Door Threshold).

Some garage doors come with a metal track that holds a replaceable rubber seal. Over time, the seal flattens and cracks. If that's what you have, replace it with a "cold weather" silicone-type seal, which remains flexible in cold weather and lasts longer. If your home center doesn't stock them, you can find one online. Lubricate the silicone seal with dishwashing detergent and slide it into the track slots.

REMOVE THE OLD SEAL

If you have a wooden garage door, rip off the nailed rubber seal. Then seal the wood with wood sealer. While the sealer dries, prepare the new aluminum track by cutting it to length and notching the ends so the track fits around each bottom roller. Next, lay down a thick bead of caulk along the leading edge of the door and attach the track setup **(Photo 1)**.

Prepare the areas between the door sections by cleaning them with a rag and household cleaner (be careful not to pinch any fingers). Then install the pressure-sensitive V-seal weather stripping **(Photo 2)**. Repeat for each section.

INSTALL THE THRESHOLD

Now move on to the threshold. Start by cleaning the concrete with degreaser and water. Rinse and let dry. Then roll the threshold into place with the hump on the inside of the garage door and cut the threshold to the width of the opening. Gently close the door onto the threshold and square up the hump to meet the door seal. Mark the edge of the threshold on the floor at each end and snap a chalk line along your marks. Next, glue the threshold into place. Close the door firmly against the threshold and leave it closed until the adhesive dries **(Photo 3)**.

INSTALL THE STOP

Pry off the old doorstop and install the new doorstop that has a sealing lip **(Photo 4)**.

1 **Install a new seal on the door bottom.** Push the track into wet caulk, tight against the door bottom. Clamp it into place. Then drill and screw the track to the back of the door using 1-in. screws.

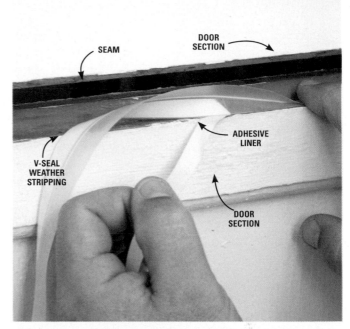

2 **Apply weather stripping in the door section seams.** Cut the weather stripping into strips the width of the door. Then fold along the crease so the V faces the outside. Insert the strip between the door sections, remove the adhesive backing and press it into place.

3 **Glue down a new threshold.** Squirt out a bead of threshold adhesive according to label directions. Then move the threshold into place and align it with the chalk line you made earlier. Close the garage door and let the weight hold it in position until the adhesive sets up.

4 **Nail on a self-sealing doorstop.** Slide the doorstop against the garage door so the vinyl seal bends at about a 45-degree angle. Then nail the stop into place with galvanized (or aluminum) 1-1/2-in. nails.

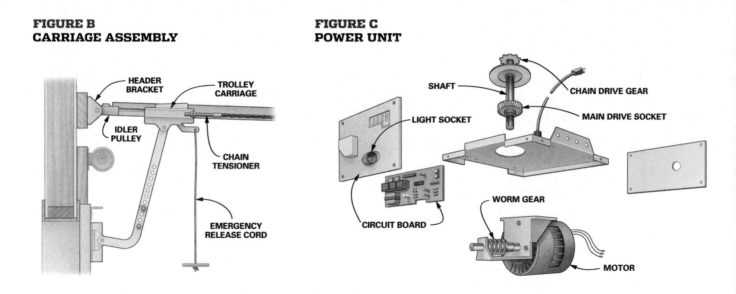

**FIGURE A
ANATOMY OF A GARAGE
DOOR OPENER**

RAIL

CHAIN

SWITCH WIRES

TO SAFETY SENSOR

WALL SWITCH

**FIGURE B
CARRIAGE ASSEMBLY**

HEADER
BRACKET

TROLLEY
CARRIAGE

IDLER
PULLEY

CHAIN
TENSIONER

EMERGENCY
RELEASE CORD

**FIGURE C
POWER UNIT**

SHAFT

CHAIN DRIVE GEAR

LIGHT SOCKET

MAIN DRIVE SOCKET

CIRCUIT BOARD

WORM GEAR

MOTOR

Garage Door Opener Fixes

Don't blow $200 on a new opener. Most repairs are cheap and easy!

Not many appliances get as much of a workout as the garage door opener. It usually gives us years of hassle-free service, but an opener can break down. When that happens, don't assume you need to replace it. There are several straightfoward repairs you can make that don't require a lot of money, a bunch of special tools or an engineering degree. We asked a garage door expert and our Field Editors for their advice and repair experiences.

Check Your Door First

With the door closed, pull the emergency release cord and lift the door to see if it opens and closes smoothly. If it doesn't, the problem is with your tracks, rollers or springs rather than your opener. This article covers opener problems only.

And Play It Safe

Work with the door down. If the problem is a broken door spring and you pull the emergency release cord while the door is in the raised position, the door could come crashing down.

Unplug the opener. That way you won't lose a finger or risk another painful injury if somebody hits the remote button while you're working. You'll also avoid, even worse, electrocuting yourself. Always take precautions and use your common sense.

Test the wall switch. Unscrew one wire and touch the other terminal with it. If the opener runs, replace the switch.

SYMPTOM A: The Remote Works but the Wall Switch Doesn't.

Fix: Replace the wall switch and wires.

If the remote works but the wall switch doesn't, you may need to replace either the wall switch or the switch wires. To determine whether the switch or the wires are bad, first unscrew the switch from the wall and unscrew one wire and touch the other terminal with it (don't worry, the wires are low voltage and won't shock you). If the opener runs, you have a bad switch. If you have an older-model opener, a cheap doorbell button might work. If you have a newer opener that has a light and a locking option on the switch, buy the one designed for your model. A new one is about $15.

If the opener doesn't run when you touch the wire, jump the two terminals on the back of the opener with a short wire. If the opener then runs, the wire that connects the opener to the switch is bad. Sometimes the staples that hold the wire to the wall pinch the wire, causing a short. Install 18- to 22-gauge wire.

Test the wires. Jump the two terminals on the back of the opener with a short wire. If the opener runs, replace the wiring.

SYMPTOM B: The Wall Switch Works but the Remote Doesn't.

Fix: Replace batteries or buy a new remote or receiver.

If the wall switch works but one of the remotes doesn't, check the batteries first—still nothing? You may need a new remote. Home centers carry a few models, and you can find a wide selection online.

If you can't find one for your opener model, you can try a universal remote or you can install a new receiver. A new receiver will replace the radio frequency of the opener with its own. An added bonus of a new receiver is that it will automatically update older openers to the new rolling code technology, which stops bad actors from stealing your

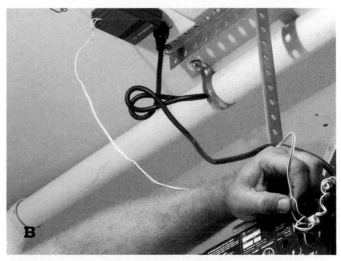

Install a new receiver. Plug your new receiver into an outlet and run two wires to the opener.

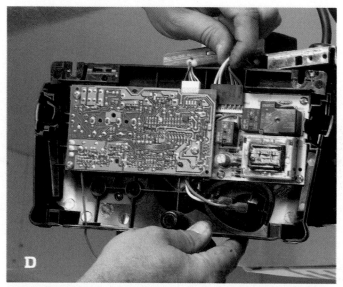

code. Just plug the new receiver into an outlet close to the opener, and run the two wires provided to the same terminals connected to the wall switch.

SYMPTOM C: The Door Goes Up, but It Only Goes Down When You Hold Down the Wall Switch.

Fix: Align or replace the safety sensors.

If the door goes up but goes down only when you hold down the wall switch, check to see that the safety sensors are in alignment. The small light on each sensor should be lit up when nothing is between them. Door sensors do go bad, so if no light is showing at all, you may need to replace them. You can save yourself some time by using the existing wires. Also, direct sunlight shining on sensor eyes can make them misbehave. A new pair of sensors sells for about $40.

SYMPTOM D: You Have Power to the Outlet, but There's No Sound or No Lights When You Push the Wall Switch and Remotes.

Fix: Replace the circuit board.

If the outlet has power, but there's no sound or no lights when you push the wall switch and remotes, you probably have a bad circuit board. Lightning strikes are the most frequent reason for the demise of a circuit board. The circuit board consists of the entire plastic housing that holds the lightbulb and wire terminals. The part number should be on the board itself.

Replacing a circuit board may sound intimidating, but it's really quite easy. It will take 10 minutes tops and requires only a 1/4-in. nut driver. Just follow these steps: Remove the light cover, take out the lightbulb, disconnect the switch and safety sensor wires, remove a few screws, unplug the board and you're done. A circuit board will cost about $80, so make sure to protect your new one with a surge protector. You can buy an individual outlet surge protector at a home center for less than $10.

SYMPTOM E: Everything Works Fine Except the Lights.

Fix: Replace the light socket.

If the bulbs are OK but don't light up, you probably have a bad light socket. To replace the socket, you'll need to remove the circuit board first. Use the same steps for fixing Symptom D to accomplish this.

Once the circuit board is removed, pop out the old socket by depressing the clip that holds it in place. Remove the two wire connections and install the new socket. Replacement sockets generally cost less than $15.

Be sure to use a bulb of the correct wattage. Using a lightbulb with a higher wattage than the socket is rated

Align or replace the sensors. Sensors are brand-specific; buy new ones made for your opener.

Remove the circuit board. All you'll need to do is unscrew a few screws and disconnect a couple of plugs.

Remove the old socket. Remove the circuit board housing to access the light socket. Then unclip the old socket and snap in the new one.

Slide on the new carriage trolley. Leave the rail attached to the opener, and install the new trolley from the other side. Clamp down the chain to make reassembly easier.

Mark the chain and sprocket. If you have to remove the chain for any reason, mark its location on the sprocket with a marker or wax pencil. The opener will require less adjusting when you put it back together.

Pull out the old gear. The shaft, sprocket and main drive gear should all come out as one piece. This procedure is best performed on a benchtop.

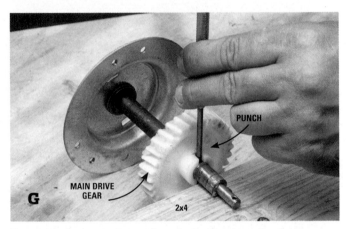

Remove the gear from the shaft. Support the shaft on a 2x4 and use a punch to drive out the pin that holds the gear in place.

will cause a socket to fail. Not only is this bad for the socket, but it can also be a fire hazard. If your light cover has turned yellow from heat, you're probably using too strong a bulb.

SYMPTOM F: The Trolley Carriage Moves but the Door Doesn't Open.
Fix: Replace the trolley carriage.

If the trolley carriage moves but the door doesn't open, the culprit is probably a broken trolley carriage. Before you pull the old one off, clamp down the chain to the rail. This will help maintain the location of the chain on the sprocket and speed up reassembly.

Once the chain is secure, separate it from both sides of the trolley. Disconnect the rail from the header bracket and move the rail off to one side. Slide off the old trolley, and slide on the new one. Reattach the chain and adjust the chain tension. Replacing the trolley on a belt drive and replacing it on a screw drive are similar procedures. A new trolley will cost $25 to $40 depending on your model.

SYMPTOM G: The Opener Makes a Grinding Noise and the Door Doesn't Move.
Fix: Replace the main drive gear.

If the opener makes a grinding noise and the door doesn't move, your main drive gear is probably toast. The main drive gear is the plastic gear that comes in direct contact with the worm drive gear on the motor. On most openers, the main drive gear is the most common component to fail.

Replacing it takes some know-how but is still well within the wheelhouse of the average DIYer. Several components need to be removed before getting at the gear. For a step-by-step description of this procedure, visit *familyhandyman.com* and search for "rebuild a garage door opener."

Once you get the gear out, you can remove it from the shaft with a punch, or you can buy a kit that comes with a new shaft. Make sure you lube it all when you're done. The gear alone will cost you around $10. A complete kit that comes with a new shaft will cost closer to $20.

Hide a Hopeless Floor

There are two general types of garage flooring: coatings and coverings. Coatings, which include things like floor paints, epoxy paints, stains and sealers, have a tendency to highlight blemishes, so if your floor has lots of cracks or pockmarks, sometimes the best option is simply to cover it up and hide the damage. Online, you'll find a huge selection of rigid plastic snap-together tiles or rollout floor mats designed to withstand vehicle traffic.

Remove a Stubborn Oil Filter

We've all done it at one time or another—overtightened an oil filter so much that it becomes an absolute bear to remove. If you think you can remove it by jamming a long screwdriver through the can and twisting, think again. The screwdriver will just rip the can open and you'll be drenched in oil. When you're done dealing with that mess, the filter will still be stuck and you'll be even more frustrated than you were at the beginning of the process.

Use one of our handy techniques to save yourself some valuable time and energy. One way to remove a stuck filter is to use a band-type wrench that you've lined with coarse-grit adhesive-backed sandpaper **(Photo 1)**. If you don't have adhesive-backed sandpaper on hand, you can also make your own by spraying adhesive on the back of conventional sandpaper. Better yet, if you're willing to shell out a little bit of money, consider buying a filter wrench with coarse grit welded to the inside of the band **(Photo 2)**. Lisle Swivel-Gripper no-slip filter wrenches are available in five sizes, and one costs about $12 at *amazon.com*. Slide the filter wrench band all the way down near the base of the oil filter. Then all you need to do is tighten it and twist. You'll thank yourself for taking the hassle out of this routine task.

1 **Add grit to get a better grip.** Slice a strip of adhesive-backed sandpaper and slip it inside a band-style wrench. Then remove the adhesive liner and press the sandpaper securely into place.

2 **Get a filter wrench with built-in grit.** Slide a Swivel-Gripper filter wrench toward the base of the filter. Rotate the handle to force the grit into the metal. Then swivel the handle and twist off the filter.

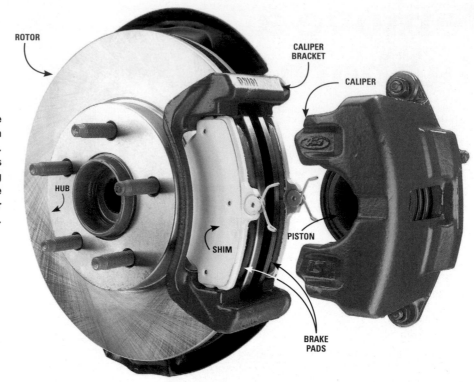

Anatomy of a brake system. Stop on a dime with three simple components. This exploded photo shows the caliper (the squeezing machine), the brake pads (the friction material) and the rotor (the part that gets squeezed).

ROTOR

CALIPER BRACKET

CALIPER

HUB

SHIM

PISTON

BRAKE PADS

Avoid the Top 4 Brake Job Rip-Offs

We lift the curtain on shady practices and show you how to avoid getting taken for a ride.

You'll buy at least three brake jobs during the life of your vehicle. And if you don't learn how to spot the rip-offs, you'll waste more than $1,000 on parts and services you don't really need. Unfortunately, brake job rip-offs happen far more often than you think. This article will cover the most common red flags and help you get a top-notch brake job every time.

1. BUYING CALIPERS WHEN YOU DON'T NEED THEM

Brake calipers work in a push-pull process to squeeze the brake pads against the rotors (see "Anatomy of a Brake System"). First, the caliper piston pushes the inboard pad outward until it touches the rotor. Then the caliper slides backward, pulling the outboard against the other side of the rotor. When you back off the brakes, the piston retracts slightly and the caliper releases pressure on the pads.

But if the caliper binds on the slide pins, the brake pads wear unevenly and quickly. Binding is a very common problem. But that doesn't mean you have to replace the calipers (to the tune of $300 per pair). Instead, the shop simply needs to replace the slide pins ($20 total parts cost) and lubricate them with high-temperature synthetic grease. So if replacement calipers are recommended, ask if they can be fixed by replacing the slide pins.

In most cases, calipers can be reused. But don't argue if you're told that the brake caliper is leaking fluid or the piston won't retract. Then it must be rebuilt or replaced.

2. PAYING PREMIUM PRICES FOR GENERIC PADS

Lots of companies build mediocre brake pads and pass them off as a premium product at bargain basement prices. They're really no bargain because they wear out quickly, chew up your rotors and increase your stopping distance.

How can you tell "real" premium pads from the impostors? First, top-quality brake part manufacturers always put their name on the box. Some well-known brands include Bendix, Raybestos, Akebono, Hawk, Wagner, NAPA/United, Carquest, Centric, Motorcraft, ACDelco, Monroe, Brembo and EBC. And even though these brands may offer several quality levels (good, better, best), their "good" pads are almost always of higher quality than a premium pad from a no-name company. Second, real premium pads usually include all the required hardware (shims, anti-rattle clips and abutment hardware) at no extra cost. So, if the shop claims it's installing premium pads but the price quote includes additional charges for the hardware, well, you can tell where this is going.

3. GETTING UP-SOLD TO CERAMIC PADS

There are lots of myths surrounding ceramic brake pads, and shops are happy to recite them to help you justify an "upgrade." They'll say that ceramic is simply the best brake pad material you can buy. Not true. Another is that ceramic pads will outlast semimetallic pads and provide better braking. Not true either. What is true is that ceramics run quieter and give off less brake dust—period.

If you haul heavy loads or do a lot of stop-and-go driving, semimetallic pads last longer and provide better braking than ceramic pads. So, before you fall for the ceramic pad upgrade routine, think about what type of pad came with your vehicle and what kind of driving you do on a day-to-day basis. If you do mainly light hauling and light braking, and you are really into the look of your aluminum wheels, then go for the ceramic pads.

4. GETTING INFERIOR ROTORS FOR PREMIUM PRICES

The brake parts market is flooded with inferior rotors that wholesale for as little as $10 a pop. Some shops buy those instead of premium rotors, charge you the higher price and pocket the difference. To the untrained eye, the generic rotors look just like the high-quality versions. But when you place them side by side, the differences are staggering. The friction surfaces on the generic rotors are noticeably thinner and they weigh about 20% less. With less metal to absorb heat and fewer cooling fins to dissipate it, the generic rotors heat up faster, warp more often (creating pedal pulsation), make more noise and simply wear out faster. They're a lousy choice all the way around—even if you're trying to save money.

Just as with brake pads, ask the shop for a quote that's based on brand-name professional grade (as opposed to service grade) rotors.

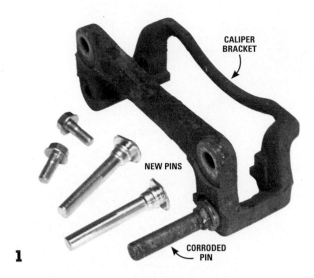

1

New caliper pins save you $300. Fix a binding caliper with new slide pins and high-temperature synthetic grease. That'll save you a fortune, and the caliper will slide freely for another 40,000 miles.

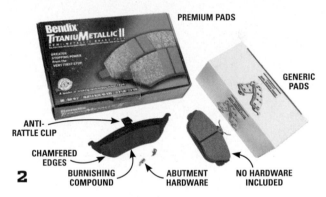

2

You get what you pay for. Demand brand-name parts. Top-quality manufacturers are proud to put their name right on the package. Generic brake parts are almost always packaged in plain white or yellow boxes. Brand name? Nowhere.

4

Less metal is a bad idea. Compare the weights of these two rotors for the same vehicle. The generic rotor weighs 20% less than the premium brand.

The Art of Car Cleaning

For the best results, you'll need to think and shop like a pro.

Detailing your own vehicle saves a lot of money (about $175) and can even produce better results than a professional job. But let's not kid each other. You can't get pro results with just a bucket of suds, old rags and a bottle of wax. And you can't whip out a pro-level job in just a few hours—it's a full-day commitment. We'll share tips from the pros and steer you away from common mistakes. When you're done, you'll have a vehicle that sparkles inside and out—and you'll be the envy of the neighborhood.

WASH FIRST—WITH THE RIGHT SUDS

Even though hand dishwashing liquid is a great degreaser, it's not the thing to use on your vehicle's finish. Yes, it removes dirt, grease and old wax. But it also sucks important oils right out of the paint's finish. Use it repeatedly and you shorten the life of your paint job. Instead of dish soap, use a cleaner formulated for vehicles (available at any auto parts store).

Once you've mixed the suds, go one step further—fill a second bucket with clean rinse water. Use it to rinse the wash mitt often **(Photo 1)**. That'll remove most of the road grit from the mitt to prevent scratches. When you're finished, throw the mitt in the washing machine.

PLUCK THE FINISH

A car hurtling down the road at 60 mph becomes a dartboard for any crud in the air. Your vehicle's clear coat deflects some of it but can hold the sharper grit. Washing removes the surface dirt, but clay-barring is the only way to pluck out embedded stuff. A clay bar kit (one brand is Meguiar's

G1016) includes a lubricating spray and several pieces of synthetic clay. The job is time-consuming, but pulling out all those "darts" helps you get a glass-like finish.

Buy a clay bar kit and prepare the clay (**Photo 2**). Then spray on the detailing spray lubricant from the kit and wipe the clay over a small section at a time (**Photo 3**).

POLISH THE FINISH

Many car owners confuse polishing with waxing, but each is a separate step. Polishing removes small surface imperfections and scratches, and buffs the finish to a shine. Waxing adds more gloss and protects the finish from the elements. Most DIYers skip polishing because they don't want to invest the money for a polisher or the elbow grease for a hand polish. But polishing your vehicle's finish is the key to getting the best gloss (pros would never skip it).

You can buy an entry-level variable-speed dual action (DA) polishing kit (machine and pads) for about $150 at an auto parts store. Don't confuse these polishers with inexpensive high-speed rotary buffers, which will burn paint if you apply too much pressure or rest on one spot too long. DA polishers are easy to use and paint-friendly, and do a great job. Apply a dollop of polish to the pad and wipe the pad across a 2 x 2-ft. area. Then run the polisher (**Photo 4**). Wipe off the final haze with a microfiber cloth.

GET A MIRROR FINISH WITH SYNTHETIC WAX

Some people swear by carnauba wax. It produces a deep, warm shine. But we prefer the wet-gloss look of synthetic polymer waxes (also known as paint sealant). We tried a newer synthetic wax for this story (Meguiar's Ultimate No. G18216). It's pricier than some other synthetics, but it doesn't leave a white film on plastic or trim—which is a real advantage. Plus, it's really easy to apply (**Photo 5**).

MOVE TO THE INTERIOR

Most DIYers start cleaning the interior by shampooing the carpet. That's a mistake—you'll just get it dirty again as you clean the upper surfaces. Instead, start at the top and work your way down. Vacuum the headliner, dash, console and door panels. Then clean all the glass, and dust the nooks and crannies (**Photo 6**).

Once the dust is gone, clean all the plastic components (dash, console and door panels) with an automotive vinyl cleaner (household cleaners remove vinyl softening agents, causing premature cracking). Then apply a vinyl protectant to condition the vinyl and protect it against UV sun damage. Use a glossy spray if you prefer a wet look, but don't use it on the top portion of the dash (**Photo 7**).

Finish off the interior by vacuuming and shampooing the upholstery and carpet. But first, raise the nap (**Photo 8**).

1 **Rinse before you reload.** Swish the wash mitt in clean water before you reload it with fresh suds. Dump and refill the rinse bucket with clean water before you start washing the opposite side of the vehicle.

2 **Make a clay pancake.** Tear a piece of clay into four sections. Flatten one section into a small pancake in the palm of your hand and store the other sections in a clean place until you need them.

3 **Wipe and knead.** Rub the clay over the paint with a back-and-forth motion. Fold the clay against itself, knead it and reflatten it until the clay turns gray. Then toss it and get a fresh piece.

4 **Polish with a light touch.** Run the polisher at a slow speed to spread the compound over the entire area. Then boost the speed and let the polisher do the work for you. Quit when there's just a light haze.

5 Apply synthetic wax. Apply the wax to the foam applicator and rub it into the finish with a swirling motion. Then wipe off the haze with a microfiber towel. Swap in a clean towel as soon as the first one loads up.

6 Suck it up while you dust. Sweep the dust out of the cracks with a detailing brush. Catch all that crud right away with your vacuum.

7 Protect without reflection. Prevent glaring dashboard reflections in your windshield by using a matte-finish vinyl protectant.

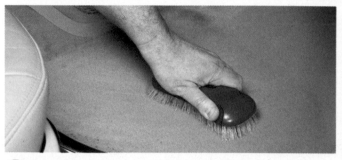

8 Brush and vacuum. Use a stiff brush to "raise" the matted carpet and upholstery fibers. That will loosen trapped dirt so you can vacuum it away.

9 Spray smoke neutralizer. With the fan on high, switch the system to recirculate mode (if you don't have that option, use "max AC"). Find the intake by holding a tissue near the blower motor. Spray mist into the opening.

10 Inject mold-killing foam. Thread the plastic hose into your AC evaporator housing. Then shake the can and depress the valve until the can is empty. Replace the drain tube and any other parts you removed.

Then use spray shampoo and a brush, or rent an extractor machine. Whichever method you choose, don't overdo the soap. Soap residue actually attracts more dirt in the long run.

DESTINK THE INTERIOR

The two most common car smells are tobacco smoke and that gym-socks "aroma" coming from your AC ducts. We've got the fixes for both offenders.

To neutralize smoke, buy an aerosol can of Dakota Non-Smoke ($14 from *dakotaproducts.com*). Holding the can 12 to 14 in. away from fabrics, lightly spray the headliner (don't soak it), seats, door panels and carpet. Then spray the rest of the can into the heating system (**Photo 9**). Leave the windows closed for at least one hour. Your vehicle will smell like baby powder for a while, but that'll go away.

To kill off mold and mildew in your AC system, buy a can of Kool-It Evaporator & Heater Foam Cleaner (about $15 at *amazon.com*). Find the rubber drain tube from the evaporator coil (usually located under the dash) and remove it from the evaporator housing. Following the product directions, shoot the entire can into the evaporator housing (**Photo 10**). The foam expands to coat the evaporator coil, killing the stinky culprits. After 15 minutes, turn the blower fan to low and let it run for five minutes. Bye-bye, locker room smell.

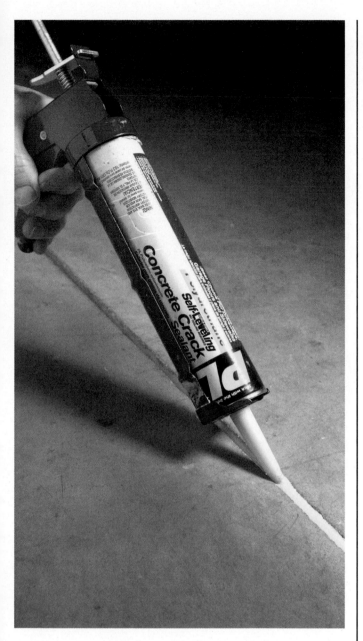

Hang It High for Finishing

Dave Munkittrick is an expert furniture builder with a plethora of practical finishing advice. When he finishes flat workpieces such as frames, plywood panels or doors, he hangs them aloft from pieces of light chain hooked to screws stuck in a board along the ceiling. To ensure a secure hold, he drives screw hooks into the project where the holes won't be noticed. With the pieces suspended in midair, he can finish both sides at the same time, and no dust settles on the vertical surfaces during the drying process.

Perfect Crack Filler

If you've ever tried to fill a crack in concrete with regular caulk, you know what a mess it can be. Self-leveling concrete crack filler solves this problem. Just fill the crack and a few minutes later the caulk settles to form a perfectly smooth joint. For wide cracks, insert lengths of foam caulk-backer first to create a better caulk joint and reduce the amount of caulk needed. Self-leveling caulk is available at home centers and hardware stores. Look for "self-leveling" on the tube.

Circ Saw Savvy

**Circular saws can do so much more than crosscut and rip wood.
Here are a few tricks to put in your carpenter quiver.**

Circular saws are the go-to tool for crosscutting and ripping lumber and plywood. And we can teach you a lot of tricks to help you make those cuts more efficiently. But a circular saw's strengths don't stop there. You can cut nearly anything with a circular saw, provided you use the right blade. We'll show you a few of our favorite techniques for cutting practically anything.

But first, a word about safety. Cutting wood is dangerous enough. When we start talking about dicing up metal, shingles and nails, you'd better take the safety glasses and hearing protection very seriously. A face shield is an even better idea than simple safety glasses, and gloves and long sleeves will protect your skin from shrapnel.

A. 8d RIPPING ASSISTANT

Whenever you have to rip boards and there's no table saw around, nail the board down to the top of the horses with 8d nails—just keep the nails away from the cut. It's much safer than holding the board with one hand while you cut with the other. And you'll get a straighter cut. When the cut is complete, pull the board free, tap out the nails to expose the heads and jerk them out.

B. WORK OFF THE STACK

Don't pick up sheets of plywood and place them on horses every time you have a cut to make. Save your back and your time. Get down on your knees and work off the stack. Slip a couple of 2x4s beneath the sheet undergoing surgery, make your marks and then cut. It's that simple. By the way, a drywall square is the perfect tool for marking crosscuts on plywood.

C. CUTTING THROUGH STONE AND MASONRY

Forget about those throwaway abrasive masonry blades. Diamond blades have dropped in price in recent years, and they're the key for this task. Find a volunteer to hold a slow-running garden hose right at the cut while you saw your way through. That'll keep the blade cool, speed up the cut and eliminate dust. And don't worry: It's safe as long as you're plugged into a GFCI-protected outlet.

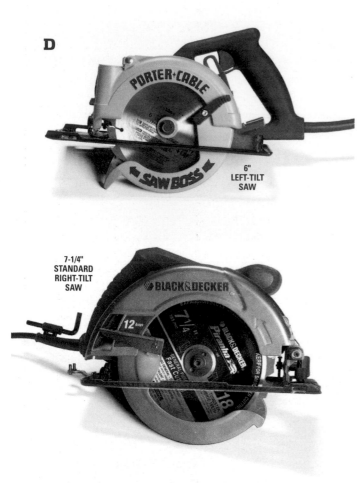

D

6"
LEFT-TILT
SAW

7-1/4"
STANDARD
RIGHT-TILT
SAW

E

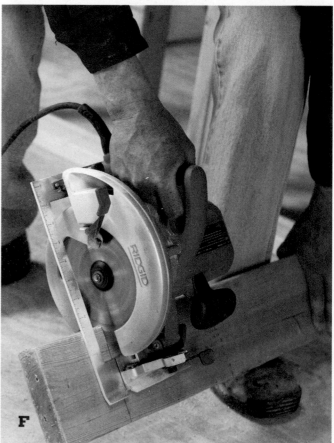

F

D. MINI CIRC SAWS

If you have a yen for an extra circular saw, consider buying a mini saw with a blade in the 5- to 6-in. range. You'll love it. It's much lighter than a standard 7-1/4-in. saw, yet you can still cut 1-1/2-in.-thick material at 90 degrees. But here's the big reason: On most mini saws, the blade is on the left side of the motor (called a "left-tilt saw"). Sometimes, this saw will fit in places where a larger saw won't. Other times you'll need it to cut bevels that are awkward or impossible with conventional right-tilt saws.

E. NONBINDING COMPOUND CUTS

Cutting steep angles, especially if they're compound (cuts with a bevel and an angle), requires one special step. That's pulling the guard back from the blade as you begin the cut. Skip this step and your guard will get bound up as you enter the cut, making it impossible to continue.

F. YOUR FOOT AS A SAWHORSE

Master this trick and you won't have to lug lumber to the sawhorse for every cut. It is simple and saves countless trips back and forth. It's also perfectly safe as long as you keep your foot at least 12 in. away from the cut. Just prop the board on your foot with the other end resting on the floor or ground. Tilt the board up and make the cut.

G

G. CUTTING THIN METAL

With a metal-cutting blade in your circular saw, metal roofing cuts as easily as aluminum foil. No magic to it—just place the show side down for a nicer finish. If you have metal to get rid of, like old exterior doors or even old metal tanks, you can cut them up into small chunks that'll fit in the trash can or make them easier to haul to the dump.

H. STEEP BEVEL CUTS

Most circular saws will make bevel cuts of only 45 degrees, but there's a trick for cutting bevels that exceed 45 degrees. Let's say you need a 55-degree bevel. Subtract 55 (or whatever bevel you're after) from 90 and set your saw at that bevel (in this case, 35 degrees). Next, clamp or screw a block even with the end of the board to support the saw base while you cut. The blade probably won't complete the cut, but it's easy to finish it with a handsaw or reciprocating saw. This trick works for compound cuts as well. Cut the angle first with the saw at 90 degrees, and then use the off-cut to support the saw while you cut.

I. CUTTING CURVES

If you grab your jigsaw whenever there's a curve to cut, next time try your circular saw instead. It'll do a sterling job for long, gradual curves in a fraction of the time a jigsaw will. Plus, you'll get a much smoother cut. If you're cutting plywood, set the saw to cut just deep enough to cut through the wood. The deeper the blade, the harder it'll be to make the cut because it'll get bound in the kerf. If you're cutting thicker material, cut halfway through on the first pass and then make a second, deeper final cut that

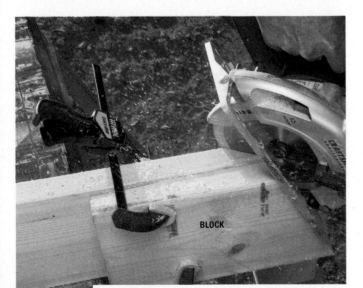

BLOCK

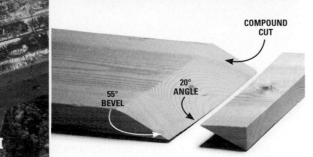

COMPOUND
CUT

55°
BEVEL

20°
ANGLE

H

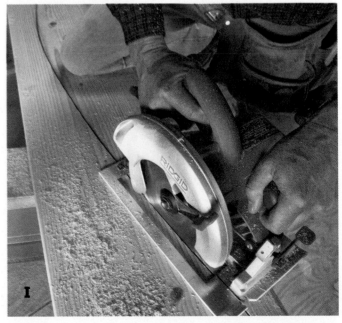

I

follows the original cut. This trick isn't for supertight curves, though. If it's too hard to push the saw through the cut, you'll just have to go with the jigsaw—sorry.

J. DEALING WITH PIPE

A circular saw makes short work of pipe—any kind but cast iron. Use a fine-tooth carbide blade for PVC, ABS or copper. Choose a metal-cutting blade for cutting up steel such as fence posts and metal plumbing pipe.

K. ONE-STEP ROOF CUTS

Sometimes you need to cut a hole in a roof for roof vents, chimneys, skylights, whatever. You don't have to remove shingles before you cut. Just stick an old carbide blade in your saw and plunge-cut right through the shingles and decking.

L. PERFECT, PAINLESS SAFE SIDING CUTS

Cutting lap siding is tough because it's awkward to "four-wheel" the saw over the laps. Next time you're faced with cutting through siding, make a plywood cutting jig. Screw the guide right to the siding with the edge of the plywood directly over the desired cutting line, and set the cutting depth to cut just through the siding, including the thickness of the jig. The saw's base will ride on the flat surface and you'll get a perfect cut every time. With a diamond blade, this trick works great for stucco, too.

Build a jig. Screw a 1x3 or 1x4 fence about 6 in. from the edge of a 12-in. strip of plywood. Then rip off the excess plywood.

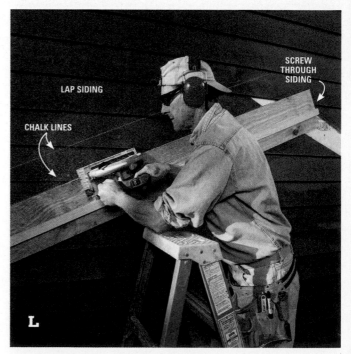

Screw it to the wall. Snap guidelines on the siding, then align and screw the jig to the siding so the edge follows the cutting line. Make your cut.

The Right Lube

Everything you need to know about the slippery stuff.

Your local home center probably carries at least a dozen kinds of lubricant. Ever wonder why so many? We did. So we interrogated the guys in white lab coats and learned this: A lube formulated for a specific job usually provides far better results and wear protection than a general-purpose product or a product designed for a different job. And a specialty product usually lasts much longer. So by using

the right lube, you'll lubricate less often, avoid frustrations, and save time and money.

We'll walk you through all the different specialty lubes and explain where to use each one. But don't worry about memorizing it all: There's a chart on p. 97 that breaks everything down. Keep it handy and you'll soon be the neighborhood source for lube advice.

USE THE RIGHT LUBRICANT EVERY TIME

Dry PTFE Lubricant

"Dry" lubricant actually goes on wet. But once the solvent dries, it leaves a thin film of dry polytetra-fluoroethylene (PTFE)—the same product used to make nonstick frying pans. The main advantage of dry PTFE is that dust doesn't stick to it. That makes it a great lube for dirty environments like your garage or shop. PTFE bonds to metal, wood, rubber and plastic—so it stays put. It's a light-load lubricant, so it's not the best lube for equipment that carries a heavy load or transmits high torque. And it doesn't have any anticorrosive properties (although some manufacturers spike theirs with an antirust additive), so don't use it on outdoor metal. Dry PTFE lube is available in both aerosols and squeeze bottles. Check the label to make sure the solvent won't harm the material you're lubricating. Note: Not all "dry" lubes are PTFE. Some are silicone, which is a different ball game.

Synthetic Grease

Synthetic grease is the best choice for gears, axles and bearings that carry heavy loads, transmit high torque, operate at high temperatures or are subject to shear stress. Synthetic grease has less rolling friction than the petroleum-based grease you'll see next to it on store shelves. It resists thermal break-down and shear, too, so it lasts much longer than other types of grease.

Marine Grease

Like lithium grease, marine grease is formulated to lubricate high-load items. But it's thicker and far more water resistant than lithium grease, so it does a fantastic job of inhibiting rust and preventing metal parts from welding themselves together with rust. Use marine grease to lubricate items that are directly immersed in water or constantly exposed to the elements. Like any grease, it's a tacky magnet for dust and dirt.

Garage Door Lube

Garage door hardware operates in an environment that's often dirty and damp, sometimes hot and sometimes cold. That's why there's a special lube for it. Garage door lubes are formulated to penetrate deep into hinges, rollers and springs but dry to a fairly tack-free finish to resist dust and dirt buildup. Many brands also contain anticorrosive additives to protect against rust.

Rust-Penetrating Oil

Other products will free up stubborn nuts and bolts—eventually. But they won't do it nearly as fast or as well as oil formulated just for that job. Rust-penetrating oil contains an aggressive solvent to penetrate the rust. And it contains a special low-viscosity, low-surface-tension lubricating oil that flows into micro cracks in the rust to get lube deep into the threads. But don't use it for purposes other than stuck stuff; it does a poor job of keeping things slippery.

Silicone Lubricant

Silicone is the slipperiest of all lubricants, so it's a great choice for items that slide against one another. Silicone repels water, but not water vapor, so you can use it to dry out electrical connectors but don't rely on it as a sealant in humid conditions. Use silicone to lubricate metal, wood, rubber and plastic. However, dust and dirt stick to silicone, so use it sparingly or use a "dry" version in dirty environments.

The biggest downside to silicone lubricant is that once you apply it to an object, you can never paint or stain it. And since the spray drifts, it can contaminate nearby walls and floors. If you ever plan to paint anything in the surrounding area, tape off a spray zone before you spray.

White Lithium Grease

Grease is the lube of choice for higher-load items like bearings and axles because it cushions parts. And unlike oil, which tends to seep away, grease stays in place and lasts much longer. White lithium is a great all-around grease for lubricating light- to medium-load items like tools and garden equipment. It comes in aerosol cans and in tubes. Aerosols are easier to use because the solvent helps the grease seep into tight spaces. That can save you the trouble of disassembling components to grease them.

Chain Lube

Chain lube penetrates deep into roller chain links and doesn't fly off when the chain is in motion. To use it, clean off the old lube with spray solvent and a brush. Apply the chain lube and slowly rotate the chain to allow it to work into the links. Then leave it alone until the solvent evaporates. Chain lube resists water, dust and dirt better than ordinary oil. Use it for chains on bicycles, motorcycles, scooters, garage door openers and outdoor power equipment. But never use aerosol chain lube in place of a bar chain oil on chain saws.

A

NAME-BRAND OFF-BRAND

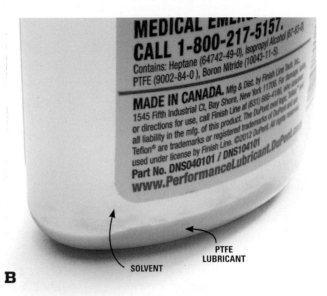

B

SOLVENT PTFE LUBRICANT

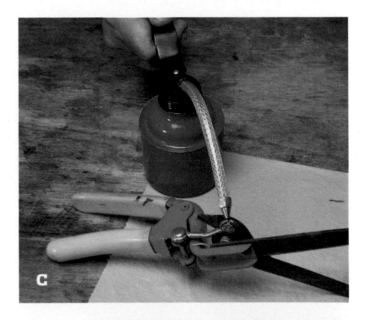

C

D

A. AVOID THE OFF-BRANDS

Cheap brands cost less for a reason—they contain less of what matters. The beakers above show how much silicone was left after the solvents and propellants evaporated from a name-brand product and a cheaper no-name one. The cheaper stuff cost less but contained far less lubricant.

CLEAN OUT THE OLD LUBE

Adding fresh lube to old, degraded oil and grease is a prescription for equipment failure. To get the full advantage of fresh lube, always clean out the old lube with a rag and spray solvent (aerosol brake cleaner works well).

B. SHAKE BEFORE USING

All spray and squeeze bottle lubes contain solvents along with the actual lubricant. If you don't shake the product before application, you'll get a lot of solvent and very little lube.

C. DON'T FORGET PLAIN OLD MOTOR OIL

That leftover can of 30-weight motor oil isn't the very best lube for all jobs, but it's a handy and acceptable friction fighter for most. Heavyweight motor oil is thicker than most spray oils, so it provides a stronger film cushion. And motor oil has built-in anticorrosive additives to resist rust. Since it doesn't have any solvents, a full drop is really a full drop of lube. And it's cheap—a quart should last a lifetime.

D. PREVENT SEIZING

Apply a thin coat of marine grease to a trailer hitch ball mount to prevent it from rusting and welding itself to the receiver.

E. CHOOSE DRY LUBE FOR DUSTY SITUATIONS

Dusty and dirty conditions call for a lube that isn't tacky. Dry PTFE is a good choice for this vacuum cleaner. It dries tack-free and bonds well to surfaces, so the spinning parts won't throw off lubricant.

F. LITHIUM GREASE FOR GARDEN EQUIPMENT

Lubricate heavy garden equipment wheels with spray lithium grease. It'll stand up to the load better than oil, silicone or PTFE. Take the wheels off and spread grease on by hand or shoot it on with aerosol white lithium grease. Spin the wheels to work the lube into the axles before the solvent evaporates.

G. GREASE, NOT OIL, FOR HIGH LOADS

Reduce wear on gears and bearings with a heavy-duty synthetic grease. Spread it on all surfaces and rotate the parts by hand to distribute the grease. Never pack the gear case completely full unless directed by the manufacturer.

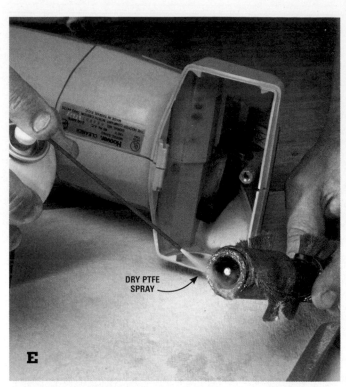

DRY PTFE SPRAY

E

F

SYNTHETIC GREASE

G

QUICK-USE CHART FOR LUBRICANTS

LUBE TYPE	BEST USES	ADVANTAGES	DISADVANTAGES
All-purpose lube	Frees up lightly rusted tools and dissolves light rust. Lubricates light-duty mechanisms (e.g., drawer slides, hinges). Dissolves some adhesives and removes scuff marks from floors. Removes pressure-sensitive adhesive labels.	Safe for wood, metal and plastic. Works fast. Dissolves gummed-up old lube and relubricates. Flows quickly and penetrates deeply into tight spaces. Protects against corrosion.	Lubrication and rust protection don't last long— you may have to reapply often. Not for use on rubber items. Not for heavy loads or high-torque applications. Attracts and retains dust and dirt. Works slowly to free up nuts and bolts.
Dry PTFE lube	Light-load lubrication for drawer slides, rollers, hinges, hand tools, window tracks/ mechanisms, latches and lock cylinders.	Won't gather dust or dirt. Once solvent evaporates, product stays in place (won't drip). Safe for wood, metal, most types of plastic and rubber.	No corrosion protection. Not for heavy loads or high-torque applications.
Spray silicone	Light-load lubrication for things that slide or roll— drawer slides, hinges, hand tools, window tracks/ mechanisms, electrical connectors, etc. Prevents sticking on snow blower chutes and mower decks.	Slipperiest of all lubes. Repels liquid water (not water vapor). Stays wet and continues to spread with every sliding movement.	Remains tacky, and holds dust and dirt. No corrosion protection. Once applied, the surface is unpaintable. Overspray makes floors dangerously slippery.
Lithium grease	Medium- to high-load applications like axles, rollers, bearings, spinning shafts on shop and garden equipment, and hinges that carry a heavy load. Any job where the lube must stay in place.	Lasts far longer than oil. Stays in place and doesn't drip. Aerosol versions allow grease to seep into tight places so you don't have to disassemble items to apply grease. Protects against corrosion.	Remains tacky, and holds dust and dirt. Washes off in heavy rain.
Marine grease	Trailer bearings, shafts, rollers and gears immersed in water or exposed to the elements. Prevents rust and seizing of metal parts.	Handles high loads and torque. Stays in place. Most water resistant of any grease.	Remains tacky, and holds dust and dirt.
Synthetic grease	High-load, high-torque lubricant for axles, bearings, gears or spinning shafts in power tools and equipment.	Lowest friction of all greases. Most resistant to breakdown under high heat. Stays in place. Dissipates heat well.	Remains tacky, and holds dust and dirt. Most expensive of all consumer-type greases.
Chain lube	Bicycle, motorcycle and scooter drive chains. Garage door opener chain and outdoor power equipment chains.	Penetrates deeply into roller links when first applied. Becomes tack-free and sling-free once dry; holds less dust than other lubes.	Doesn't spread once dry. May harm plastic or rubber (check the label before spraying chains that contain nonmetal parts).
Garage door lube	Garage door hinges, rollers, cables, reels and springs.	Penetrates, lubricates and protects against corrosion. Less tacky, so less likely to hold dirt.	May harm plastic or rubber parts.
Penetrating oil	Frees up rusty tools, tracks, slides, nuts and bolts.	Fastest option to break up rust and free fasteners. Dissolves grease and old, gummy lubricant.	Not a good permanent lubricant. Some formulas may dissolve paint or damage finishes.

Fiber Cement Board Tips

To install it, you need just a few special tools and techniques.

NAILING BASICS

Fiber cement siding can be hand-nailed, but because it's so much harder and more brittle than wood, you have to predrill holes near any edge. You can save yourself a bunch of time by using a pneumatic coil siding nail gun. Unfortunately, a siding gun will set you back twice as much as a 15-gauge trim gun, and it's only half as versatile, so if installing fiber cement isn't your full-time gig, you may want to rent one (about $110 a week). Every manufacturer has specific nailing guidelines, but here are some basic rules:

■ Use 6d galvanized or stainless siding nails and install them no more than 16 in. apart.

■ Nail lengths should be chosen so that they penetrate a minimum of 1-1/4 in. into the solid wood (wood sheathings such as OSB and plywood count toward the 1-1/4 in., but "soft" sheathings such as fiber board and foam do not).

■ Don't drive nails into the siding at an angle.

■ Fastener heads should be snugged up against the siding, not driven into the surface.

■ The end of each plank making up a butt joint needs to be fastened to a stud.

■ Nail butt joints last. That way you can tweak the ends of each plank so the bottom edges line up perfectly.

A. HOLD THE STARTER 1/4 IN. DOWN

Find your most beat-up pieces of siding and rip them down into 1-1/4-in. starter strips. These strips, installed at the bottom, will make your first row of siding angle out to match the rest of the rows. Snap a line 1 in. above the bottom of the wall sheathing as a guide. Install these fragile starter strips with a 15-gauge trim gun. Snap another line for the bottom row of siding, positioning it so it will hang down an additional 1/4 in. from the starter.

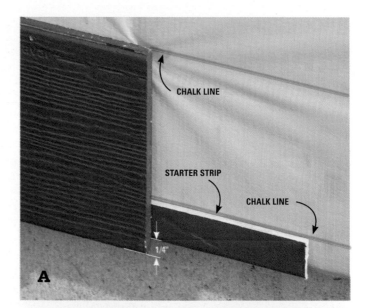

B. PREASSEMBLE THE CORNERS

It's a lot easier to preassemble corners on a flat surface. To do this, we recommend that you use 2-1/4-in. galvanized nails in a 15-gauge trim gun. You can then use the same size nails to install the corners on the wall. And if you're tempted to use a framing gun or try to hand-nail the corners together, don't do it—that's a good way to break the trim boards. Also, the trim nails look much better where nails will be exposed, especially on a prefinished corner board. So, if you don't have a 15-gauge trim gun, let these tasks serve as the perfect opportunity to go buy one at your local home center. The results will be worth your investment in the proper tools.

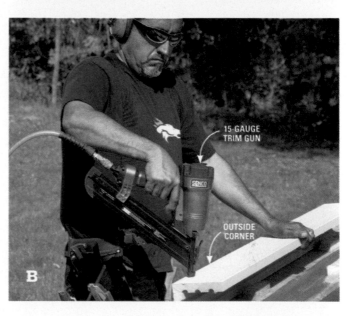

C. REMOVE THE PLASTIC LAST

Prefinished fiber cement boards come with a protective plastic coating. To protect the paint from getting scratched during installation, leave the plastic on and make your cuts right through it. Peel away the plastic after the board has been fastened to the wall.

D. FLASH THE BUTT JOINTS

Caulking butt joints is unnecessary, and some manufacturers prohibit it. However, you should flash behind the joints. You can use metal, house wrap or any other approved WRB (weather-resistant barrier), but we prefer to use 30-lb. felt paper. It's easy to work with and cheap, and it isn't noticeable if a seam happens to open up a little. Tack it to the wall so it doesn't get knocked out of place when you install the second piece of siding.

E. WINDOWS NEED DRIP CAP AND A GAP ON TOP

Whether or not you're installing trim boards around your windows, you'll need to install a drip cap over each window. You'll also need to leave a 1/4-in. gap (no caulking) between the top of the window and the plank or trim board directly above it. This is to allow any water that may have gotten behind the siding to weep out. Tape the drip cap to the wall, but don't tape all the way to the bottom of the drip cap because it will be visible through the 1/4-in. gap. The top trim board will also need its own drip cap and 1/4-in. gap. Treat the tops of doors the same way.

D

30-LB.
FELT

WINDOW
FLASHING TAPE

DRIP CAP

DRIP CAP

1/4" GAP

E

F. IT'S A TWO-PERSON JOB WITHOUT SIDING GAUGES

Fiber cement siding is heavy and breaks if it's bent too much. Installing it by yourself is tough, but it's possible with the aid of siding gauges. These tools create the proper reveal (the part of the siding that shows) between rows and actually hold the planks in place while you nail. Even if you do just one fiber cement job, siding gauges are worth the money. A pair of SA902 Gecko Gauges costs about $85 at *amazon.com*, but cheaper versions are available. Most gauges are adjustable to accommodate reveals from 5 to 8 in.

G. CUT THE PLANKS WITH A CIRCULAR SAW

Tons of fiber cement cutting gadgets are available, but most jobs can be handled with just a steady eye and a standard circular saw fitted with a fiber cement blade. If you plan to hang a lot of fiber cement, though, you'll want a chop saw with a proper blade that will allow you to cut several pieces at once. You can buy fiber cement blades sized to fit any saw style or size at most home centers. When you're cutting this stuff, a dust mask is the bare minimum protection, and this is not a casual warning: The silica dust generated by cutting fiber cement can be bad news for your health!

H. VINYL MOUNTING BLOCKS WORK BEST

Most fiber cement manufacturers make mounting blocks for lights, electrical receptacles, AC lines, PVC venting, etc. We prefer to use the vinyl mounting blocks typically used with vinyl siding. They're cheaper and easy to install, and you can cut the proper-size hole in a plastic mounting block with a utility knife or a snips. With fiber cement blocks, you have to use a jigsaw or a hole saw.

MountMaster is one brand of blocks sold at Home Depot and many lumberyards. It's available in a variety of colors, but you can order paintable blocks if you want an exact match with your siding or trim.

PAINTED VS. PRIMED

We decided to use a prefinished product in this story, but the other way to go is simple primed siding. That material is primed and ready for you to paint. Here are some facts to consider when making your decision.

The advantages of primed: Primed products cost half as much as prefinished products. On-site painting looks better up close because the touch-up paint and caulked areas are less noticeable. Primed products are easier and cheaper to install.

The advantages of prefinished: The color on a prefinished product won't fade nearly as fast. Some finishes come with a 15-year warranty. And the biggest plus? After installation, you're done and not faced with painting an entire house.

VINYL MOUNTING BLOCK

I. PAINT, PRIME OR CAULK ALL CUT EDGES

Every time you cut a plank, you create an exposed surface that has no primer or paint to protect it from the elements. If a cut edge is going to butt up against a corner post or trim board, caulk it. If the cut edge is part of a butt joint in the middle of a wall, it needs to be painted (try to use factory edges on all butt joints). Planks that have been cut to fit over windows and doors also need paint. Order paint kits and caulking to match both the trim and the siding colors. Your siding supplier should have access to both.

J. DONT SKIP KICK-OUT FLASHING

Kick-out flashing is essential for preventing water from running down a roof and behind the siding on an adjacent wall. You'll fail your inspection if the inspector doesn't see it on your job. It's a pain to work around, but it helps if you don't nail the flashing tight until you have your siding cut to size. It's much easier to get a proper fit for a plank if you can shift the flashing beneath it.

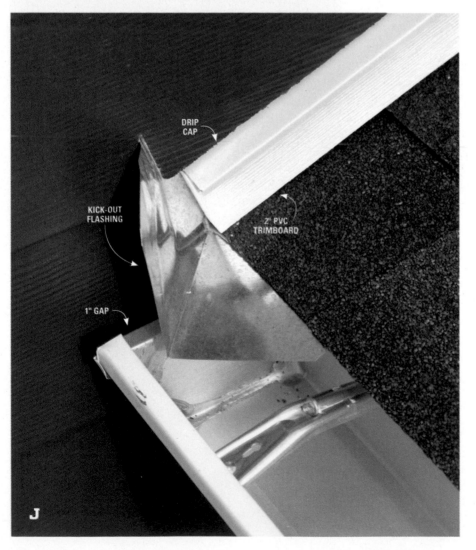

The Lowdown on Clearances

Fiber cement siding is not bulletproof—it will deteriorate if exposed to water for a long time. It's imperative that you honor the proper spacing between the siding and the roof surfaces and between the siding and the horizontal surfaces, such as the ground or cement slabs and decks. Check with your specific manufacturer before you start. Here are some general guidelines.

Leave:

- 1/8 to 1/4 in. between siding and trim
- 1/4 in. between siding and horizontal flashing
- 1 in. between the gutter and an adjacent wall
- 2 in. between siding and roofing, decks, patios, driveways, steps and walkways (using PVC trim boards is a good way to accomplish these clearances)
- 6 in. between the siding and the ground.

Generator Smarts

In the dark about using a generator? These tips will help you avoid the most common mistakes.

DON'T GET BURNED BY WATTAGE RATINGS

Every generator lists two capacity ratings. The first is "rated" or "continuous" watts. That's the maximum power the generator will put out on an extended basis. And it's the only rating you should rely on when buying a generator. The higher "maximum" or "starting" rating refers to how much extra power the generator can put out for a few seconds when an electric motor—like the one in your fridge—starts up. If you buy a generator based on the higher rating and think you can run it at that level, think again. It will work for a little while, but soon your new generator will be a molten mass of yard art and you'll be shopping for a replacement. Our advice? Ignore the higher rating and select a generator based on its "rated," "running" or "continuous" watts.

A. STOCK UP ON OIL AND FILTERS

Oil-change intervals for generators are short: Most new generators need their first oil change after just 25 hours. Beyond that, you'll have to dump the old stuff and refill every 50 or 60 hours. So to keep your generator humming through a long power outage and get the most out of your investment, you need to store up enough oil and factory filters to last a few days (at least!). Running around town searching for the right oil and filter is the last thing you want to be doing right after a big storm.

B. RUNNING OUT OF GAS CAN COST YOU

Some generators, especially low-cost models, can be damaged by running out of gas. They keep putting out power while coming to a stop, and the electrical load in your house drains the magnetic field from the generator coils. When you restart, the generator will run fine, but it won't generate power. You'll have to haul it into a repair shop, where you'll pay a fee to reenergize the coils. So keep the tank filled and always remove the electrical load before you shut down.

CHILL OUT BEFORE YOU REFILL

Generator fuel tanks are always on top of the engine so they can gravity-feed gas to the carburetor. But that setup can quickly turn into a disaster if you spill gas when refueling a hot generator. Think about it—spilled gas on a hot engine, and you're standing there holding a gas can. It's no wonder generators (and owners) go up in flames every year from that mistake. You can survive without power for 15 minutes, so let the engine cool before you pour. Spilling is especially likely if you refill at night without a flashlight.

C. OLD FUEL IS YOUR WORST ENEMY

Stale fuel is the No. 1 cause of generator starting problems. Manufacturers advise adding fuel stabilizer to the gas to minimize fuel breakdown, varnish and gum buildup. But it's no guarantee against problems. Repair shops recommend emptying the fuel tank and the carburetor once you're past storm season. If your carburetor has a drain, wait for the engine to cool before draining. If not, empty the tank and then run the generator until it's out of gas. Always use fresh, stabilized gas in your generator.

D. STORE GASOLINE SAFELY

Most local residential fire codes limit how much gasoline you can store in your home or attached garage (usually 10 gallons or less). So you may be tempted to buy one large gas can to cut down on refill runs. Don't. There's no way you can pour 60 lbs. of gas without spilling. Plus, most generator tanks don't hold that much, so you increase your chances of overfilling. Instead, buy two high-quality 5-gallon cans. Consider spending a bit more for a high-quality steel gas can with a trigger control valve.

E. BACKFEEDING KILLS

The internet is full of articles explaining how to "backfeed" power into your home's wiring system with a dual male-ended extension cord. Some of our Field Editors have even admitted trying it (we'll reprimand them). But backfeeding is illegal—and for good reason. It can (and does) kill family members, neighbors and power company line workers every

A head lamp helps for tank filling. After the engine cools, strap on an LED head lamp so you can actually see what you're doing. Pour slowly and avoid filling the tank to the brim.

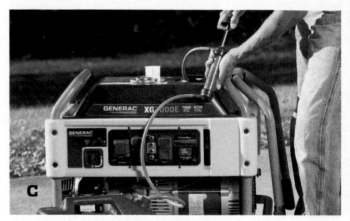

Out with the old. Empty the tank with a hand pump before running the carburetor dry. Reload with fresh gas next time you run the generator.

A better gas can means less spillage. The trigger valve on this gas can (Justrite No. 7250130) gives you total control over the fill. There's a separate refill opening so you never have to remove the spout.

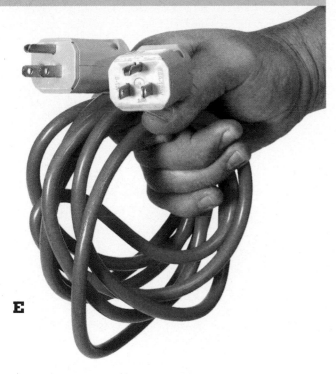

E

Prevent shocks and stop crooks. Protect yourself from accidental electrocution by connecting the generator to a grounding rod. Then secure the unit to the eye bolt with a hardened steel chain and heavy-duty padlock.

year. In other words, it's a terrible idea. If you really want to avoid running extension cords around your house, pony up for a transfer switch (around $300). Then pay an electrician about $1,000 to install it. That's the only safe alternative to multiple extension cords. Period.

F. LOCK IT DOWN

The only thing worse than the rumbling sound of an engine right outside your bedroom window is the sound of silence after someone steals your expensive generator. Combine security and electrical safety by digging a hole and sinking a grounding rod and an eye bolt in concrete. Encase the whole thing in 4-in. ABS or PVC drainpipe with a screw-on cleanout fitting. Spray-paint the lid green so that it blends in with your lawn. If you don't want to sink a permanent concrete pier, at least screw in ground anchors (four anchors, No. WI652775; about $29 from *globalindustrial.com*) to secure the chain.

G. USE A HEAVY-DUTY CORD

Generators are loud, so most people park them as far away from the house as possible. (Be considerate of your neighbors, though.) That's OK as long as you use heavy-duty 12-gauge cords and limit the run to 100 ft. Lighter cords or longer runs mean more voltage drop, and decreased voltage can cause premature appliance motor burnout.

Long cords let you get some sleep. Invest in some long extension cords to put some distance between you and the noisy generator. But don't exceed 100 ft. between the generator and appliances.

CHAPTER **FOUR**

LAWN, GARDEN & OUTDOORS

Planting a Tree

The key to a thriving, beautiful, mature tree is knowing what you're doing on planting day. Here are 10 of the best tips for planting and caring for your new tree so you can enjoy it for years to come.

1. DON'T ADD SOIL AMENDMENTS

For years, experts recommended adding soil amendments such as compost, peat moss or fertilizer to the planting hole. However, most now agree that you shouldn't backfill with anything other than the original soil from the planting hole (despite what the plant tag might say). This is because soil amendments in the planting hole can discourage the tree roots from spreading into the surrounding soil and can cause poor water drainage. Also, in some instances, fertilizers can kill young roots.

2. DON'T CHOOSE A PROBLEM TREE

You'll be living with this tree for a long time, so make sure you plant one you won't grow to detest in a few years. Trees to avoid include cottonwoods, which have invasive root systems (as shown), messy mulberries and stinky female ginkgoes. Before you buy a tree, research its benefits and potential negatives so you won't resent it later on. Contact your local extension service for a list of trees recommended for your area.

3. DON'T PLANT TOO CLOSE TO A BUILDING

Plant a tree with its mature size in mind. Many arborists suggest planting a tree no closer to a structure than one-half of its expected mature canopy spread. "I actually like to provide even more room," says tree expert Jeff Gillman, an associate professor at the University of Minnesota and the author of five books on gardening. "Tree roots and branches need space. When a tree is planted too close to a structure, pruning it to keep it from damaging your roof, foundation or siding can damage or disfigure the tree."

Also, some trees develop large surface roots that can crack or lift driveways, patios and sidewalks. If that's a concern, plant well away from these surfaces or choose a tree less likely to produce aboveground roots. Also, watch out for overhead power lines—most shade trees will grow at least to the height of residential power lines. Choose shorter, ornamental trees for these areas.

4. MATCH THE TREE TO THE PLANTING SITE

Plant a tree that will grow well given your hardiness zone, existing soil conditions (test if you're not sure), sun exposure and available moisture. "Tree species that are native to the place you live are probably well adapted to the climate in your part of the country," says Jeff. "If you're planting a non-native species, research its site requirements carefully." One of the best ways to check how trees will do on your land is to observe species growing naturally in the vicinity and in the same conditions.

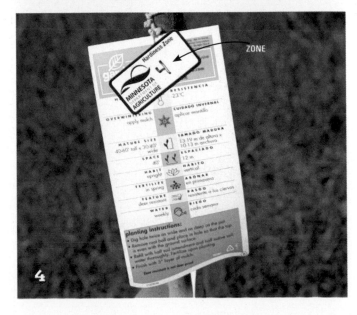

5. DON'T PLANT TOO DEEP

"If you plant the root ball of a tree too deep," says Jeff, "new roots can girdle the trunk, and they may also suffer from a lack of oxygen." Instead, plant your tree so the root collar—where the uppermost roots attach to the trunk—is about an inch above the soil level.

"In many cases, containerized trees from nurseries are planted too deep," he says. "Don't go by the soil level in the container. Dig down into the planting medium to find the root collar so you know how deep to plant the tree."

If you're planting a bare-root tree, leave a cone of soil at the bottom of the planting hole and set the root system on top. Place the handle of your shovel flat across the hole from one side to the other to make sure the crown is level with the surrounding soil. You should be able to partially see the root collar, or trunk flare, after the tree is planted.

6. DIG A SHALLOW, BROAD HOLE

Dig a saucer-shaped hole three to five times the diameter of the root ball (or the spread of the roots for a bare-root tree). This allows the roots to easily penetrate the softened backfill and properly anchor the tree.

If you will be planting your tree in clay or wet soil, use a garden fork or your spade to roughen the bottom and sides of the planting hole to avoid "glazing."

"Glazing happens when the sides and bottom of a hole become so smooth and compacted that water can't pass easily through the soil," says Jeff. "In extreme situations, it could block roots from penetrating the sides of the planting hole."

7. PLANT IN FALL OR EARLY SPRING

The ideal time to plant a tree is in early spring before bud break or in the fall before the tree goes dormant. Cool weather allows the tree to establish roots in its new location before new top growth puts too much demand on it. Trees that establish better if planted in early spring include oak, pine, dogwood, American holly, willow and black gum trees. Avoid planting any trees during the summer when they are in full leaf and particularly susceptible to heat stress.

CAUTIONARY INSTRUCTIONS
A few days before you dig, call 811 to have your underground utilities marked. Visit *call811.com* to learn more.

8. MULCH WIDE, BUT NOT DEEP

Mulch holds moisture, moderates soil temperatures, reduces competition from grass and weeds, and prevents lawn mowers and trimmers from nicking the trunk. Make a 3-ft. (or larger) circle of mulch 2 to 4 in. deep around the trunk. But don't mulch too deep. This can create surface drainage problems and deprive roots of oxygen. Keep the mulch 3 or 4 in. from the trunk to avoid disease, rot and pest problems. Some good mulch choices are shredded bark or composted wood chips. "Don't use woven or plastic landscape fabric or other weed barriers underneath the mulch," cautions Jeff. "These can cause major problems later on as seeds grow roots down through these materials and anchor themselves in the barriers."

9. SET THE ROOTS FREE

Cut away all rope, twine, wire, staples and burlap before backfilling (you can leave natural burlap underneath the root ball if you can't cut it all away). "If the roots circle the root ball but none is thicker than a pencil, use your fingers to tease the root ball apart," says Jeff. But if the tree is severely root-bound and has circling roots larger than a pencil in diameter, a newer method called box cutting is recommended: "Use a pruning saw to shave off all four sides, creating a root ball that is square," says Jeff.

10. WATER CAREFULLY

You'll need to water your newly planted tree until the root system is well established. Don't rely on a "rule of thumb" for watering. The right amount of water depends on the weather conditions, your soil and the planting site. The most reliable method for knowing when to water is to stick your finger 2 to 3 in. into the ground. You want to keep the soil at the level of the root ball moist but not wet. Allow the soil's surface to begin to dry out between waterings.

For the first few weeks, you may have to water every few days depending on the weather. After that, longer (deeper), less frequent watering is much better than shorter (shallower), frequent watering. To help the tree create deep roots to resist drought and wind, Jeff suggests encircling it with a soaker hose a few feet out from the trunk and running it at a trickle for an hour.

Ultimately, watering is all about balance. According to Jeff, "Overwatering can be as bad or worse than underwatering. If you're watering more than twice a week, there's a good chance you're overwatering."

Water Your Grass
Deeply but Less Often

Heavy watering every few days develops deep roots that tap into subsurface nutrients. Frequent light watering does just the opposite, encouraging grass to stay healthy only under ideal conditions. To give your lawn the right amount of water, start with this test: Water for 30 minutes, then dig into the soil with a spade. If the soil is wet to a depth of less than 6 in., you need to water longer. If the moisture depth is more than 6 in., you can water for a shorter period. How often you water depends entirely on your soil and climate. In most areas, two to four times per week is best.

Calibrate Your Lawn Spreader

If you have a broadcast spreader, there's a trick to getting the most uniform application of fertilizer with it. First, clean your driveway. Then fill the spreader, dial in the appropriate setting and spread some fertilizer on your driveway at your normal walking pace. Measure approximately how far the fertilizer is spread on both sides (it's common for one side to be wider than the other). Write the measurement on a piece of duct tape on the top of the spreader and use the information to guide your application. Sweep up the fertilizer on your driveway and discard or reuse.

Sharpen Your Shovel

Your shovel will slice through dirt and roots more easily if it has a sharp edge. If the point of your shovel is ragged with dents or chips, start by smoothing it with a grinder **(Photo 1)**. Then switch to a mill bastard file **(Photo 2)** to file a bevel. You don't want to give your shovel a knifelike edge. Instead, just bevel the top edge at a 70-degree angle to the back. That's pretty blunt compared with the 25- or 30-degree angle used for knife sharpening.

1 **Grind the edge smooth.** Use a metal grinding disc in an angle grinder to remove nicks and create a smooth profile. Keep the grinder moving to avoid overheating the metal edge.

2 **File a bevel.** Hold the file at a 70-degree angle to the back of the shovel. Apply pressure while pushing the file. Lift the file to return for the next stroke. Files cut on the forward stroke only.

6 Backyard Headaches and How to Fix Them

Lawn and garden experts weigh in on real-world yard woes.

HEADACHE #1: Seasonal Swamp

"I have a low spot in my yard that fills with runoff from our downspouts during rainstorms. It's not a constant problem, but it's a real bear to grow grass there."

Expert input: If you have workable soil (not clay) in your yard, a rain garden is an easy and effective solution for a short-term, isolated drainage problem. "Building a rain garden means that you don't have to fight a losing battle to grow turf," says Douglas Owens-Pike, plant ecologist and owner of EnergyScapes, a Minneapolis landscape design firm. "It's also a great way to treat rainfall as a resource rather than a problem."

All you need is a shallow depression with the soil amended to ensure that it drains quickly. Make sure your rain garden is located at least 10 ft. from your foundation. That way, you won't have any seepage problems in your basement. Plant the rain garden with shrubs and perennials that tolerate pooling water as well as periods of drought (type "rain garden" into your online browser and you'll find tons of plant lists with suitable options). The amended soil and water-loving plants capture the excess water, which slowly percolates into the earth instead of running into the storm sewer or sitting on the surface of your lawn.

And, according to Douglas, rain gardens aren't limited to just flowers or areas with full sun. "Partially shaded areas planted with lower-growing trees and shrubs can create wonderful rain gardens that provide wildlife habitat and become perfect nesting areas for birds," he says. (For detailed instructions on building your own rain garden, visit *familyhandyman.com* and search for "rain garden.")

HEADACHE #2:
"Gumbo" Soil Won't Drain

"Our clay soil is mush when wet and like concrete when dry, and nothing will grow in it."

Expert input: According to Steve George, a horticulturist at the Texas A&M AgriLife Extension Service, clay soil that is heavy and sticky when it's wet and that gets deep cracks when it's dry in the summer can benefit from expanded shale. Plants don't grow well in clay soil because they don't get enough oxygen, and expanded shale creates cavities in the soil to hold both air and water. Steve recommends adding 3 in. of 1/4 to 3/8-in. shale, along with 3 in. of compost, and tilling them into your soil 6 to 8 in. deep. Then cover your garden bed with a 3-in. layer of mulch.

The good news about expanded shale is that, unlike with other amendments such as compost or fertilizer, you need to add the shale to your garden beds only once. After that, you'll never need to add compost or commercial fertilizer again. The bad news is that expanded shale costs more than compost (about $10 for a 40-lb. bag; slightly less if you buy it in bulk). But according to George, it's worth it. "Using expanded shale is just so much better. It makes it fun to garden in clay."

BEFORE

AFTER

HEADACHE #3:
Heavy Shade Kills Grass

"I have tried to grow grass many times over the years. But thanks to the heavy shade cast by our oak trees, by midsummer our backyard consists of small, lonely tufts of grass surrounded by bare earth."

Expert input: A shade garden can be a beautiful way to deal with mature trees. However, planting a garden at the base of a tree can be challenging for both the plants and the tree. Shade isn't the only issue: "The plants will also need to cope with dry soil and root competition," says Doris Taylor, a plant information specialist at the Morton Arboretum near Chicago. "And many trees are sensitive to having their roots disturbed." Doris offers these suggestions for planting a successful shade garden near a tree without harming the tree:

- Consult online resources and the local extension service to choose drought- and shade-tolerant plants for your zone.
- Newly established plants of any kind (even drought-tolerant plants) need supplemental water the first year. If the tree hates having its feet (roots) consistently wet, spot-water your new plants.
- Most tree roots are in the top 12 to 18 in. of soil and extend past the canopy. Don't cover existing tree roots with more than 1 in. of soil or they can suffocate. Tilling near a tree can destroy the fine root hairs that take up water. Instead, plant in the pockets of soil between larger roots and add slow-release organic compost to the individual planting holes.
- Don't plant closer than 12 in. from the trunk. Plant shallow-rooted perennials that don't require frequent division, such as hostas, sedums and liriope.
- Shallow-rooted trees, like oaks, lindens, magnolias and many maples, are sensitive to disturbance and can be easily damaged. Consider adding a bench or planters near those trees instead of a shade garden.

HEADACHE #4:
Multiplying Mushrooms

"We have so many mushrooms in our lawn that they make the weeds seem easy to control. We must have six different kinds, and they're worst after it rains. Those mushrooms are disgusting. Also, we've got a dog and grandkids—I'm worried someone's going to eat one."

Expert input: There's good news and bad news if you have this problem. The good news, according to retired University of Minnesota turf expert Bob Mugaas, is that while mushrooms can look unsightly (and they are worse in years with a lot of rain), they're actually beneficial to your lawn. "They're part of the breakdown of organic material in the soil, and they help recycle nutrients," he says.

The bad news, as this homeowner has already discovered, is that mushrooms are nearly impossible to get rid of. They're actually the fruit of an extensive underground root system. (They are like the tip of an iceberg.) So even if you remove the visible mushrooms or use fungicides, the source is still there.

According to Bob, you have several options. "You can certainly pull them," he says. This won't permanently rid your lawn of mushrooms, but it can give you temporary relief.

You can also make your lawn less hospitable to fungi by correcting drainage problems and eliminating decaying organic matter. Grind down stumps, rake up grass clippings, dig up buried lumber, replace old mulch, aerate and dethatch.

The easiest option (or maybe the hardest) is to make peace with your mushrooms. Their numbers will increase and decrease depending on the season. Teach children never to eat mushrooms from the lawn, and keep a close eye on your pets during cool, wet periods.

HEADACHE #5: Boggy Backyard

"Our house is at the bottom of a slope, and every time we have a hard rain, everything becomes a muddy mess. We get water in the crawl space and in the basement. We can't grow anything since it all just gets washed away. Our backyard is like a wasteland."

Expert input: One option is to build a French drain that doubles as a gravel walkway. "This is a creative solution for invisibly controlling a lot of water," says landscape architect Susan Jacobson. A French drain is similar to a dry creek bed, except the water flows underground through a drainpipe enclosed in a gravel-filled trench. It's effective because water flows through gravel much more quickly than through soil. The water migrates into the trench and flows out of the drain at its end point. The net effect, according to Susan, is that your lot dries out. "This solution works well if you have a place to dump the water safely, such as a sandy area or a side yard that slopes away from your foundation," she says.

If you don't have a place for the water to go, try creating a small holding pond that actually takes advantage of the excess water. "The idea," says Susan, "is to work with the natural features of your yard rather than against them." Another alternative is to build a dry well. This is essentially a holding tank for a large amount of water runoff that will slowly drain into the surrounding soil. (For step-by-step instructions, visit *familyhandyman.com* and search for "yard drainage.")

HEADACHE #6: An Eroding Slope

"Our beautiful backyard slope is washing down onto our patio with every rain. It's only a matter of time before the whole hill comes tumbling down!"

Expert input: "A dry creek bed can work well to control erosion if there's a place for the water to go, such as a sandy area somewhere else on your property," says landscape architect Susan Jacobson. In its most basic form, a dry creek bed is simply a gully or trough filled with rocks that directs the flow of water to prevent erosion. To control larger volumes of water, pin landscape fabric in the gully and mortar the rocks into place. Constructing the creek bed with rocks of several different sizes gives it a natural look and maximizes its water-carrying abilities—you'll likely notice it filling dramatically during the next heavy rain. Plus, a dry creek bed can often be an attractive addition to your landscape.

But Susan says that building a dry creek bed won't work in every situation. "You'll create a bigger problem (and a potentially illegal situation) if you direct the water into the street or into your neighbor's yard," she says. "And if the slope is too steep, you might just end up with the rocks tumbling down the hill."

To control erosion on a particularly steep slope or when there's no reasonable place for the water to flow, consider these suggestions:

- Terrace the slope with boulders, stone retaining walls or landscape timbers to gradually flatten the incline and slow the water drainage.
- Use layered plantings of deep- and shallow-rooted trees, shrubs and ground covers to prevent water runoff.
- Don't use plastic, straw, mulch, grass or shallow-rooted ground covers alone to control erosion on a slope, because they won't be stable over the long term.

CRABBY
GNOMEOWNER

HAPPY
GNOMEOWNER

Give Hopeless Grass a Fresh Start

Sometimes it's worth it to kill off the old grass and seed a healthy new lawn.

Let's get this straight right from the get-go: A healthy lawn doesn't get taken over by weeds. So if it looks as if you're raising weeds in your lawn instead of grass, that's a sign of a more serious problem. And solving that problem may mean killing off the existing grass and starting over. It's a big project that'll take several weekends and may cost you up to 25¢ per sq. ft. for equipment rentals, soil conditioners and seed. If you're willing to spend a bit more money, you can lay sod instead of planting seed, but don't skip the steps of soil testing and remediation.

Are you ready for a fresh start? Just follow our guide and you'll be the happiest gnomeowner on your block.

ARE WE TALKING ABOUT YOUR GRASS?

Total destruction shouldn't be your first option. Instead, start with spot applications of weed killer, dethatching and core aeration. But if you still see more than 60% weeds at the start of the next growing season, your lawn is too far gone to save. Your best option is to kill the grass and replant it.

STEP 1: Get a Soil Analysis

Don't even think about replanting until you get the results of a soil analysis (the cost is usually less than $20). Contact a local extension service or search the Internet for a soil-testing lab near you. Select three different locations around your lawn and collect samples. Mix them together and scoop the soil into a container. Note on the lab form that you'll be planting new grass. Also note whether you bag the clippings when you mow or return them to the lawn. In a couple of weeks, you'll get a report with recommendations about which fertilizers or soil treatments to add.

STEP 2: Kill Everything

You can kill the grass with chemicals such as Roundup or Killzall. But if you hate the idea of using chemicals and you have a large area, rent a sod cutter to remove the lawn surface. Or kill the grass by blocking out its sunlight with black poly film (4 mil or thicker; about $100 for a 28 x 100-ft. roll). Remove the poly when the grass is dry and brown (two to three weeks or longer, depending on the weather).

STEP 3: Remove the Dead Stuff

Now comes the upper body workout: Rake up the dead grass and weeds before you amend the soil. Yup, it's got to be done.

STEP 4: Improve the Soil

Don't think you can fix bad soil just by adding a few inches of black soil on top of the old stuff. Instead, rent a tiller (usually about $45 per day) to till in the soil conditioners recommended by the soil analysis.

1 Collect samples for a soil test. Plunge your spade about 6 in. deep and pull out a plug of soil. Then slice off a section of the plug (top to bottom). Remove the grass and rocks and mix all the samples together.

2 Kill the grass with plastic. Lay the poly film over the lawn and secure it with rocks or stakes. **Or kill it with herbicide.** Cover nearby plants with a tarp. Choose a calm, windless day and hold the spray head close to the grass to prevent overspray.

3 Rake off the dead grass. Rip up all the dead grass and weeds with a rigid tine rake—and lots of muscle.

4 Till in the soil conditioners. Spread the conditioners across the entire lawn. Then till them into the soil to a depth of about 5 in.

5 Rake the soil. Level and smooth the soil with a broom rake. Then drag the rake (tines up) to create furrows.

6 Jump-start the seed with lawn starter fertilizer. Spread the fertilizer into the furrows with a spreader. Don't overdo it.

PRO TIP

When to Plant

There are good and bad times of year for starting a project like this. In cold climates, plant new grass seed in early spring when the lawns are just coming out of winter (early to mid-April) or in late summer (from about mid-August to mid-September). In warm-weather climates, plant in late spring or early summer. If you're not sure, contact your local extension service to get planting advice from a turf expert.

STEP 5: Smooth the Soil

Grass seed needs smooth and level ground to get the best germination. And it needs good seed-to-soil contact. So first remove all rocks and debris, then smooth the soil with a rake.

STEP 6: Add a Starter Fertilizer

A starter fertilizer gives grass seeds the nutrients they need to germinate and grow quickly. Consult with a local nursery to find the best starter fertilizer for the type of seed you select. When you apply the fertilizer, follow the instructions on the bag for the proper spread rate for a new lawn.

STEP 7: Pick the Seed to Match Your Site

Consult with the grass expert at a garden center to select a type of grass seed that matches your site conditions, lawn care preferences and budget. Ask about the newer low-maintenance and drought-resistant varieties.

Purchase grass seed by the bag or in bulk by the pound. But buy just what you need. Don't apply the leftover seed—extra seed actually reduces the germination rate.

STEP 8: Prepare the Seed

To avoid applying too much seed, mix the seed in a 4:1 ratio with a fertilizer/bulking agent (Milorganite is one brand; about $15 for a 36-lb. bag).

8 Mix the seed. Pour the seed and fertilizer into a plastic bucket and mix it thoroughly.

9 **Cover the seed.** Turn the broom rake upside down and drag it from side to side over the furrows until only 10 to 15% of the seed remains uncovered. **Compact the soil.** Fill a sod roller halfway with water and roll the area to pack the soil-and-seed mixture.

10 **Spread seed accelerator.** Set the spreader to the widest setting and walk quickly to get a light application of the pellets.

11 **Water regularly.** Place an impact sprinkler in the corner of the lawn and set it to spray in a quarter arc. Then move it to the other corners.

12 **Make the first cut.** Mow the new lawn once it reaches a height of 3 in. Use a new or newly sharpened blade—it's healthiest for the grass. Cut just 1/2 in. per mowing.

STEP 9: Spread the Seed

Load the seed into a spreader and apply it. Make sure it doesn't fly into nearby gardens. Rake to cover the furrows as shown. Then compact the soil with a sod roller (rent one for about $20 per day) to get good seed-to-soil contact.

STEP 10: Add Mulch or Grass Seed Accelerator

Cover the soil with compost mulch to retain water during germination. Or apply a type of grass seed accelerator (GreenView, *greenviewfertilizer.com*, has one for about $30 for 38 lbs., covering up to 760 sq. ft.). The accelerator absorbs more moisture than either mulch or hay and then slowly releases it. It also degrades naturally, eliminating cleanup.

STEP 11: Water, but Not Too Much

Water the new lawn generously right after the mulch application, but be sure to stop as soon as you see puddles forming. Then keep the soil moist to a depth of 4 to 6 in. for the best germination. Keep watering the lawn regularly as the seedlings appear and grow. Gradually reduce the watering over a six-week period. Then switch back to your normal watering routine.

STEP 12: Cut the Grass with TLC

Set the cutting height to 2-1/2 in. Use a new or sharpened blade in order to make sharp, clean cuts. Avoid using a dull blade to mow—it rips the grass, setting up the conditions for disease.

Kill Your Crabgrass!

Don't let a few stubborn tufts sidetrack your quest for the perfect lawn.

If you have a lawn, chances are you've battled crabgrass. The most effective way to control it is to use preemergent herbicides, but they work only if you use them right. Follow these tips from a turf pro and you'll be on your way to winning the war on crabgrass.

1. FERTILIZE YOUR LAWN AND KILL CRABGRASS AT THE SAME TIME

The most cost-effective way to apply a preemergent herbicide is to use a fertilizer with crabgrass preventer added to it. These combination products are readily available in the spring and cost about $20 for a 5,000-sq.-ft. bag at garden centers. Apply it when you would normally apply your first application of fertilizer, and do it just before it rains to work both the fertilizer and the herbicide into the soil. The fertilizer will help thicken the turf. Thicker turf helps to squeeze out crabgrass plants missed by the herbicide. Common brands include Fertilome Weed-Out, Sta-Green Crab-Ex Plus and Scotts Turf Builder Halts.

2. CHECK THE KEY INGREDIENT

There are many different trade names for "weed and feed" products on the market. Chemical names can be confusing. Look carefully at the ingredients panel for pendimethalin, prodiamine or dithiopyr. These active ingredients, which are sold under brand names such as Dimension and Barricade, will kill crabgrass in most areas of the United States and in many kinds of turf. However, it's always wise to ask your local extension service which chemicals are best for your area and turf species.

3. DON'T SKIP A SPRING

Killing crabgrass this year doesn't mean you're off the hook next year. Crabgrass seeds can lie dormant in the soil for several years and will germinate once they make their way to the soil surface. Don't be lulled into a false sense of perfect turf security. Make a habit every spring of applying a pre-emergent herbicide to prevent seeds from getting established. And if your lawn is overtaken by crabgrass now, applying a preemergent herbicide every spring will eventually wipe it out and prevent those seeds from germinating in the future.

4. TIME YOUR APPLICATION BY WATCHING YOUR SHRUBS

Crabgrass germinates when soil temperatures reach 55 to 60 degrees F, which could be as early as February or as late as May depending on where you live. Applying your preemergent herbicide at the right time is critical, because it works by killing germinated crabgrass seeds before they sprout. If you apply it too early, it will lose its potency before the crabgrass sprouts. If you apply it too late, it won't do any good. In the North, a good rule of thumb is to apply preemergent herbicide when lilacs or forsythias are blooming; in the South, it's when dogwoods are blooming. You can also buy an inexpensive soil thermometer (about $15 at garden centers) to monitor soil temperature.

5. SPOT-KILL CRABGRASS THAT COMES UP

To kill crabgrass that appears later in the summer, spot-spray infested areas with a postemergence herbicide designed specifically to kill crabgrass and other annual grass weeds—quinclorac is the most common active ingredient. Typical broadleaf herbicides, like the ones that kill dandelions and clover, will not take out crabgrass. The best time to start spot-spraying for crabgrass is when the plants are mature, usually in early to mid-July.

6. KEEP YOUR LAWN HEALTHY

A weak lawn that is poorly cared for is simply an open invitation to crabgrass and other weeds. The best way to stop crabgrass is to shade it out with a dense, healthy lawn.

The key to maintaining a healthy lawn? Proper care. That means watering, mowing, fertilizing, core aerating, top-dressing with compost and reseeding thin spots. For detailed step-by-step instructions on all these topics, visit *familyhandyman.com* and search for "lawn care."

7. TWO APPLICATIONS ARE BETTER THAN ONE

Most preemergent herbicides are designed to provide weed control for about eight to 10 weeks. But during unusually hot summers, the herbicides don't last that long because warmer soil temperatures degrade them. This means that your lawn might be vulnerable to crabgrass again by midsummer. To prevent this, use a lawn fertilizer that contains a preemergent herbicide during your second lawn feeding as well as the first. Doing so will extend your crabgrass control into early fall and prevent crabgrass from sneaking back into your lawn during late summer. That way, you can sit back and enjoy your summer barbecues without getting "crabby" over a new patch of crabgrass.

8. RESEED OR KILL—NOT BOTH

It's important to remember that herbicides formulated to kill crabgrass will also kill desirable grasses such as bluegrass, ryegrass and fescue. If you treat your lawn with a preemergent herbicide, you cannot seed. And if you seed, you cannot use a preemergent herbicide. The solution is to control crabgrass in the spring and do your seeding in late summer or early fall, making sure to keep these two chores at least eight weeks apart. A few preemergent herbicides, such as Tupersan, are compatible with newly established seed, but they are expensive and can be hard to find.

9. APPLY A DOUBLE DOSE NEAR HOT SPOTS

Grassy areas near driveways, sidewalks and curbs or on south-facing banks absorb a lot of heat during the summer months, which makes them more susceptible to crabgrass.

You can effectively limit crabgrass growth in these areas by doing a targeted double treatment. After you've treated your entire lawn, go back and make another pass, about 6 to 8 ft. wide, along these areas (and make sure to sweep the herbicide off hard surfaces afterward). This will help keep crabgrass from taking hold along these heat absorbers.

10. KNOW WHEN TO THROW IN THE TOWEL

Sometimes a lawn becomes so overrun by crabgrass and other unwelcome weeds that it makes more sense to start over rather than try to save it. If weeds occupy more than 50% of an area, it's best to start over by destroying the entire lawn and reseeding it or sodding it over. You'll thank yourself in the long run. Late summer or early fall is the best time of year to take on this project. For step-by-step instructions on how to start a lawn from scratch, see "Give Hopeless Grass a Fresh Start" on page 118 or visit *familyhandyman.com* and search for "seed a lawn."

Consider Chemical-Free Control Methods

Preemergent herbicides are the most effective and economical way to control crabgrass. But if you'd rather not use herbicides, you can try hand-weeding individual crabgrass plants in late spring before they get too big. They can be pulled easily from soft ground after a rain.

Corn gluten meal (CGM), a corn by-product, is another method used to control crabgrass and broadleaf weeds such as dandelions and clover. It releases a protein that slows the development of weed seedlings' roots. CGM requires a heavy application rate (20 lbs. per 1,000 sq. ft.), which makes it expensive and cumbersome to use. It costs about $30 for 25 lbs. at garden centers.

The Art of Felling a Tree

We'll show you how to make it fall where you want it to.

It would be hard to name a more dangerous DIY project than felling a big tree. There's the obvious risk of getting crushed by the falling tree, but you also could have your melon crushed if a big limb were to shake loose from above. Trees can twist as they fall and make all kinds of other unexpected moves. Add a chain saw to the mix, and—well, you get the idea. It's not a job for the careless, the reckless or the faint of heart.

Here, we'll detail some commonsense precautions you should take and techniques you should employ to make tree

felling as safe as possible. We'll also tell you how to analyze the situation so you'll know when it's best to call in a pro.

Besides a chain saw, a stiff dose of common sense and a bit of courage, a few other things are required to properly fell a tree. They include safety gear (see "The Right Stuff" on p. 127) and two plastic felling wedges to keep your saw from getting pinched in cuts on larger trees. You can find everything you'll need at any outdoor power equipment store that carries chain saws. Don't bother looking for these items at home centers.

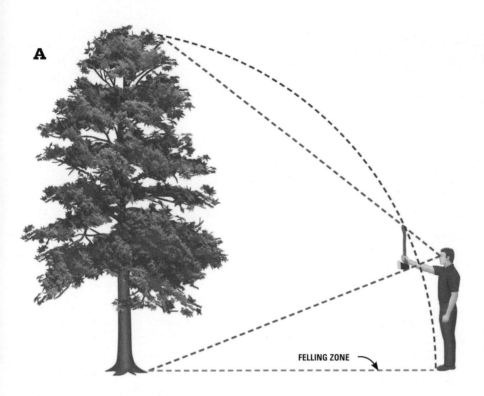

A

FELLING ZONE

A. ESTIMATE THE FELLING ZONE

Trees are taller than you think they are, and they reach farther on the ground than you might expect (maybe all the way to your shed or garage). Luckily, you can estimate where a tree will fall by using the "ax handle trick." Hold an ax handle at arm's length, close one eye and back away from or move toward the tree until the top of the ax handle is even with the treetop and the bottom is even with the base. Your feet should be about where the treetop will rest after falling. It's just an estimate, though, so allow extra room if there's something nearby that the tree might fall on!

B. SIZE UP THE TREE

Start by studying the crown of the tree. Look for dead branches that are broken but attached, or ones that are actually broken off and supported by other branches. Don't even think about cutting down the tree yourself if you see any danger upstairs. You're bound to knock a branch loose and have it fall on you.

Next look at the lean and the branch loading. If the tree is obviously leaning in one direction or heavily loaded with branches on one side, that's the way it's going to fall. Forget the myth that pros can drop a tree on top of an empty beer can. If the tree is perfectly straight and evenly loaded, maybe they'll get close. But if it's unevenly loaded or leaning, they won't have a chance.

Are there any buildings, fences, power lines or other things you care

B

The Right Stuff

Safety isn't a throwaway word when it comes to felling trees and running chain saws. You must take it seriously. There are a few absolutely essential pieces of safety gear you need to wear for any chain saw work:

Loggers helmet: The helmet protects you from falling branches, a major cause of logging injuries. Earmuffs and a face screen protect your ears and eyes. Safety glasses keep the dust out—you don't want something in your eye in the middle of dropping a 4-ft.-diameter cottonwood.

Kevlar chaps: Kevlar fibers will stop a chain instantly should you happen to drop the bar against your leg. It's the best logging safety device developed in the past 30 years, and it's a rare (and foolish) pro who doesn't wear them.

Felling wedges: These wedges will prevent your saw from getting pinched during a cut.

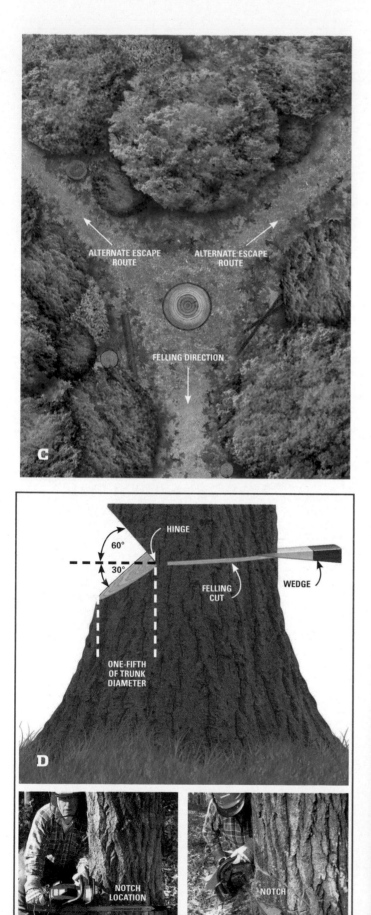

about in the felling zone? If so, that's your sign to skip the felling and call a pro.

C. CLEAR A CUTTING ZONE

Once you're sure which way the tree is going to fall, cut away any brush around the trunk and clear two escape routes on the "nonfalling" side of the tree. They should be about 45 degrees away from each other in opposite directions. You don't want to trip while walking away from a falling tree.

D. ANATOMY OF A PROPER NOTCH

The depth of the notch should be one-fifth of the tree trunk's diameter. The goal is to make the angles as shown in the diagram (or as close as you can). The felling cut should meet the point of the notch. When the tree starts to fall, the hinge will help guide the tree to fall in the desired direction.

Plan the notch You're going to be cutting a notch on the "fall" side of the trunk. Sight along the handle and adjust the saw until it's pointing toward your fall direction. The spot where the bar touches the bark will be the center of the notch. Before cutting, lay out the notch by marking with chalk or by scoring the bark with the chain saw. Make the notch at a comfortable working height. (You can always shorten the stump later.)

Cut the notch Make the top cut first and then the bottom cut. When you're making the bottom cut, adjust your hand to control the throttle with your thumb. If you meet the top notch perfectly, the wedge you cut will drop out of the notch. But most likely you'll have to extend the cuts from either the top or the bottom so the wedge can drop free.

E. USE WEDGES ON BIG TREES

If your tree has a diameter of more than 18 in., go ahead and make your notch cut and begin the felling cut. Stop cutting

as soon as you've penetrated far enough to pound felling wedges behind the bar. Leave the bar in the cut with the saw running, but lock the chain brake and tap in the wedges. Then finish the cut. The felling wedges will keep the saw from getting pinched in the cut if the tree leans back.

F. MAKE THE FELLING CUT

Score a line connecting the apex of the notch on both sides for a cutting guide. The back cut should be parallel and even with the apex of the notch. Then make the felling cut. As soon as the tree begins leaning, pull the saw free, set the chain brake and walk away along one of your escape routes, keeping an eye on the tree so you can react in case it doesn't fall the way you planned. Never take your eye off a falling tree.

G. A LOOKOUT MIGHT SAVE YOUR LIFE

Ask an assistant to stand a few feet behind you, watch the top of the tree for any falling branches, and let you know when the tree starts to fall. Have your assistant tap you on the shoulder with a stick to alert you when it's time to vacate the area. If it's early in the cut and you get the tap, leave the saw and walk away immediately. That means a branch is falling. Near the end of the cut, a tap means the tree is beginning its descent.

FELLING CUT

Wisdom on Tree-Dropping

- Never cut on a breezy day.
- You'll have an easier time cutting up a fallen tree if you do it when the leaves are missing.
- Grab the chain saw handle with an encircling thumb on your right hand and never release it during a cut.
- Stay away from hollowed-out trees, especially if they're big. These trees are very unpredictable and dangerous to fell.
- Gas up the saw before beginning a cut. Never run out of gas halfway through a cut.
- Once you start working, don't stop until the tree is down. You don't want the tree to fall while you're taking a break.

Pressure Washer Smarts

One of these cleaning machines can be a great investment. Make it last (and get the most bang for your buck) by caring for it properly.

Once you've used a pressure washer and seen the results, you'll wonder how you ever got along without one. In fact, you'll find new uses for it every time you fire it up! We talked to several manufacturers and a few power washer fanatics to learn the best tips for using and maintaining a pressure washer. And we learned how to avoid the most common mistakes DIYers make, like leaving water in the pump through winter, using the wrong nozzle for the job and letting the engine idle for more than a few minutes. Read on to find out for yourself.

1. MAKE YOUR PUMP LAST LONGER

Leaving water in the pump can result in mineral buildup and corrosion, which can wear out the pump seals and pistons (a $200 repair). So it pays to flush the pump after every use—a quick job. Pick up a can of pump lube/antifreeze solution (such as Briggs & Stratton 6151 Pressure Washer Pump Saver; about $10 at home centers). Screw the garden hose adapter onto the pump inlet and press the trigger until you see foamy liquid shoot out the other port. That means the pump is fully lubed and protected against freeze damage.

2. PREP THE ENGINE FOR WINTER STORAGE

The small engines on consumer pressure washers have a limited life span (sometimes less than 200 hours). But you can extend the life of the engine by following these simple prestorage tips.

- Even if you have only a few hours' use on the crankcase oil, drain the oil and refill with fresh oil (follow the manufacturer's recommendation for viscosity and type). Then run the engine for a few minutes to coat all the internal parts with clean oil and fresh anticorrosion additives. That will provide the best protection during storage, and you'll be ready to rock and roll at the start of the next season.

- Whether you run the engine dry or fill the tank to the brim, always run the engine with fresh gas treated with fresh fuel stabilizer first. Run the engine for a few minutes so the treated gas fills the carburetor. Then drain the tank and run it dry. Or fill the tank to the brim.

- As we covered above in tip 1, be sure to flush out the pump before putting it away for the winter. If you live in a freezing climate and you leave the pump full of water, your pump will be destroyed.

3. BUY AN EXTRA HOSE TO SAVE TIME

Most consumer pressure washers come with a 25-ft. hose. That means you have to lug the machine up stairs to wash your deck or constantly shut down the engine so you can move the machine as you work. Phooey on that! Just add a 50-ft. extension hose to your 25-ft. factory hose and leave the pressure washer in one spot. (You can buy a 50-ft. extension hose and a hose-to-hose coupler, No. ND10040P, at *northerntool.com* or any home center.) The extra hose will cause a slight drop in pressure and volume, but you'll still have enough power to clean most surfaces.

Flush after every use. Attach the lubricant can to the garden hose port. Press the trigger for about two seconds until water and lube shoot out the other port.

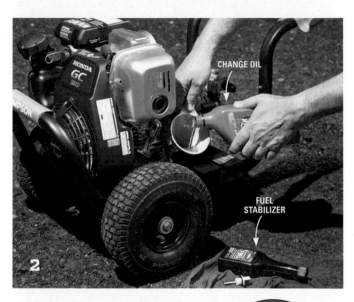

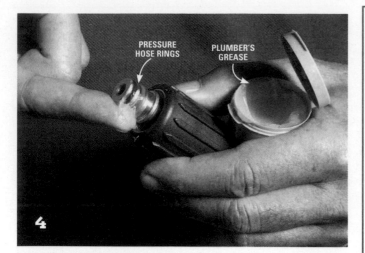

PRESSURE HOSE RINGS

PLUMBER'S GREASE

4

5

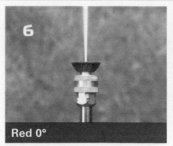

6

Red 0°

A zero-degree nozzle produces a concentrated pencil-point spray with no fan. Use it to blast mud or debris off surfaces from a distance or to remove weeds from cracks in concrete.

Yellow 15°

A 15-degree nozzle produces a spray with a slight fan pattern. Hold the nozzle at a 45-degree angle to use it like a scraper when you're removing peeling paint or dislodging other coatings.

Green 25°

A 25-degree nozzle produces a wider fan pattern that's perfect for removing dirt and grime. This nozzle can also be used as a water broom to sweep debris off a driveway.

White 40°

A 40-degree nozzle produces the widest fan pattern. Use it to wash delicate surfaces like deck boards, glass and vehicle exteriors.

4. LUBRICATE THE HOSE CONNECTORS WITH SILICONE

Dry O-rings in a hose connector can twist slightly and tear as you make the connection, causing them to fail. Since regular oil washes off when it gets wet, buy a small container of silicone plumber's grease instead. It doesn't wash off and it's compatible with all types of O-ring materials. Tape the container to your machine so you'll always have it handy. Then apply a new coating every five uses or anytime the O-rings look dry.

5. USE CLEANING FLUIDS DESIGNED FOR PRESSURE WASHERS

Pressure washer soap dispensers are designed for dedicated pressure washer fluids only. General-purpose degreasers, heavy-duty cleaning liquids, bleach and acids can destroy the pump. Even if the soap is rated for pressure washer use, make sure it's the right soap for the job—the soaps aren't interchangeable. Vehicle wash soap, for example, won't clean concrete, and the chemicals in concrete soap can discolor alloy wheels and bright metal trim pieces if used to wash

your car or truck. For the best results, let the soap set for the recommended time and scrub heavily soiled surfaces with a brush before you rinse them.

Finally, never leave soap in the dispenser when you store the machine—it can dry into crystals and cause pump damage. Flush the soap dispenser after each use and pull the gun trigger to run clear water through the pump before you shut it down.

6. USE THE RIGHT NOZZLE FOR THE RIGHT JOB

Nozzle tips are color coded to denote their spray pattern. A zero-degree nozzle provides the most power for really stubborn stains. But that force can etch concrete and brick, blast holes in wood siding, break windows and even rip trim off your car. So test the area first and back the tip away from the surface if you notice any etching or damage.

The soap nozzle (which is black) has a large opening to allow maximum water flow through the pump. The high water flow is needed to siphon soap out of the dispenser nozzle. The soaping function won't work with any other nozzle.

7. PULL THE TRIGGER FIRST

When using a gas-powered pressure washer, before you yank the starter rope, pull the gun trigger (or have someone else do it). This will relieve pump pressure and lower engine resistance, making it easier to start.

8. TARP THE AREA BEFORE YOU REMOVE PAINT

Lay down tarps before using your pressure washer to remove peeling paint. When you're done, just grab the corners and pour the chips into a container for disposal or recycling.

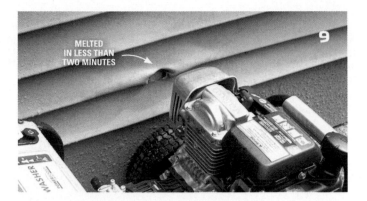

MELTED IN LESS THAN TWO MINUTES

9

9. THREE WAYS TO KEEP FROM WRECKING STUFF

- Don't park the unit too close to structures. Hot exhaust can melt vinyl siding and start fires. The damage shown here **(Photo 9)** was caused in less than two minutes.
- Never run a gas-powered pressure washer in the garage while you clean the garage floor. Move it well away from the house (at least 5 ft.) to prevent dangerous carbon monoxide poisoning.
- Never use a strong spray to remove caulk around windows. The stream can force water behind siding, causing extensive water damage.

10. BUY THESE ACCESSORIES TO GET THE MOST OUT OF YOUR PRESSURE WASHER

- Replacement O-ring kit with filtering screens ($7 at home centers).
- Quick-connect adapters and couplers ($30 per set at home centers). Convert your screw-on pressure washer hose to quick-connect fittings and you'll never have to worry about potential O-ring damage or cross-threading.
- Gutter cleaner attachment ($30 at home centers). Snap this attachment onto a telescoping extension wand. You'll be able to blast the gunk out of your gutters without climbing a ladder.
- Adjustable pressure regulator (less than $30 at home centers). Snap one end onto the hose and the other end onto the gun. Set the pressure to 1,000 psi to protect any delicate items you want to wash.
- 6-in-1 dial nozzle ($30 at home centers). Stop fiddling around with individual nozzles. If your hose uses quick-connect nozzles, just snap this on and you're done.

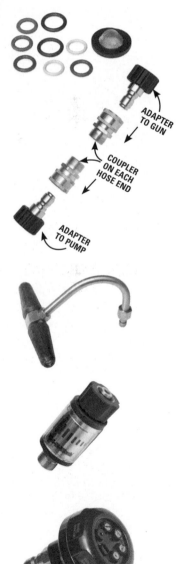

ADAPTER TO GUN

COUPLER ON EACH HOSE END

ADAPTER TO PUMP

Reviving a Wood Deck

Rejuvenating a wood deck that's dirty, stained and covered with mildew and mold is easier than you might think. Here are some tips to make your outdoor space attractive and ready to enjoy again.

A. A POWER WASH WILL WORK WONDERS

You could scrub with a deck brush, but it's far smarter to rent, borrow or buy a pressure washer. You'll need to spray with at least 2,000 psi, and that usually calls for a gas-powered unit— few electric ones possess the power. Choose the 15-degree spray tip and then experiment. The trick is to hold the wand just far enough away to avoid tearing up the wood but close enough to remove all the ugliness. You'll get the feel pretty quickly, but it's best to start in an inconspicuous area. If your washer is capable of distributing detergent, you can use it to speed things up.

B. CLEANERS & BRIGHTENERS

If your deck has black or green stains, choose a cleaner that's formulated to remove mildew. If you just want to brighten a deck with a dull finish, try a simple deck brightener, which will remove a thin layer of aged wood fibers. You can apply either product with a plastic pump sprayer. Scrub the deck while the brightener or mildew remover is still wet, then rinse the residue immediately. Feel free to experiment, though—sometimes a pressure washer can handle both the scrubbing and the rinsing.

C. CHOOSING A STAIN

You have to balance how much traffic your deck gets, the condition of your deck and how much maintenance you can stand. Here are the choices:

Transparent: It goes on easy as pie, but you'll see every little flaw on an old deck since it has less pigment than semi or solid stains. Transparent stains don't wear as well either, so you will be down to bare wood in a year or two and will have to reapply it if you want a fresh finish. You'll need to clean it again, but that and the recoat go pretty doggone fast.

Semitransparent: Because there's more pigment in semitransparent stains than in transparent ones, they last longer and wear better under foot traffic. They offer more UV protection, too. Depending on how long you wait to recoat the deck, you may have to use a stripper first.

Solid stains: If you want a finish that lasts three to four years, a solid stain may be the best choice—but there is a dark side. If you're not meticulous with the prep work or if your deck gets lots of foot traffic, solid stains can start to peel, which means extra work. Peeling (which is typical of a failing solid stain but not of the other two) is especially unsightly and obvious because it exposes the bare wood beneath the finish.

Still, solid stains mask flaws well and help blend in any newer wood you've installed to replace bad deck boards. Choose a solid stain if hiding surface flaws is what matters most to you, there's little foot traffic and you're willing to do extra work when it's time to refinish your deck.

D. SOMETIMES DECKS NEED STRIPPING

If a thoroughly cleaned deck has leftover finishes, especially solid stains, you'll have to get busy with a deck stripper. It's not as arduous as it sounds. Stripper typically dries in about 15 minutes, so work in sections, spreading a heavy coat over a small area that you can scrub before it dries. Then rinse it off and recoat any areas that have stubborn spots. You may have to use a stripping disc in an angle grinder to knock off any really rough areas.

STRIPPING DISC

E. CLEAN OUT THE CRACKS

Don't leave all that organic stuff in the cracks between the boards. You can make your own cleaner for the cracks by screwing a utility hook into the end of a broom handle or board, and use it to plow out all that junk. We used a grinder to make the hook thinner so it would fit into tighter cracks.

F. APPLY DECK STAIN FAST WITH A PAINT PAD

Before you begin, cover anything beneath the decking that you want to protect from stain drips. Start your stain application by cutting in around posts and areas next to the siding with a brush. Stain the adjoining deck areas before the cut-in stain dries. You can spray or roll on the finish on the main deck section, then back-brush it to even it out. Or use a paint pad on an extension handle. Always overlap the previous board and maintain a wet edge as you go. The goal is to prevent lap marks. Avoid staining on hot days, and never apply stain when the deck is in direct sunlight.

Tape off and cover fascia and trim boards, even if you plan to stain them; any drip marks will show up noticeably darker. Each additional row of stain should be applied while the previous row is still wet; this helps blend the finishes. To gauge the open work time before the stain dries, you'll have to consider how much cut-in work you're doing, the weather conditions and the particular product you're using.

D

E

F

PRO TIP

Read Product Directions

When you're using liquid restoration or finishing products on decks, be sure to read the label at least twice. Some products need diluting, some are very sensitive to temperature and some require completely dry wood. All that labor you're putting into this project could go to waste because of a simple application mistake. So remember: Study the directions carefully, then follow them!

7 Roof Problems and What to Do About Them

Rusting, rotting and leaking—oh my! Identifying and addressing common roof issues before they get worse will save you time, stress and money in the long run.

Your roof covers the largest asset you own, so it pays to know the signs of trouble. Fortunately, many of the danger signals are easy to see—you can sometimes even spot them from the ground. (Tip: binoculars help!)

A small leak can go undetected for years, causing massive damage before you notice anything's wrong, so it's a good idea to inspect your roof regularly. Many contractors offer free inspections. But even if you have to pay, it's better than finding leaks after the damage is done—your wallet will thank you down the line. Ask inspectors, and they'll tell you that they've made thousands of inspections and revealed thousands of looming problems. Here are a few of the most common and easily recognized ones.

SHINGLES USUALLY AREN'T THE PROBLEM

Shingles rarely leak, even if they're crumbling and long overdue for replacement. In reality, most leaks occur where the shingles stop: at chimneys, walls, vents or valleys. So although you shouldn't ignore aging shingles, you should look for trouble in other areas first.

1. ROOF CEMENT

Metal flashing prevents leaks where shingles meet other surfaces, like walls and chimneys. Proper flashing work takes time and know-how, so sloppy roofers sometimes slather on roof cement instead. It seals out water long enough for them to cash your check, but the cement soon hardens, cracks and leaks. In the end, all it does is make a proper repair more difficult. So if you see heavy "tar" patchwork on your roof, fix it—before it leaks and leads to interior damage.

2. NO CHIMNEY CRICKET

A wide chimney forms a dam on your roof. Debris can then build up behind that dam and hold moisture, which leads to rusted flashing and wood rot. Any chimney wider than 30 in. needs a "cricket," or "saddle": basically a small roof built behind the chimney. A properly installed chimney

"Tar" means trouble. Roofing cement may seal out water for a few months, even a few years. But it's sure to fail eventually.

A dam on the roof. A wide chimney traps debris, which stays wet and causes rust or rot. A cricket diverts debris. This miniature roof behind the chimney will channel water and debris away from the chimney.

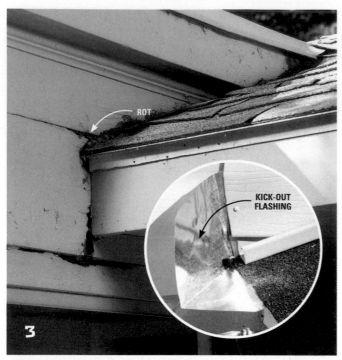

Water gets into walls. Without kick-out flashing, water flows down the wall and seeps behind siding and trim. Water may enter the walls close to the roof as shown here, or at any point downhill from the roof. **Kick-out flashing is simple.** It consists of a bent section of step flashing that diverts water away from the wall.

Shortcut flashing. Instead of several sections of flashing covered by counterflashing, the side of this chimney has just two pieces of flashing. Big leaky gaps have opened at the ends of the flashing. **Good flashing.** Proper flashing includes many parts, including counterflashing to cover the step flashing. Counterflashing may be a single piece or several.

cricket will direct water and debris around the chimney and off the roof. If your chimney doesn't have one, watch for holes rusting through the flashing. If you're getting a new roof, be sure the contractor's bid includes a cricket.

3. MISSING KICK-OUT FLASHING

Kick-out flashing is critical where a roof edge meets a sidewall. Without it, roof runoff flows down the wall and possibly into the wall. This is worst when there is a door or a window below and water can seep behind the trim. You might not notice it for years, but eventually rot will destroy sheathing and framing. In some cases, by the time an inspector arrives the stucco is the only thing holding up the wall! Don't wait for that to happen to you and your home. To see how to add kick-out flashing, go to *familyhandyman.com* and search for "kick-out flashing."

4. BAD CHIMNEY FLASHING

Good chimney flashing includes sections of step flashing (which runs up the sides of a chimney) and counterflashing (which fits into grooves cut into the chimney and covers the step flashing). Cutting, fitting and installing all those parts takes time and effort, so sloppy roofers tend to take shortcuts.

Improperly flashed chimneys cause lots of rotting roof sheathing and framing members. Chimneys need to be properly step-flashed and counterflashed so water can't run down the face of the chimney and into the attic. Inspectors commonly discover chimneys with no flashing, or bad flashing that relies on caulk or roof cement. If you suspect your flashing is shoddy, crawl into the attic after a heavy rain. Look for signs of water around the chimney and downhill from it.

5. MISSING GUTTER APRON

When water flows off the edge of your roof, some of it clings to the underside of the shingles and dribbles toward the fascia. If you have gutters but no gutter apron to stop the water, it will wick behind the gutter. Eventually the fascia, the soffits and even the roof sheathing will rot. You may see water stains below the gutter on the fascia and soffit. This is a sure sign that gutter apron is missing.

The best time to add gutter apron is when you're getting new shingles. But it is possible to slip gutter apron under existing shingles. A dab of roof cement every couple of feet will "glue" it to the shingles and hold it in place. You'll have to remove gutter brackets or straps and then refasten them after the apron is in place. Gutter apron is available at home centers in 10-ft. lengths (about $5 each).

6. VENT FLASHING FAILURE

Your plumbing system includes "vent" pipes that pass through the roof. And like any other roof penetration, that sometimes means trouble. There are two kinds of flashing used to seal

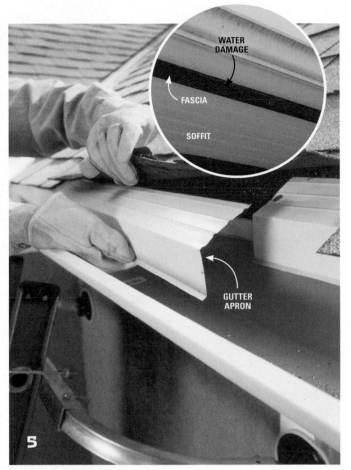

Water gets behind gutters. If there's no gutter apron, water seeps behind gutters, damaging fascia and soffits.

5

Gutter apron retrofit. Adding gutter apron under existing shingles is easiest on a warm day, when shingles are more flexible. If you need a new roof, make sure the contractor's bid includes gutter apron. **Water gets behind gutters.** If there's no gutter apron, water seeps behind gutters, damaging fascia and soffits.

6

Rubber boots can crack. After years of exposure to sun and weather, the seal around this plumbing vent cracked and tore open. **Metal flashing isn't bulletproof.** The lead collar on metal vent flashing usually outlasts the shingles. But it can corrode, crack or even fall victim to gnawing squirrels.

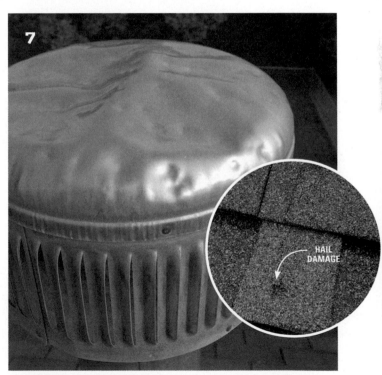

7

Damaged metal is a clue. Any hailstorm that was harsh enough to dent metal probably damaged the shingles, too. Look for dents in metal vents, siding, gutters and flashing. **It doesn't look that bad.** You may not even notice hail damage at first. But the spots where granules are missing will grow as sunlight degrades the shingles.

vents: a "boot" that relies on a snug rubber seal, and all-metal flashing with soft lead that can be bent over and into the pipe. Some versions are made completely from lead; others are galvanized steel with a lead collar. When any type of vent flashing fails, the best solution is to replace it. To see how this works, go to *familyhandyman.com* and search for "plumbing vent flashing."

7. HAIL DAMAGE

When a large hailstone hits an asphalt shingle, it can tear or even puncture the shingle. But usually the hailstone just knocks granules off the surface. While that impact may seem less severe, it can still cause plenty of issues. When a shingle loses its protective layer of granules, UV rays from the sun begin to destroy it. More granules fall off around the damaged spot, and the bruise grows larger. The damage may not be obvious at first, so if you suspect hail damage, get an inspection from a roofing contractor. Most offer free inspections to check for hail damage.

CHAPTER FIVE

FLOORS, CEILINGS, WALLS & TRIM

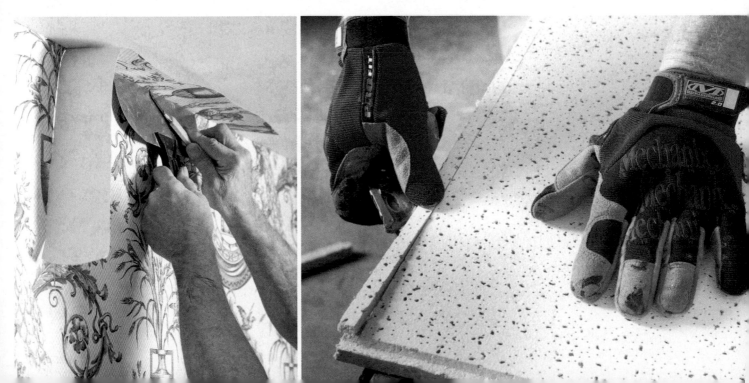

Laminate Floor Clinic

Follow these pearls of wisdom for a DIY project done right.

A. SHEAR—DON'T CUT

Cutting laminate with a miter saw is a noisy and dusty affair. And walking back and forth to your miter saw isn't very efficient. Why not cut the planks with a laminate shear—quietly and cleanly—right where they're going to be installed?

Laminate shears cost anywhere from $60 to $1,000. The lower-end models are available at most home centers. Higher-end models are found at flooring specialty stores or online. A Bullet Tools 13-in. EZ Shear was used here.

B. GRIND DOWN THE HIGHS, FILL IN THE LOWS

Laminate floor systems don't function well on uneven surfaces. Before starting any flooring work, inspect the subfloor. Crawl around with a straightedge to find any areas that are more than 1/8 in. high or low. Subfloor seams are the usual suspects.

A belt sander sporting a coarse-grit belt will knock down seams pretty fast, but you may have to rent a commercial floor sander to grind down severe peaks.

A dip in the floor will cause a soft, spongy section in the laminate floor. Most dips can be taken care of with a trowel and some vinyl floor patch. Buy a fast-drying variety if you want to start laying the floor the same day.

"Avoid self-leveling floor compounds, especially on older homes," says flooring expert Jay Heise, who works for his family's flooring business. "An out-of-level floor could take a whole truckload of self-leveling compound to flatten. And oh, yeah—this is the time to screw the plywood to the joists anywhere there's a squeak."

C. USE THE PROPER TAPE

All underlayment seams need to be taped. It's tempting to use whatever tape you find in the pickup, but don't do it. Some packing tapes and house wrap tapes are too rigid and may cause an annoying crinkling noise when they're stepped on. Use the tape that's recommended by the underlayment manufacturer, or buy an underlayment that has built-in seam tape.

Heise recommends installing underlayment perpendicular to the way the planks will be installed. The underlayment will be less likely to "bubble" as you lay the flooring. And he suggests installing only a few rows of underlayment at a time to avoid tearing it up with your boots.

D. RIP DOWN THE STARTER ROW IF YOU MUST

It's tempting to find the longest, straightest wall and start slapping down planks. The problem is that when you get to the opposite wall, you may end up ripping down a sliver-thin row of flooring. That won't look good and will be tough to install.

Plan ahead by snapping together a section of four or five pieces, put it against one wall and make a pencil line on the outside of the connected piece, then slide the section toward the opposite wall, lining it up with the pencil line. Walk your way across the room like this to determine whether you should start with a ripped row and how wide it should be.

Heise says, "It's not an exact science, but it's a quick way to get a good idea of how wide that last row is going to be without doing a bunch of math."

E. SNAP IN A WHOLE ROW AT ONCE

If you read the instructions on most laminate flooring (that's a big "if," I know), the pieces are supposed to be snapped in consecutively. Some flooring (usually the cheap stuff) is almost impossible to install that way without damaging the planks.

If you're having problems, snap the butt ends of a whole row together, then snap in the row as if it were one long piece.

F. USE TRANSITION STRIPS UNDER DOORS

If you're installing flooring that continues through a doorway, you'll be better off leaving a gap to receive a transition strip between rows (rather than snapping together the flooring). Position the gap directly under the door so the transition strip will make visual sense. A transition strip lets you treat each room as a separate project. This allows for greater flexibility on your layout.

G. IS THE ROOM SQUARE?

When figuring out the size of your starter row, you also have to make sure the walls are parallel. You may find yourself installing laminate in a room that is 6 in. narrower at one end than at the other. That means you'll have to rip a severely tapered last row and it'll look ugly.

Unless one side of the room will be forever covered with furniture, you're better off splitting the difference and tapering both the first and the last rows so neither side will be so noticeable.

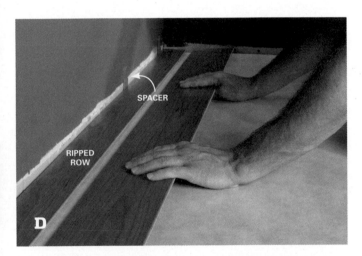

D — SPACER — RIPPED ROW

E

F — TRANSITION STRIP

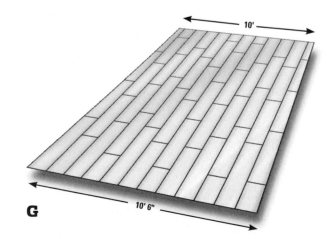

G — 10' — 10' 6"

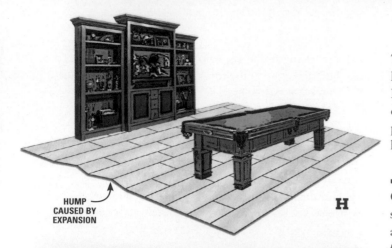

HUMP CAUSED BY EXPANSION

H

I

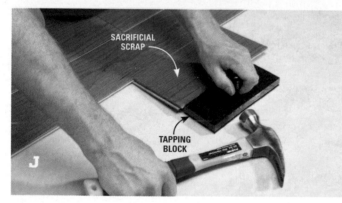

SACRIFICIAL SCRAP

TAPPING BLOCK

J

H. BEWARE OF HEAVY FURNITURE

Laminate floors expand and contract with variations in humidity and temperature. So before starting any laminate job, pay attention to the furniture in the room. Heavy furniture like a pool table or a fully loaded bookshelf can pin down the laminate, causing it to either push up as it expands or separate as it contracts. The trouble really starts when you have two heavy pieces of furniture directly across from each other, trapping the floor. You'll have to either lose one of the furniture pieces or go with a different flooring material to avoid trouble. How much weight will trap a floor? A good rule of thumb is that a typical laminate floor can still move properly under a fully stocked refrigerator.

I. BUY GEL-FILLED KNEE PADS

The hard-shell knee pads worn for roofing and landscaping are not the knee pads you should wear to install a floor.

There's no question about it: Flooring is hard on the knees, and the wrong knee pads will scratch laminate floors. Flooring installation calls for pads that have a cloth, foam or soft rubber material on the business end. "Gel-filled pads are probably the most comfortable, because the gel helps distribute the weight," Heise says.

J. TAP ON A SACRIFICIAL PIECE

Occasionally it'll be necessary to tap a plank into place or snug together an uncooperative one. Yes, you should use a tapping block, but to avoid damaging your brand-new floor, snap in a sacrificial scrap, and tap on that to prevent wrecking the edge of the new flooring.

START BY THE MOST DOORS

Flooring around doorways is one of the thorniest issues you'll deal with. Simplify it by starting on the wall that has the most doorways. You'll still have to undercut jambs and trim, but it's a lot easier starting at a doorway than ending up at one.

ENDING AT DOORWAYS

Often, there's no avoiding ending up at a doorway. When that happens, it's a bit tricky because you have to slide the flooring under both jambs. **Photo 1** and **Photo 2** below show how to handle it.

DOOR-STOP

SECOND PIECE

FIRST PIECE

1 **Lift to fit.** Plan on a seam in the middle of the doorway. Notch and cut the first piece to fit and then slide it completely under the jamb. Notch the second piece so it'll be just short of the doorstop when it's in place. Lift the flooring to get it around the corner and under the casing, then snap it in.

2 **Slide both pieces over.** Once the two pieces are connected, slide them both over just far enough so that both jambs cover the flooring ends.

Cookie Cutter Carpet Patch

Are you tired of looking at that wine stain your brother-in-law so graciously gifted you last Christmas? Before replacing the carpet in the entire room, first try a cookie cutter repair kit for around $30. They're available online (search for "cookie cutter carpet tool") and at flooring supply stores. The idea is to cut out the stain from the highly visible area and replace it with a patch cut from a remnant, or from carpet in a closet or under the sofa.

An adhesive pad holds the new piece in place. Some adhesive pads require ironing. For a stronger bond, use carpet seam sealer around the perimeter to fuse the backing of the patch to the backing of the surrounding carpet. You can buy seam sealer for less than $10 at home centers.

The kit we tried came with thorough instructions, but here are a few things to keep in mind: You'll need to cut out the stained portion first so you can cut out a replacement piece with an identical pattern. Even if your carpet appears to have no pattern, it does. Before installing the new piece, examine the backing on the carpet. It should look like a grid of sorts (you may have to lift it up a bit). The orientation of the grid on the patch should line up with the surrounding carpet.

Try to clear a path for the cutting knives. The fewer carpet fibers you cut, the better. This is harder to do with looped-pile carpeting like Berber. If you're lucky enough to have a remnant, try a practice run on that. As with most seams in carpeting, it might take a while for the patch to blend in, but it will be less noticeable than the eye-grabbing merlot stain.

1 Cut out the stain. Twist to slice out the damaged area. Do the same in a closet to cut a perfect patch.

ADHESIVE PAD

2 Stick in the patch. Lay in an adhesive-backed pad to secure the carpet patch. Make sure the nap direction of the patch matches the nap of the surrounding carpet.

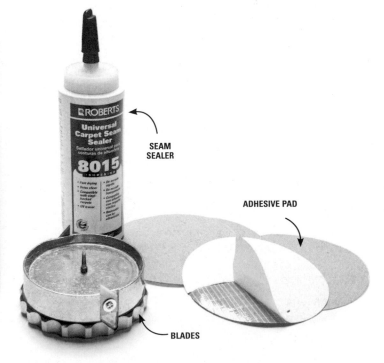

SEAM SEALER

ADHESIVE PAD

BLADES

1 **The oscillating tool method.** Chuck up either a 1/16- or 1/8-in.-wide blade (depending on the grout width) and go to town. Rotate the blade and rechuck it to maneuver into tight corners.

2 **The recip saw method.** Install the carbide-grit grout blade into your recip saw so it points down while the saw handle is pointing up. Apply power and "saw" out the grout.

Two Great Ways to Remove Grout

The worst part of regrouting is the incredibly tedious, tough hand-scraping to get the old stuff out. Now you have two much better options. If you already own a variable-speed reciprocating saw, try a Milwaukee Carbide-Grit Grout Blade (No. 48-08-0415). It works really well. Just make sure to use the slowest speed until you get the feel of the process.

If you don't have a recip saw and you're dying to get your hands on a new oscillating tool, this is now your chance.

An oscillating tool **(Photo 1)** is a bit easier to control than the recip saw **(Photo 2)** because it's smaller and has a much shorter blade stroke. Plus, you can rotate the cutting head, so it's a tad more versatile.

With either tool you'll need to be careful not to chip the tile. We've tried both systems and they work equally fast. The oscillating tool does get you a bit tighter into corners. With either method though, you'll still have to scrape some areas by hand.

Replace a Stair Spindle

It's true: The spindles on your old stair railing weren't installed with the notion that they would someday need to be replaced, but don't be intimidated—they can be, even if the spindles are trapped in holes at the top and bottom.

First, you need to remove the damaged spindle. If the spindle isn't completely broken in half, finish the job with a saw. Then persuade both pieces out of their respective holes.

Next, find the proper size spade or Forstner bit, and overdrill the top hole. Be careful not to punch all the way through the rail. Mark your bit with masking tape if you have to. Overdrilling the hole in the handrail will allow you to push the new spindle up into the railing and then back down into the hole at the base.

You may need to cut down the new spindle to make it fit, but mind which side you trim down. If you cut too much off one side or the other, the shape of the replacement spindle may not line up exactly with the existing spindles. If the old spindle was glued in and the bond is still strong, you may have to cut the damaged spindle out flush and bore two new holes. If you think that the damaged spindle may be held in with a brad nail, don't use your most expensive Forstner bit to bore the new holes.

To find a matching spindle, start local. Try the lumberyard closest to your house. There's a good chance the builder of your home purchased it there. If not, the folks working there may know where it came from. Otherwise you could try an online source. Here are a few: *cheapstairparts.com*, *stairpartsnow.com* and *stairwarehouse.com*. If you can't find a new one, you may need to have one custom made by a local woodturner.

1 Yank out the broken spindle. Wiggle while you pull and make sure you don't break off the end of the spindle in the hole. You may need a big pair of pliers to do the job.

2 Deepen the upper hole. Extra depth lets you insert the top of the spindle far enough to get the bottom end of the spindle into the lower hole.

3 Test the fit. Don't go for the glue until you're sure the new spindle fits. Insert the upper end, then drop the spindle into place.

Flawless Floor Sanding

Do it yourself with these important pro tips for an absolutely smooth job from start to finish.

Sanding hardwood floors might seem like a pros-only project. It's a big job that creates big disruptions in your household. And then there's that big, scary sanding machine…

But it's really not that difficult. Hundreds of homeowners (some of them complete DIY novices) successfully prep their floors for new finishes. Here are some of the most important tips for smooth sanding.

GOODBYE, BASE SHOE

If a room has quarter-round molding (aka "base shoe") at the bottom of baseboards, pry it off and reinstall it later. Here's why: Edge sanding slightly lowers the floor and leaves the baseboard standing on a little plateau. You think you won't notice this, but you will. Edge sanding also scuffs up base shoe, which means touch-up work later.

Removing the base shoe sidesteps both problems. Label the base shoe as you remove it to avoid confusion when you reinstall it. Exception: If the base shoe is bonded to the baseboard by decades of paint buildup, leave it in place. If

you have newer baseboards and no quarter-round, leave the baseboards in place but expect lots of the aforementioned touch-ups.

PET STAINS ARE FOREVER

Water stains usually disappear after a couple of passes of the sander. But stains caused by pet urine often penetrate so deep into the wood that you just can't sand them out. Bleach formulated for wood floors may be worth a try, but the results can be mediocre at best, and at worst, the wood is left pitted and blotched.

Often, the only solution is to replace the wood—or finish over the stain and think of it as a permanent memorial to a beloved pet.

How do you tell water from pee? Pet stains are darker (deep gray, almost black around the edges) and often look like a map of Indonesia, with big and small islands covering a large area. To see how to replace a section of wood floor, go to *familyhandyman.com* and search for "patch wood floor."

A. PREP THE ROOM

Some of the prep work is obvious, such as removing all the furniture and covering doorways with plastic. Here are some steps DIYers often don't think of:

- Cover or plug air grilles to keep dust out of ducts. Turn off the HVAC system at the thermostat; less air movement means less dust traveling around your house.
- Remove all window coverings and any art on the walls (unless you want to clean them later).
- Remove doors that open into the room. You can't completely sand under doors, even by opening and closing them.
- Raise low-hanging light fixtures; just tie two links of the chain together with wire. Otherwise, you're guaranteed to bump your head. Repeatedly.
- Nail down any loose boards with finish nails.
- When you're sanding, nail heads will rip the sanding belt (which costs you money) or gouge the sanding drum (which costs you more money). So countersink all nails by at least 1/8 in.

B. SCRAPE OUT CORNERS

When the sanding is done, use a paint scraper to attack spots that the machines can't reach. A sharp scraper will leave a super-smooth glazed surface that won't take finish the same as the surrounding wood. So rough up scraped areas with 80- or 100-grit paper.

C. RENTAL TIPS

You'll need two rental machines: a drum sander to sand most of the floor and an edger to sand along baseboards. Here are some tips:

- Rent from a flooring specialty shop rather than a general rental store. You'll get expertise at no extra expense.
- Measure the room. Knowing the square footage will help the crew at the rental store estimate how many sanding belts and discs you'll need.
- Prep before you rent. The prep work will take longer than you think. Don't waste money by picking up the sanders before you're ready to use them.
- Get a drum sander that uses a continuous belt or sleeve, not one that requires you to wrap a strip of abrasive around the drum. That's tedious and often leads to chatter marks on the floor.
- Think twice before you rent any flat-pad sanders (aka "orbital" or "square-buff" sanders). Sure, they're easier to use, but they're just not aggressive enough to bite into finishes or hardwoods.

Choose a sander that has a lever to raise and lower the sanding drum. That makes graceful stops and starts easier—and reduces gouging.

D

E

PICK A STARTING GRIT

It takes coarse abrasive to cut through a finish and into hardwood. But determining just how coarse isn't always easy for a DIYer. So try a trial-and-error process: Start with 36-grit. If that doesn't completely remove the finish in one pass, step down to 24-grit. If 24-grit doesn't remove at least three-quarters of the finish in one pass, go to 16-grit. Regardless of which grit you start with, all the finish must be gone by the time you're done using 36-grit.

NIX THE STRIPPER

DIYers often think that paint stripper is a good way to get rid of the finish before sanding. But don't waste your time. Sanding is faster. And cheaper.

D. CHANGE BELTS OFTEN

Using dull belts is a strategy you'll regret. Here's the problem: After the floor finish is gone, you can't see whether the sander is doing its job. So you keep sanding. The machine is raising dust and everything seems fine. But the dull paper isn't cutting deep enough to remove the scratches left by the previous grit. And you may not discover this until you put a finish on the floor. A dull edging disc is even worse, since it won't remove the ugly cross-grain scratches left by the previous disc.

Even if sandpaper feels sharp, it may be beyond its prime. So the best way to judge is by square footage covered. The belts can cover about 250 sq. ft., and edger discs can be spent after about 20 sq. ft. That varies, so ask at the rental store.

E. EDGER EDUCATION

The edger is basically a sanding disc mounted on a big, powerful motor. A simple tool, but not so simple to use. Here are some tips to help you master the edger and minimize the inevitable swirls left by the spinning disc:

- Follow up each phase of drum sanding with edging. After you've drum-sanded at 36-grit, for example, edge with 36-grit.
- Place a nylon pad under the sandpaper. This cushion minimizes gouges and deep swirls. Get pads at the rental store.
- Replace the sandpaper when it's dull. Dull paper won't remove swirls left by the previous grit.
- At the end of the job, lay a flashlight on the floor to highlight any leftover swirls. Then hand-sand them out with 80- or 100-grit paper.
- A warning to woodworkers: You'll be tempted to edge with your belt sander, but even the biggest belt sander can't cut half as fast as an edger. You'll also be tempted to polish out swirls with a random orbit sander. But beware: That can overpolish the wood so it won't take finish the same as the surrounding wood. Hand-sanding is safer.

F. DON'T SKIP GRITS

The initial coarse grits remove the finish and flatten the wood. But that's not enough. You need to progress through every grit to polish off the scratches left by the previous grit. On most jobs, the sequence is 24-36-60-80 for coarse-grained wood like oak. On fine-grained wood like birch or maple, scratches are more visible, so go to 100-grit.

G. CLEAN UP BETWEEN GRITS

Sweep or vacuum the floor before you move up to the next grit. Even the best abrasives throw off a few granules while sanding. And a 36-grit granule caught under a 60-grit belt will leave an ugly gash in the floor. Wrap the vacuum nozzle with tape to avoid marring the floor.

H. SCREEN THE FLOOR

After you've finished with the sanders, the floor will look so good that you'll be tempted to skip this step. But don't. "Screening" blends the edge-sanded perimeter with the drum-sanded field and polishes away sanding scratches. You can do it with a rented buffing machine or with a sanding pole (like the one used for sanding drywall). Either way, the abrasive to use is 120- or 150-grit sanding screen (again, just like the stuff used on drywall).

DOES DIY MAKE CENTS?

DIY floor refinishing typically costs about $1 per sq. ft. Hiring a pro costs from $3 to $8 per sq. ft. On average, especially on jobs that are larger than 500 sq. ft., DIYers can save $1,000 by doing it themselves. Not bad for a weekend of work. Keep in mind that pro prices vary a lot, so it's worth making a few calls to check on pro rates in your area.

G

H

F

Hire the Best Carpet Cleaner

Regular cleaning doesn't just make your carpet look better; it makes it last longer too. Most carpet manufacturers recommend professional hot-water extraction as the primary cleaning method for synthetic carpets. The best strategy is to hire a professional every year or two and clean the carpet yourself between pro cleanings. Here are some hiring tips:

■ Hire a pro who uses truck-mounted equipment rather than portable steam-cleaning equipment. Truck-mounted equipment exhausts the dirty air and humidity outside. Its stronger suction leaves carpets drier too.

■ Ask for a high-pressure rinse. This agitates the pile and neutralizes the carpet's pH.

■ Ask the pro to set furniture on blocks or pads after cleaning. This prevents stains from transferring from furniture legs to the damp carpet.

■ Make sure the estimate includes everything—such as furniture moving, vacuuming (some pros charge extra for this, so check), routine spot removal, preconditioning and deodorizing—as part of a standard cleaning package.

Buy a High-Quality Pad

The right pad will extend the life of your carpet, but the wrong pad can cut the life of your carpet in half. The quality of a carpet pad is determined by its density, not its thickness. A good-quality pad will be 3/8 to 1/2 in. thick and have a density/weight rating of at least 6 lbs. (the residential standard). In most cases, a cheap low-density pad will last only a few years before it needs to be replaced. For high-traffic areas, get a thinner carpet pad with a density of 8 lbs. or more.

ADJUSTMENT SCREWS

Stop Leaks Under Doors

If you can feel the breeze or see daylight under your entry door, that's bad news. The good news is that you can adjust most thresholds up or down just by turning a few screws. Turn all the screws equally until the door opens and closes without much drag—and without letting in a draft.

Suspended Ceilings— Do's and Don'ts

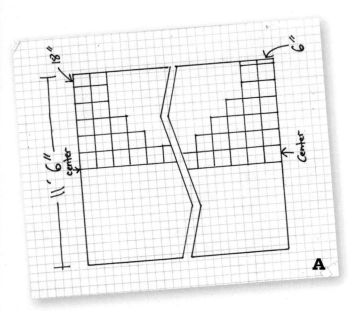

A

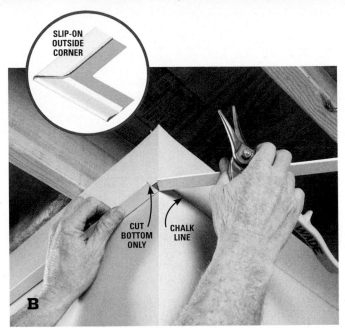

SLIP-ON OUTSIDE CORNER

CUT BOTTOM ONLY

CHALK LINE

B

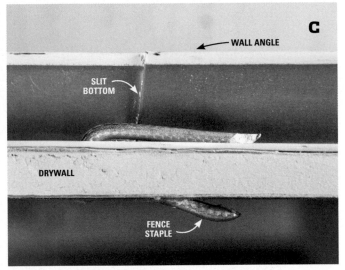

WALL ANGLE

SLIT BOTTOM

DRYWALL

FENCE STAPLE

C

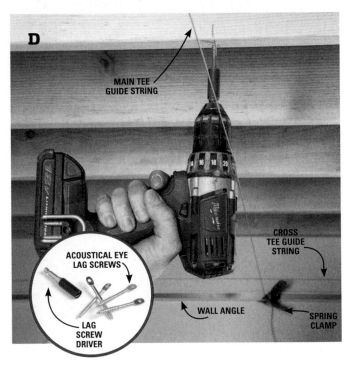

D

MAIN TEE GUIDE STRING

ACOUSTICAL EYE LAG SCREWS

LAG SCREW DRIVER

CROSS TEE GUIDE STRING

WALL ANGLE

SPRING CLAMP

A. LAY IT OUT ON PAPER

Even the pros use graph paper to lay out the ceiling grid for each room. It helps not only with your materials list but also with getting equal-size panels at each side of the room. Include items like light fixtures and heat registers. The room should be bisected at the center by either a main tee or a centered row of tiles. Expert tip on ordering materials: Order by even numbers. If a room is 9 x 11 ft., order enough for a 10 x 12-ft. room.

B. NAIL UP THE WALL ANGLE

Pick a height so the ceiling tile will clear the lowest ceiling obstruction, like plumbing lines or ductwork. Snap a chalk line marking the top of the wall angle. Nail the wall angle at every stud with 1-1/4-in. drywall nails. Try to avoid nailing on or near the corner beads—it's a sure way to cause nail pops and cracks. Instead, run the wall angle long, snip the bottom and then bend it around the corner. Finish it with a slip-on outside corner.

C. USE FENCE STAPLES TO HOLD THE ANGLE TIGHT

Use fence staples to secure the wall angle between the studs, especially where there's a gap between the wall and the angle. If there's a severe bow in the wall, you may have to cut the lower part of the channel so it will flex and follow the contour.

D. RUN GUIDE STRINGS AND DRIVE IN THE HANGING SCREWS

Use strings as a guide to position the hanging screws (lag screws) and to keep the main tees straight while hanging. Offset the strings 1/2 in. so they line up with the sides of the tees rather than with the center. We wrapped the end of the strings around a nail and used a spring clamp to secure them to the wall angles. Sight along the string to position and drive in the hanging screws—they don't have to be perfectly centered. These acoustical eye lag screws require a special driver, which can be purchased at the home center where you get your other ceiling materials and tools.

E. LINE UP THE CROSS TEE SLOTS

Once you've figured out the size of the border row, measure back from the cross tee slots and cut your main tees to size. Don't assume the wall is straight. Instead, run a string and use that as a guide to make sure all the cross tee slots line up.

F. USE POP RIVETS TO HOLD THE GRID SQUARE

Once you've hung a couple of main tees and locked in 8 to 12 ft. of cross tees, it's time to square up the grid. Check the diagonal measurements of at least a couple of

the openings. When everything is square, rivet the main tees and cross tees to the wall angle. This can be where most people get in trouble. If things are out of whack in the beginning, the problem will telegraph out across the room. Before you're done, you may end up trimming full panels instead of just plopping them into place.

G. MAKE RIVET HOLES WITH A GRID PUNCH

Drilling your rivet holes works fine, but it's slow going. If you've got more than one suspended ceiling project in your future, a grid punch will save you a bunch of time. You can buy one at *amazon.com* for less than $30.

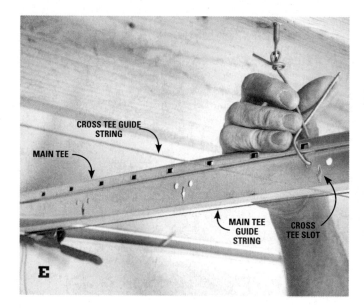

CROSS TEE GUIDE STRING

MAIN TEE

MAIN TEE GUIDE STRING

CROSS TEE SLOT

E

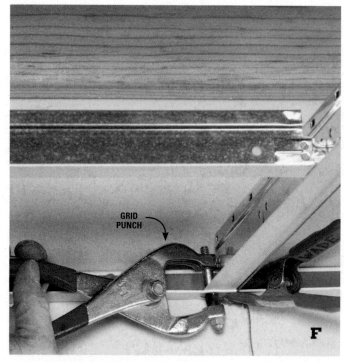

GRID PUNCH

F

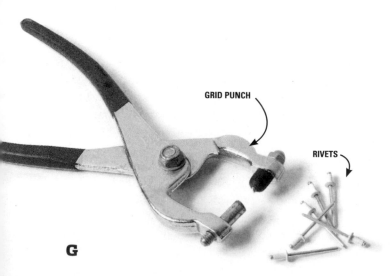

GRID PUNCH

RIVETS

G

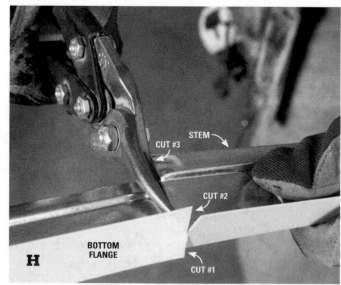

STEM

CUT #3

CUT #2

BOTTOM FLANGE

CUT #1

H

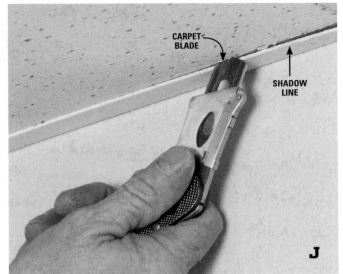

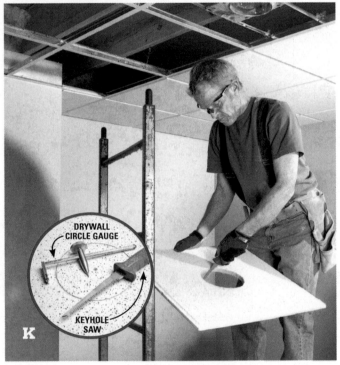

DRYWALL
CIRCLE GAUGE

KEYHOLE
SAW

K

CARPET
BLADE

SHADOW
LINE

J

L

J. SCRIBE EACH SHADOW LINE WITH A CARPET KNIFE

Cut the border panels to length, then rest them in the track and score the shadow line with the knife. Then take the panel down to cut the shadow line.

K. MARK YOUR HOLES WITH A DRYWALL CIRCLE GAUGE

Scribe holes with a drywall circle gauge, then make the cuts with a drywall saw. With just these two tools, you can cut a wide variety of hole sizes.

L. REPAIR PANELS WITH FLAT LATEX CAULK

When a panel gets damaged, use a little white caulk to patch it up. Make sure you use a flat latex caulk—shiny silicone will stand out worse than the hole. If the damaged area is bigger than a pencil eraser, you may want to set that panel aside to be used as a partial in another location.

H. CUT THE FLANGES FIRST

The cleanest way to cut the main tees to length is to cut the bottom flange first from both directions. Then cut the stem last. That'll give you a clean, flat cut. Our cutting tool of choice is a pair of high-quality straight-cut aviator snips.

I. USE FINGER AS A DEPTH GAUGE

Follow the scribe to cut halfway through the face of the panel first, and then finish it by cutting through the side. Use your finger as a depth gauge. Gloves will prevent the oil in your hands from making smudge marks on the panels—and, of course, will protect your hands.

INSIDE OF FRAMING

TRUSS FINDER

BETWEEN FRAMING

DRYWALL SAW

1 **No power saws for this step.** Probe with a nail to find the framing on either side of the breakout. Mark the cut between the framing, then make those two cuts until you hit the framing. Then cut alongside the framing at the sides.

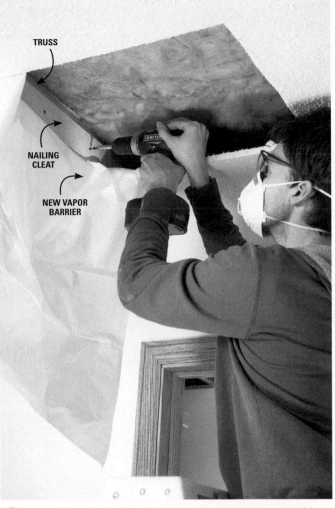

TRUSS

NAILING
CLEAT

NEW VAPOR
BARRIER

2 **Patch the hole.** Screw 3/4-in.-thick cleats to the sides of the trusses and replace or repair the vapor barrier. Then patch in a fresh piece of drywall.

6" DRYWALL
KNIFE

MUD PAN

SPRAYER WITH
WATER

3 **Reapply texture.** Wet the texture on the edges of your patch and allow water to soak in for several minutes before you scrape. Tape the joints and then reapply texture.

Patch a Textured Ceiling

We're not going to ask how you managed to step through your living room ceiling. But we can tell you that pros fix that mistake quite often, charging several hundred dollars to patch the hole and retexture it. But you can do the job yourself for a lot less. You'll have to paint the entire ceiling afterward, and even then the patched area won't match perfectly; even a pro can't achieve that. Perfection calls for scraping off and retexturing the entire ceiling after the patch is complete.

You'll need a small piece of drywall and a couple of scraps of any 3/4-in.-thick wood or plywood, plus standard taping supplies and materials. And you'll need to rent a texture gun. But first, scrape off a small sample of your texture material and find a match for it at a home center. If a home center doesn't carry it, try a local drywall supplier.

Start by cutting out the damaged area **(Photo 1)**. Avoid cutting the vapor barrier, or reseal it with red moisture barrier tape if it does get cut. Screw cleats above the unsupported drywall ends of the enlarged hole and install the new patch **(Photo 2)**.

Mist water over the surrounding ceiling texture in an area about 24 in. out from the patch to soften it so you can scrape it off to prep for the taping work **(Photo 3)**. Then tape, mud and skim-coat the entire patch. Sand it smooth and you're ready to spray.

Rent a professional spray texture gun and practice on scrap drywall or cardboard. Apply a light coat of texture and add more in stages until you get a match. Lightly blend it into the existing texture.

Wall Repair Simplified

We know these products work—because we use them! Give them a try on your projects.

A. WHOLE WALL COVER-UP

There are some walls that are just so bad that the best fix is to tear them out and install new drywall. Wall liner is the next-best fix. It's basically extra-thick, paintable wallpaper that acts as a big patch over the whole wall. Some versions are smooth; some have a textured or patterned surface. Fill cracks and holes in the wall using joint compound, prime the patches and then hang the liner just as you would wallpaper. You can find wall liner at home centers, paint stores and online.

B. FAST PATCH BACKING

If you're installing a drywall patch, you've got to screw the patch to something. Usually, that means installing wood backing. But here's a quicker, easier way: Screw drywall repair clips to the surrounding drywall, then screw in the patch. Then break off the tabs and you're ready for mud. Get a six-pack for about $4 at home centers.

C. MINI TEXTURE GUN

You can have some good results using texture from aerosol spray cans—and some disasters. The texture blasts out fast and heavy. One wrong move and you've got an overtextured mess.

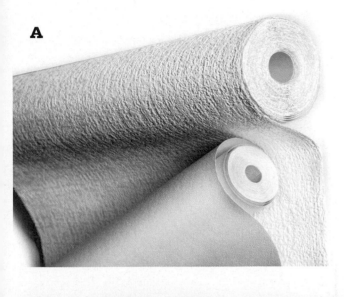

A

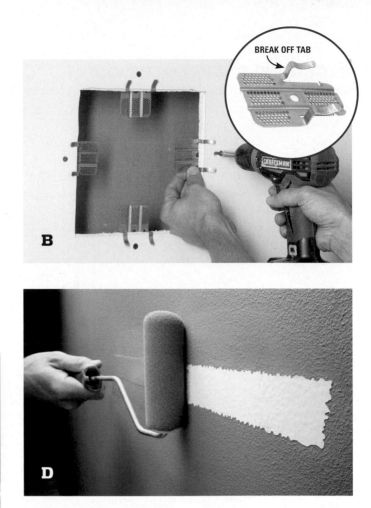

B

C

D

This little hand-pump gun is much easier to control. It spits out just a little texture with each blast, so you can spray on a light texture, then add more until it looks right. Still, it's best to practice on some cardboard first. Also have a bucket and sponge handy in case you need to wipe away a misfire and start over. We got good results matching orange peel, splatter and knockdown textures, but lousy results with popcorn ceiling texture. The gun is available at some home centers for less than $20. Or search online for "Homax 4105." The kit comes with texture packets, but watered-down joint compound works fine too.

D. SIMPLEST CRACK SOLUTION

Stepsaver Self-Adhesive Stress Crack Tape sounds like the perfect solution for cracks. Just stick it on and paint over it. So we gave it a try. The tape was still visible from across the room—even under two coats of paint. If you take a few minutes to skim over it with joint compound, the tape disappears completely. But it's possible the tape may stretch and stay stuck through seasonal crack movement.

Stepsaver Self-Adhesive Stress Crack Tape is available at Sherwin-Williams and The Home Depot, as well as online at *stepsavers.com*.

E. BIGGER COVER PLATES

"Oversized" plates cover an extra 1/4 in. or so of wall on all four sides. And sometimes that's just enough to hide damage and save you the trouble of making a repair. Home centers carry oversized plates for common configurations like single and double switches and outlets.

F. CHAIR RAIL

The walls in kitchens can get banged up from decades of kids and grandkids slamming their chairs into the walls in their hurry to get away from the table. We talked about repairing the damage, but isn't that what a chair rail is for? So we just covered up the dings. Looks great.

G. TEXTURE IN A TUB

For small repairs on popcorn ceilings, dab on this stuff. Start with a light application, let it dry and add more if needed. With some careful brushwork, you can perfectly match the surrounding texture. A quart costs about $6. If you don't find it at a home center, search online for "Homax popcorn ceiling patch."

H. CEILING STAIN SOLUTION

If you have a water-stained ceiling, a stain-blocking primer is mandatory to prevent the stain from bleeding through a fresh coat of paint. You could roll on primer, but there are two spray-can products you should consider first: Kilz Upshot and Zinsser Covers Up are both stain-blocking primers, and both have nozzles that shoot upward—perfect for ceiling work. Upshot is tinted to match aged, unpainted ceiling texture. Covers Up is a lighter shade of off-white. So if you're lucky, the primer will blend in and you won't have to paint the whole ceiling. You'll find one or the other (but probably not both) at home centers and paint stores.

I. INSTANT PATCH

Every fix-it person we know—DIYer or pro—loves self-stick metal patches. Just stick one over the hole, and mud over it. Find them in sizes from 4 x 4 in. to 8 x 8 in. for around $5 at home centers.

J. PATCH AND PROTECT

If you drag your feet on fixing a doorknob crater, we have a simple solution. Cover it with a stick-on bumper. They're sold at home centers for around $5.

How to Apply Wallpaper

Anyone can hang wallpaper, but it takes a little know-how to hang it straight with tight, nearly invisible seams. Every quality job starts with careful planning and proper preparation.

MAP OUT THE ROOM

- **Use a roll to lay out the wall.** Use a full roll of paper as a guide to lay out the room. Butt a roll into the corner where you plan to start, and make a pencil mark on the wall at the edge of the roll. Slide the roll down to that mark, and make another pencil mark at the other edge of the roll. Keep doing this until you know where every seam is going to fall. You may have to cut down the first panel to avoid hanging small strips (3 in. or less) near doors and corners.
- **Work away from the door you enter.** Wallpaper seams on straight walls are butted, not overlapped, but seams are less visible if you place them at the point farthest from where the first panel was installed. Minimize the visibility of seams by starting in the area opposite the most-used entrance to the room.
- **Start with a plumb line.** Don't assume the corner you're starting in is plumb. Use a level and draw a straight plumb line about 1/4 in. past where you want the first panel of paper to end. Take into account that inside corner seams need to be overlapped at least 1/8 in. For more information, see **D** on p. 165.
- **Hide the last seam.** If you're hanging paper that has a repeatable pattern, the pattern on the last seam is not going to line up, so try to hide it in a low-visibility area like above the entry.

A. PREP THE WALLS

Start by removing plate covers, heat registers and light fixtures. Fill any holes with a nonshrinking joint compound so you don't have to wait until it dries or apply another layer. Scrape the walls with a drywall knife or sand them with 50-grit sandpaper to remove smaller imperfections.

Finally, cover the whole wall with "wall size," a primer/sizing product. We used Shieldz made by Zinsser. Don't skip this step! Using wall size will help the paper adhere to the wall and reduce the chance that the paper will shrink. It also makes it easier to remove the paper when the time comes. One gallon costs about $20 at a home center. And never hang wallpaper over unfinished drywall—it won't ever come off if you do. Make sure all the walls have at least one coat of primer.

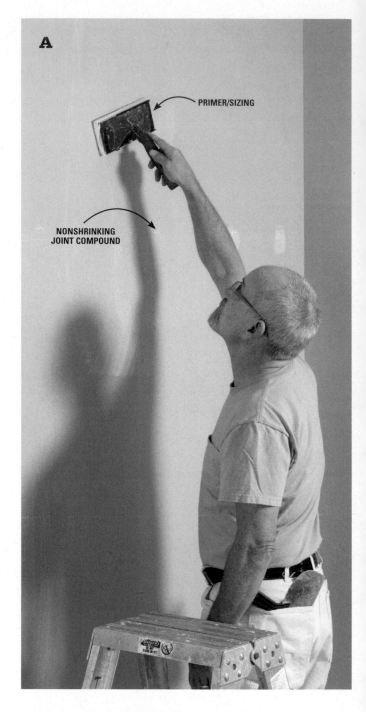

A

PRIMER/SIZING

NONSHRINKING
JOINT COMPOUND

ORDER ENOUGH PAPER

When measuring a room, you need to take into account the pattern of the paper. Sometimes the pattern on one panel needs to line up horizontally with the pattern on the panel next to it. If you're measuring a room with 8-ft. walls and the paper you're hanging has a pink poodle that repeats every 54 in., only two poodles will fit on each length of panel. If you cut off the first panel so the two poodles are centered on the wall, you'll have to cut about 1 ft. off the roll to make the poodle on the next panel line up with the first one. This means you'll be using 9 ft. of paper for every 8 ft. of wall. So in this case, you would multiply the linear feet of the room by 9 ft. instead of 8 ft.

B. ROLL ON THE PASTE—DON'T DUNK!

Use a high-quality 1/2-in.-nap paint roller cover to apply paste—the cheap ones will leave fuzz balls all over the paper. When working with prepasted products, use a paint roller to roll the water on the paper. Submerging paper in a tray is messy and doesn't guarantee uniform coverage. You can even add a little paste to the water (2 cups per gallon) to encourage stronger adhesion.

C. CHOOSE THE RIGHT PASTE FOR YOUR PAPER

There are three basic types of paste: clay, wheat and starch. Each group has several subcategories. Most wallpaper instructions will indicate which paste to use. Avoid the "universal" paste unless the paper you're hanging specifically calls for it.

D. SEAM INSIDE CORNERS

Corners are rarely perfectly straight. You'll need to create a seam at every inside corner to make the next panel plumb. The first panel installed in a corner should be overlapped onto the adjacent wall at least 1/8 in. When working your way into a corner, measure over from the last panel to the corner at the top, middle and bottom. Then cut the corner panel 1/8 in. longer than the longest of the three measurements. You can use the leftover piece to start the new wall, but you may need to cut it at a slight angle to accommodate a crooked corner. Some wallpaper won't stick to other wallpaper, so run a small bead of seam adhesive in the corner before overlapping the second piece.

USE VINYL PAPER IN HIGH-TRAFFIC ROOMS

Wallpaper made from paper absorbs moisture and can be hard to clean. Vinyl products are better suited for bathrooms, kitchens and hallways, but not all vinyl wallpapers are the same. Some are solid vinyl, others have a vinyl face with a paper backing, and some are mostly paper with a thin vinyl coating. Solid vinyl wallpaper is the most resistant to moisture and the most washable. To avoid confusion, many manufacturers have a "best uses" label on each roll.

CLAY

C

WHEAT

STARCH

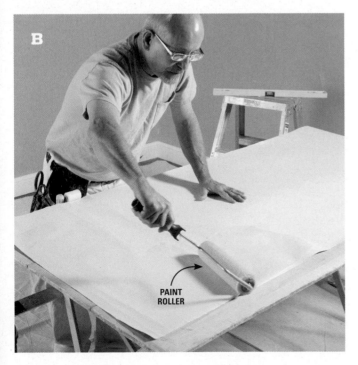

PAINT ROLLER

B

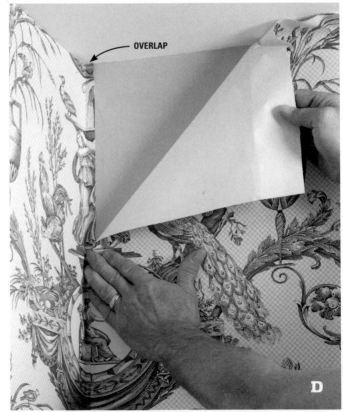

OVERLAP

D

E. BOOK THE PAPER BEFORE HANGING

Booking is the process of folding the paper in on itself. It allows time for the paste to activate and the paper to soften. Fold the paper so that when you unfold it, you'll be working with two-thirds of the panel. The longer the paper, the easier it is to get straight. Cut a bunch of pieces of paper at once, and book several at the same time. Set each roll in front of the wall where it's going to be hung. If you're a beginner, set them in a plastic bag to give you more time to work with them.

F. GENTLY SMOOTH OUT THE PAPER

Once the paper is on the wall, be sure to run a smoother over every square inch of the paper. But don't push too hard on your smoother or you'll squeeze out the paste and stretch the paper. This is especially important when you're working with prepasted paper. Stretched-out paper with too little paste behind it is guaranteed to shrink when it dries. Shrinking causes gaps in the seams—gaps are bad.

G. WIPE DOWN AS YOU GO

It's a lot easier to clean up the paste before it has fully cured, so sponge off every panel with warm water as you go. Use natural sponges, one in each hand. Swipe with the first and make a final pass with the other. Use a few drops of dish soap when working with particularly sticky paste. To avoid creating suds, squeeze out the sponges while they're still submerged in water, then give them another small squeeze above the water bucket.

H. TOOLS OF THE TRADE

Hanging wallpaper doesn't require a huge investment. You probably already own many of the tools. Our most expensive tools here were a beechwood cutting table and a magnesium straightedge. You can substitute an old door slab and a level.

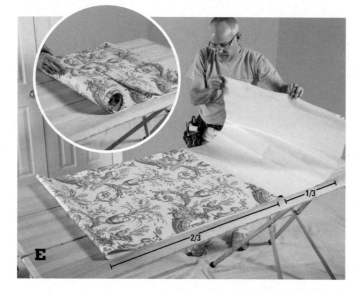

E — 1/3, 2/3

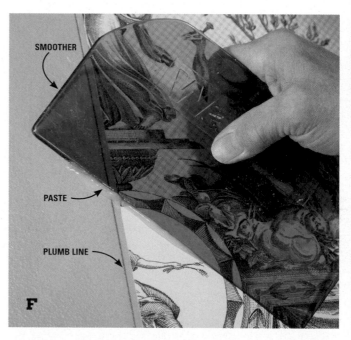

SMOOTHER

PASTE

PLUMB LINE

F

NATURAL SPONGE

G

H

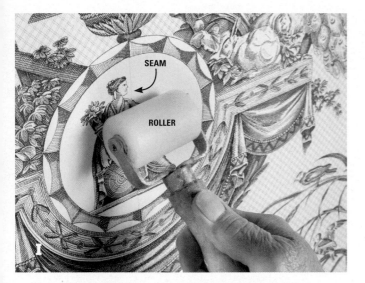

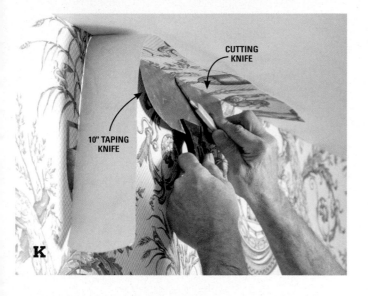

I. ROLL EVERY SEAM

To keep the edges from curling, you need to set them with a roller. But the same rule that applies to the smoother applies to the roller: Don't press too hard or you'll squeeze out too much adhesive.

J. OVERLAP AND CUT BOTH PIECES AT ONCE

Sometimes, rather than butting one panel up to another, you'll need to create your own seam. The best way to do this is to lap one panel over the other, and cut down the middle of the overlap. Then peel the two pieces apart, and pull out the small strip that was cut off the underlying piece.

If you don't have a steady hand, you can use a drywall knife as a cutting guide. Try not to penetrate the drywall paper. Angle the knife blade down low so more than just the tip of the blade is doing the cutting. We used a knife with blades that snap off. Blades are a lot cheaper than wallpaper, so we snapped off a section after every cut.

K. USE A TAPING KNIFE AS A CUTTING GUIDE

Leave an extra 2 in. at the top and bottom, and use a drywall knife as a guide to trim it. We prefer a 10-in. taping knife so we don't have to move it as often as we would a smaller one. Hold the cutting knife down close to the wall to avoid cutting into the ceiling.

L. MAKE RELIEF CUTS BEFORE TRIMMING

When you're up against trim or other obstacles, you'll need to make a relief cut before trimming the paper. You could make the cut with a knife, but scissors are better to avoid scratching the trim.

CUT DOWN
CENTER OF
OPENING

CRACK

CUT DOWN
CENTER OF
STUD

HORIZONTAL CUT
48" FROM CEILING

1 **Saw and slice the drywall around the crack.** Remove the door trim and cut the drywall horizontally (with a drywall saw or utility knife) to the nearest stud. Then use a utility knife to slice down the center of the vertical stud and also down the center above the door.

Fix a Persistent Drywall Crack

If you have a door or window with a crack on either side traveling up to the ceiling, there's probably a drywall butt joint behind it. Installers aren't supposed to seam drywall at the ends of doors, but sometimes they do. Houses settle, and wood expands and contracts, and that area is very susceptible to cracks. A taped joint just isn't strong enough to handle the stress. Patch the crack and it'll nearly always show up again. The only real fix is to cut out the drywall and put in a solid sheet spanning the crack-prone zone. The entire job costs less than $15 and takes about eight hours (spread over a few days). Sure, you'll have to repaint, but you have to do that anyway every time you repatch.

Start by cutting out the cracked drywall **(Photo 1)**. Then cut all the way through the taped joint at the ceiling. Remove the old pieces of drywall and any exposed screws and nails. Cut a single sheet of drywall to match the new opening. Screw the new sheet into place **(Photo 2)**. Then clean up all the cut edges **(Photo 3)**. Tape the new seams using paper or mesh tape, and mud them using lightweight joint compound **(Photo 4)**. To avoid repainting and patching against the ceiling, "flat tape" that seam by embedding tape in the mud against the surface **(Photo 4)**.

BEVELED EDGE

3 **Bevel the edges. Bevel all the cut edges. That will give the joint compound more "bite" and remove any jagged paper edges.**

TAPERED EDGE BUTTED TO CEILING

2 **Cut the patch and screw it on. Cut the drywall patch with the tapered side facing the ceiling. Screw it into place with a few 1-1/4-in. screws.**

4 **Mud, tape, sand, mud. Apply joint compound and tape to the vertical seams and embed the tape. Then tape the bottom horizontal seam and finish at the wall-to-ceiling seam. Follow up with sanding and two additional coats.**

Tips for Hanging Drywall

It's not all that complicated, but there is a right and a wrong way to do it. Save time and money, make taping easier and earn the confidence of your customers with our help.

A. CUT OUTSIDE CORNERS FLUSH WITH THE FRAMING

It's tempting to cut the first piece of an outside corner flush with the framing and run the perpendicular piece flush with the first. Don't do it! If you run the first piece just a little too long, the second piece will flare out. If you cut the second piece a bit too long, it will have to be shaved down to accommodate the corner bead. A good-quality metal corner bead will cover a gap and hold up as well as a perfectly flush corner—without the fuss.

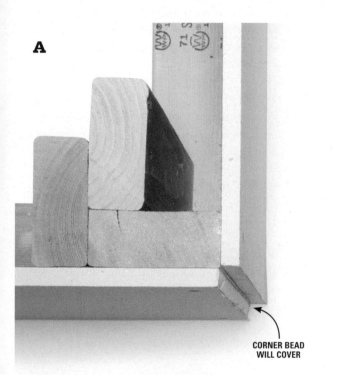

CORNER BEAD WILL COVER

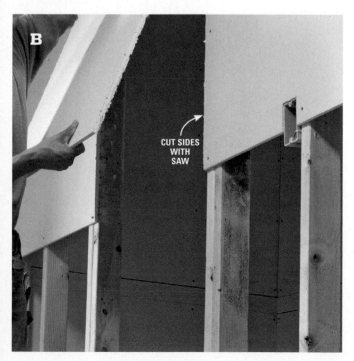

CUT SIDES WITH SAW

Master the Basics

Even pros sometimes forget a few of the basics of good drywall installation. Here are some that we think are important to know:

- Think ahead when you deliver the drywall. For example, don't bury the sheets for the ceiling behind the ones for the walls. Stack all the sheets so the finished sides are facing out. Place the drywall throughout the job site where it is most handy and won't be in the way. Order 12-ft.-long sheets whenever possible. Order 54-in.-wide sheets for 9-ft. walls. Consider having your drywall delivered; it will cost a bit more per sheet.

- Most manufacturers now offer a stiffer 1/2-in. drywall that can be used on ceilings in certain situations. Half-inch is considerably easier to hang than 5/8-in., but make sure the drywall you use conforms to the fire code in your area.

- If you use a chalk line to mark your pieces before you cut them, use blue chalk. Red, orange or any other color is likely to bleed through the finish.

- If you write down measurements or mark the stud lines with a pencil, do it very, very lightly. Even modest pressure on drywall with a pencil will show up on your finished walls.

- In our neck of the woods, screws need to be spaced no more than 12 in. on ceilings and 16 in. on walls. Nails require 8-in. spacing on ceilings and 7-in. spacing on walls. Technically, the fastening schedule code is whatever the manufacturer requires, which can usually be found online.

- Don't overtighten the screws. If a screw breaks the paper, its holding power has been compromised. And don't undertighten the screws or your taper will curse your name while finishing your job.

- Leave about a 1/2-in. gap between the drywall and the floor. You don't want drywall to wick up moisture from concrete or from an inevitable spill in an upper-level room. In addition, a gap at the floor makes it easier for carpet to be tucked under the trim.

- On a long wall, it's not always possible to steer clear of seams located directly over a window or door, but a seam that's in line with the horizontal edge of a window or door should be avoided at all costs. It's sure to crack.

B. HANG IT, THEN CUT IT

You can save time and be guaranteed a perfect fit if you cut out the door opening after you hang the sheet. Once the sheet is up, score the back of the piece, pull the scrap forward and finish it off by cutting the paper on the front side.

C. INSIDE CORNERS: MEASURE EXACT, THEN SUBTRACT

When you're working in a smaller area like a closet and have to cut a piece that's going to fit between two perpendicular walls, don't try to cut exactly. Precision is a worthy goal, but cutting the piece smaller is key. All the inside corners are going to receive mud and tape anyway. If the piece is too big and you try to force it into place (which you will do), besides scraping up the drywall on an adjacent wall, you're more than likely going to damage the piece you're trying to install.

D. USE HEAVY BOXES AND WATCH OUT FOR THE WIRES

If you have any control over which electrical boxes are going to be used on the job, buy the ones made from hard plastic. A spiral saw can cut right through boxes made from soft plastic (usually blue), sending the saw off on an unfortunate path.

Make sure wires are tucked in far enough so the spiral saw won't cut them. Fishing new wire can be an expensive inconvenience, but cutting a live wire could be worse.

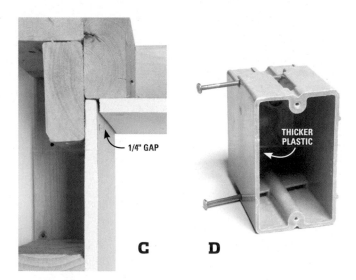

1/4" GAP

THICKER PLASTIC

C   D

E. SPIRAL SAWS—A HANGER'S BEST FRIEND

A spiral saw can save you time and money if it's used properly. Here are a few tips for getting the most out of this important drywall tool:

- Make sure you're using a sharp bit. And have extra bits handy, because they will break.
- Don't insert the bit too far into the spiral saw. About 1/8 in. of the bit's shank should be exposed. This allows the bit to flex and reduces the chance of breaking.
- Make sure the bit is adjusted to the proper depth. If the bit extends too far, you may cut right through an electrical box or nip a wire inside it. If the bit doesn't extend far enough, the tip of the bit may hop right over an electrical box or recessed light and head off in the wrong direction.
- Cut in the proper direction. Go clockwise when cutting freehand. When cutting around an electrical box or recessed light, move the spiral saw in a counterclockwise direction. The spinning motion of the bit should pull toward the object that's being cut around.
- Never overtighten the drywall screws or drive screws too close to the cutting area. The pressure will crack and tear the drywall as you're finishing the cut.

F. DON'T CUT DRYWALL TOO CLOSE TO DOOR OR WINDOW JAMBS

Door and window jambs are not always straight. Often, the jamb has to be adjusted when you install the casing. This can't be done if the drywall is cut too close to the jamb. When you're using a spiral saw, guide it with the wood that makes up the rough opening, not the window jamb itself.

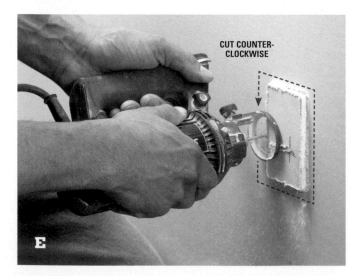

CUT COUNTER-CLOCKWISE

E

LEAVE ENOUGH ROOM TO STRAIGHTEN WINDOW JAMB

USE ROUGH OPENING AS THE GUIDE

F

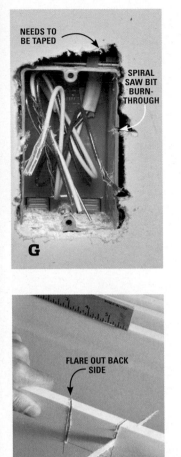

NEEDS TO BE TAPED

SPIRAL SAW BIT BURN-THROUGH

G

FLARE OUT BACK SIDE

H

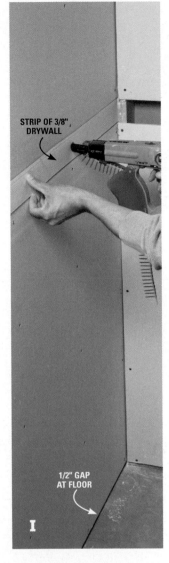

STRIP OF 3/8" DRYWALL

1/2" GAP AT FLOOR

I

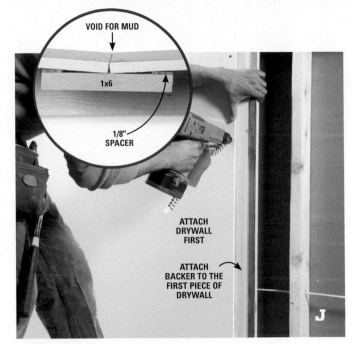

VOID FOR MUD

1x6

1/8" SPACER

ATTACH DRYWALL FIRST

ATTACH BACKER TO THE FIRST PIECE OF DRYWALL

J

G. GAPS MEAN EXTRA WORK

All tear-outs and gaps that won't be completely covered by a cover plate have to be taped and feathered out—more work. So use your spiral saw carefully (and see section **D** here about heavy plastic electrical boxes!). If a gap around an electrical box is just filled with mud and the cover plate is overtightened, the mud will crack and crumble out of the gap. The areas around outlets are particularly vulnerable because of the pressure of plugging in and unplugging electrical cords.

H. BACK-BEVELING GIVES YOU WIGGLE ROOM

Even in a world of spiral saws and screw guns, two classic tools—handsaws and keyhole saws—are still essential on any job site. One advantage of hand-sawing is the ability to create a back bevel. This allows for a little more leeway when you're sliding a piece into place, because if you need to trim, you won't have to remove as much material.

I. AVOID A LARGE GAP AT THE FLOOR

When you're dealing with a wall that is a few inches over 8 ft., two sheets of 4-ft. drywall will leave you with a large gap at the floor. While most base trim will cover that gap, the tapered edge on the bottom sheet will have to be filled with mud or it will show above the trim line, and that's a lot of extra work (and bending over!) for the taper. Instead of leaving a gap at the bottom, leave a gap in the center of the wall and fill it with a strip of 3/8-in. drywall. The thinner drywall is a snap to tape over smoothly. Your taper will thank you.

J. WHAT BUTT JOINT?

A butt joint in drywall will result in a raised layer of tape and mud because the edges aren't tapered. A good taper can minimize the ridge over a butt joint, but it's hard to eliminate it altogether. If you're installing drywall by yourself or installing in a space where it's impossible to deliver 12-ft. sheets, butt joints are going to be unavoidable. And if you're dealing with wall sconces or areas where raking light means a truly flat wall is imperative, a butt joint backer may be the answer.

A butt joint backer is basically a 4-ft.-long, 5- or 6-in.-wide board with 1/16- to 1/8-in. spacers added along the edges. You can purchase them at a drywall supply store or make your own. You could use an inexpensive 1x6 pine board and either glue or staple strips of ripped-down wood to the outside edges.

Installing the backer is easy. First, install the sheet of drywall, making sure the end doesn't land on a stud. Next, attach the butt joint backer to the back of that piece. Finally, fasten the second piece of drywall to the backer. When installed properly, the butt joint backer will cause the ends of each piece to suck in, resulting in a recess similar to the recess created by two tapered edges.

Perfect Window Trim

You don't even need a tape measure! We'll help you get it right.

Most veteran carpenters have trimmed hundreds—maybe even thousands—of windows. So trimming out a window is second nature to them. But when they see windows that were trimmed by a rookie (or when they watch rookies trim a window), they may realize it's not quite as easy for others. The truth is, most carpenters don't even use a tape measure.

Nope, it's all done by eye, using a sharp pencil, a miter saw and an 18-gauge nailer. We'll show you how to pull off a window trim job that'll look every bit as good as a trim person's—without hours of frustration. We're working with standard trim, between 3/8 and 1/2 in. thick—the types you'll find at any home center.

1 Mark the length. Cut a 45-degree angle on one end of the trim and hold it so the short end of the angle overhangs halfway, or 3/8 in., onto the jamb. Then mark the other end flush with the inside of the jamb. That'll give you a 3/16-in. reveal.

2 Get the spacing right. Hold the trim 3/16 in. away from the jamb at both ends and along the base of the trim. Nail the trim to the jamb with 1-in. brads spaced about every 6 in. Nail the thick part of the trim to the framing with 2-in. brads.

3 Check the fit, then cut to length. Cut a 45-degree miter on one end of the trim board. Adjust the miter as needed for a perfect fit. Then scribe the cut length 3/16 in. past the bottom of the jamb. Nail the trim onto the jamb first and then to the framing, as you did with the top piece.

4 Glue and pin for a solid miter. Glue and pin together the miter from both directions with 1-in. brads. Wipe the glue squeeze-out with a damp rag right away.

5 **Trim the other side.** Repeat all the same steps on the other side of the window, fitting first the top miter, and then marking and cutting the bottom one. Nail the trim into place.

6 **Fit the first bottom miter.** Cut an overly long piece of trim and cut a miter on one end. Overlap the far end to check the fit. Mark and recut the miter as needed for a perfect fit.

7 **Fit the opposite miter.** Cut a test miter on the other end and check the fit. Adjust the miter as necessary until you're satisfied with the joint.

8 **Scribe for length.** With the saw still set for the previous miter, flip the trim over and scribe the length for the end that has that miter. Transfer the mark to the front side and make the cut.

DEALING WITH PROBLEM DRYWALL

If you have drywall that's "proud" (sticking out past the jamb) or recessed behind the jamb, you have to deal with it before trimming or the trim won't lie flat. Here's what to do:

If the drywall projects more than 1/8 in., crush in the drywall with a hammer **(A)**. Just be sure that the crushed area will be covered by trim. In this situation, your miters won't be 45 degrees. You may need to go as low as 44 degrees to get a tight miter.

If the drywall projects past the jamb 1/8 in. or less and is close to the window jamb, just chamfer the edge with a utility knife **(B)**. Check to see if you've pared off enough drywall by holding a chunk of trim against the drywall and jamb. If it rocks and won't sit flush against both surfaces, carve out some more.

If the drywall's recessed behind the jamb, don't nail the trim to the framing at first. Nail it to the jamb only and pin the mitered corners together **(C)**. After the window is trimmed, slide shims behind each nail location to hold out the trim while nailing, then cut off the shims. Caulk the perimeter of the trim to eliminate gaps before painting.

AVOIDING TRIM-INDUCED HEADACHES

Here are a few tips to help you avoid a few trim hassles:

- Whenever you can, cut with the thick side of the trim against the miter saw fence. You'll be less likely to tear out the narrow tapered edge that way.
- Cutting right up to the pencil mark almost always leaves pieces too long, so remove the pencil line with the blade. You'll most likely still have to shave off more.
- Sneak up on cuts by starting long and dipping the saw blade into the wood while you work your way to the cutoff mark.
- Trim out the biggest windows first. That way, you can reuse miscuts for the smaller windows and not run out of material.
- When nailing 3/4-in.-thick trim, use 15-gauge 2-1/2-in. nails for the framing and 18-gauge 2-in. brads for nailing to the jamb.
- To prevent splitting, avoid nailing closer than 2 in. from the ends.

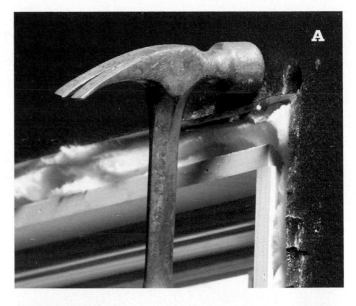

Real-World Advice
for Hanging Doors

A simple job can get complicated; we have the answers.

You already know the standard approach to hanging a door: Set it in the rough opening, then level, shim and nail it. This traditional approach works fine in a perfect world where walls are always plumb, floors are level and you have plenty of time to fuss with the fit. But in the real world, some nonstandard tricks can help you finish the job faster and better.

Shim the easy way. Mark the location of the hinges on the drywall alongside the opening so you'll know where to place the shims. Place shims at the top and bottom hinge locations using a long level, or a straight board and a short level. Then add the center shims.

A. SHIM BEFORE THE DOOR GOES IN

The usual method of holding the door frame in place while you shim behind the hinge side is awkward. It's a lot easier to shim the hinge side of the rough opening before you put in the door frame. After that, it's a simple job to set the frame in place, screw or nail it to the shims, and then shim the strike side. Measure the width of the rough opening before you start shimming to see how much shim space is available. Usually the rough opening allows for about 1/2 in. of shimming on each side of the frame. If the rough opening is extra wide, you can use fewer shims by tacking scraps of 1/2-in. plywood at the hinge locations first, and then adding shims to plumb the jamb.

B. MAKE SURE YOUR EXTERIOR DOOR CLEARS THE RUG

Most of the time, you can simply set your new exterior door frame directly on the subfloor and the door will easily clear carpeting or a throw rug. But if you're replacing an old door with a thick sill—or if the floor will be built up with tile, thick carpet or an extra layer of wood—you could have a problem. And there's no easy solution after the door is installed. You can't simply trim the bottom, because then the door won't seal against the sill. To avoid this problem, add a spacer under the door before you install it. The key is to determine where the top of the tile, carpet or throw rug will be, and then raise the door frame to leave about a 1/2-in. space under the door.

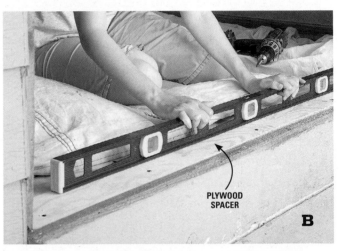

Avoid clearance problems. Screw a strip of plywood to the bottom of the rough opening to raise the door and prevent it from rubbing on the floor inside.

C. SET INTERIOR JAMBS ON SPACERS

If you set the doorjambs directly on the subfloor, there's a good chance the door will rub against the carpet later. Of course, you can cut off the bottom of the doors, but it's easy to avoid this extra work by planning ahead. Find out the thickness of the finish floor and then calculate where the bottom of the door will be. Plan the installation so there will be about 1/2 to 3/4 in. of space under the door. Usually setting the doorjambs on scraps of trim 3/8 to 1/2 in. thick will put the door at the correct height.

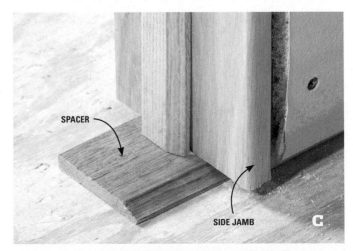

Avoid trimming door bottoms. Raise doorjambs with scraps of trim to make sure the door will clear the carpeting.

D. HIDDEN SCREWS MAKE EXTERIOR DOORS STRONGER

There are many benefits to using screws rather than nails to install exterior doors. They can be adjusted and won't easily pull out or loosen. But you don't want to leave the painter with the task of filling big, ugly screw holes. The trick is to hide the screws under the weather stripping on the latch side. On the hinge side, you can simply replace one screw in each hinge with a matching 3-in.-long screw. Always start by drilling a clearance hole that allows the screw to slide freely in and out of the hole. This ensures the screw will pull the jamb tight to the shims, and it allows for adjustment if needed. Don't let the spinning screw rub against the weather strip—it will slice right through.

E. TUNE UP THE ROUGH OPENING

Twisted or out-of-plumb rough openings raise havoc with door installations. If you install the jambs to follow the walls, the door is likely to swing open or shut on its own. On the other hand, if you plumb the jambs against the out-of-plumb rough opening, the trim will be hard to install.

As long as the bottom of the wall isn't held in place by flooring, there's a simple solution. Just move the studs on both sides of the opening back to plumb. Don't think you can do this with your trim hammer, though. You'll need a maul or a sledgehammer.

Hide the screws. Pull back or remove the weather strip on the latch side of the door frame, then drive screws where they'll be hidden.

Check for plumb. Check both sides of the door opening. If they're more than 1/4 in. out of plumb, adjust them before you install the door. **Nudge the wall.** Protect the wall with a 2x4 scrap while you move the bottom of the wall over with a sledgehammer. When the wall is plumb, toe-screw the bottom plate to the floor to hold it in place.

Troubleshooting Tips

- **Door won't latch.** Out-of-plumb jambs or a warped door can cause this. If the door won't latch because it's hitting the latch-side stop on the top or bottom, the fix is to move the stop. If it needs only a little adjustment, you can just tap it over with a hammer and a block of wood. Otherwise, pry it off carefully and (with the door closed and latched) reinstall it against the door.
- **Door binds and resists closing.** If the door isn't rubbing against the jamb but there's tension when you try to close it, then it's binding on the hinge jamb. Usually this means you haven't shimmed correctly and the jamb isn't at a right angle to the wall. Fix this problem by adjusting the hinge-side shims to twist the jamb back to a right angle with the wall.

Install a Door in 4 Easy Steps

1. Plumb the hinge jamb. The hinge side of the door has to be plumb or the door will swing open or closed on its own. Start by shimming the hinge side of the rough opening. First make marks to indicate the centers of the hinges. Then use a long level or a long, straight board along with a short level to plumb the shims. Tack a pair of tapered shims at the top hinge. Then install the bottom shims and finally fill in the middle.

2. Screw the hinge-side jamb to the stud. Remove the door from the frame and set it aside. Remove the hinge leaves from the jamb. Set the door frame in the opening with the jamb resting on the finished floor or on a spacer. Drive 3-in. screws through the jamb where they'll be hidden by the hinges.

3. Adjust the gap along the top. Slide shims between the floor and the latch-side jamb until the head jamb is level. Now reinstall the door hinges and the door. Adjust the shims under the latch-side jamb until the gap between the top of the door and the top jamb is even.

4. Shim and nail the latch-side jamb. Shim behind the latch-side jamb to make an even gap between the door and the jamb. Usually three or four sets of shims, evenly spaced along the jamb, are plenty. Drive two finish nails into each set of shims to hold the jamb in place. Cut off the protruding shims with a fine-tooth saw or a utility knife.

F. TRIM THE BOTTOM TO LEVEL THE TOP

Old houses are notorious for having sloping floors. Even some newer houses settle in unexpected ways. If you don't cut the jamb to compensate for the out-of-level floor, you could have a problem getting an even space between the top of the door and the head jamb. This is critical if you're installing a door over existing flooring where the jambs have to fit tightly to the floor. Photos for **F** show how to trim the jambs to fit a sloping floor.

G. HIDE SCREWS BEHIND THE HINGES

Screws are better for securing the hinge jamb, because nails can work loose. You can easily replace one of the short hinge screws with a long screw, but it can be difficult to find a strong screw that matches the other screws. Here's a trick we learned. Hide the screw behind the hinge. It takes only a minute or two to remove all the hinges and gain access to this area. Then you can drive a self-drilling screw through the jamb with ease. Make sure the jamb is straight and plumb before you reinstall the hinges.

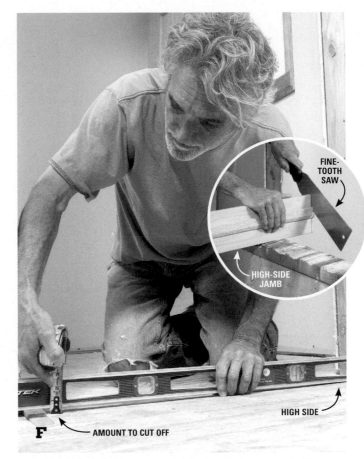

F   AMOUNT TO CUT OFF   FINE-TOOTH SAW   HIGH-SIDE JAMB   HIGH SIDE

Check with a level. Level across the opening and shim up one side until the bubble is centered. The distance between the level and the floor tells you how much to cut off the jamb. **Cut the high-side jamb.** Trim the jamb with a fine-tooth saw. A Japanese-style pull saw cuts fast and leaves a clean cut.

SHIM   HINGE MORTISE   3" SCREW   **G**

Use screws, not nails. Screw through the jamb in the hinge mortise. The screws will hold better than nails and will be hidden by the hinges.

Wipe the test area in a backward S pattern with a moist cloth, picking up dust to use as a sample.

Test for Lead Paint

If your home was built before 1978, it may contain lead paint. Most lead-paint poisoning occurs by exposure to lead dust. Testing the dust will determine if you have a lead hazard. The test kits, available at home centers and hardware stores, include step-by-step instructions for collecting the samples, bags for the samples, plastic gloves and an envelope

to send the samples to an EPA-certified lab for analysis. Results, mailed back in about two weeks, will tell if the samples contained a potentially harmful level of lead. If you have a lead hazard, contact your local health department or the Environmental Protection Agency (*epa.gov/lead*) for remediation guidelines.

Working with Steel Studs

Learn about using these in your next DIY project.

How would you like to be able to frame a perfectly straight wall each and every time, using studs that won't split or crack, and that are so light you could carry 20 of them at once? If this sounds good to you, consider using steel studs for your next project. When you add in steel's other benefits—it won't burn or rot or get eaten by insects—we're confident that these pro tips will make you think about steel.

PRO TIP

Finding Steel Studs

Drywall supply companies furnish lumberyards and home centers with steel studs. So if you're having trouble finding them, go directly to the source.

DOOR OPENING

TRACK

TAPCON SCREW

A

RAFTER SQUARE

B

C

A. DON'T LAY TRACK OVER A DOOR OPENING

There are two basic steel framing components: studs and tracks. The track functions as the top and bottom plates. Lay out your walls and openings just as you would with wood, but when you install the bottom plate, don't run the track across the door openings. You can't use your recip saw to cut the opening out later, as you can with wood. Concrete screws (Tapcon is one brand) work well to attach the track to concrete.

B. TO CUT, SNIP BOTH SIDES, THEN SCORE

Most home centers sell circular and chop saw blades designed for cutting studs, but we prefer a quieter and less messy approach. Cut both sides with snips and score a line on the back. After bending the stud back and forth a few times, you end up with a burr-free cut. No need for hearing protection and no metal shavings sticking to your boots. Caution: Steel studs and tracks are sharp. You should wear gloves, unlike our pro here.

C. USE A STUD TO LOCATE THE TOP PLATE

Unlike wood, steel studs are reliably straight. Cut one stud to size and use that, along with a level, to mark the location of the top plate at both ends, then snap a line to guide placement. Don't worry about cutting your studs to fit perfectly. It's completely unnecessary. This is a great advantage if you're working on an uneven floor. You can cut steel studs about 1/4 in. shorter than the actual measurement.

D. USE THE TRACK FOR BLOCKING

Top plates that run parallel to joists often need to be fastened to braces. You could use wood, but we prefer to use scrap pieces of track instead. Just cut the sides of the track and fold them out. Then fasten the track to the underside of the joist with drywall screws.

E. PROTECT YOUR CORDS AND YOURSELF

Accidentally stepping on an extension cord that's draped over a sharp track is a perfect way to cut your cord. To avoid potentially shocking developments, take a scrap chunk of track, flip it upside down and put it under the cord.

F. CUT A KERF IN THE BLOCKING

Like doors, cabinets and other heavy objects need extra support. You can use plywood or 2x4s, but make sure you cut a kerf to accept the lip on the inside of the stud. If you don't, that lip of the stud will press against the support board and twist the stud, creating a bow in the wall.

G. LAY OUT STUDS FROM THE BACK OF INSIDE CORNERS

Drywall is hung a little differently on steel framing. Drywall sheets don't butt up to each other at inside corners. One of the sheets will be slid all the way to the back of an inside corner (see **L**). So, when you lay out the stud locations, slide your tape measure all the way to the back of the track. We clamped our tape into place with a spring clamp. Clamp it several inches away from the end to avoid damaging the tang (steel tab).

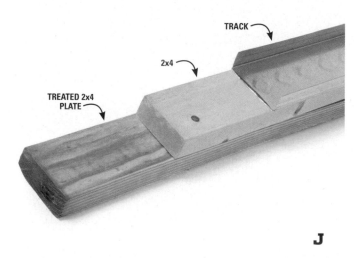

H. INSTALL TRACK AS A HEADER

Use a section of track as a header on those interior openings that aren't load bearing. Cut the track 3 or 4 in. wider than the opening, cut the sides and use a rafter square as a guide to bend them back. Have the open side of the track face up so you can slide in the cripple studs if you need them.

I. USE WOOD BUCKS TO HANG A DOOR

It's a hassle to hang a door directly onto steel studs. Instead, frame the openings 3 in. wider and 1-1/2 in. higher and use drywall screws to fasten 2x4 bucks on the inside of the steel opening, then hang your door from the wood bucks. The bucks are also there for nailing on the casing. Slide a plastic shim under each side 2x4 if the wood is going to be in direct contact with a concrete floor.

J. BUILD UP THE BOTTOM PLATE

Base trim can still be installed with trim screws. If you don't like the look of the screw heads, you can install two layers of 2x4 plates instead of steel track. With 3 in. of wood under the track, you'll be able to nail all the base trim just as you would a wood-framed wall. Over concrete, make sure you use treated wood for the bottom plate.

K. CHOOSE THE RIGHT SCREWS

Don't use drywall screws to screw your studs together—they're not designed for that. Panhead framing screws work best. Concrete screws work great to attach the bottom track to the floor. And be sure you use fine-threaded drywall screws to hang the drywall.

L. LEAVE THE LAST STUD LOOSE AT INSIDE CORNERS

The proper way to drywall an inside corner is to slide the first sheet all the way into the inside corner and then fasten the last stud on the wall adjacent to the drywall. To do this, you'll need to leave that last stud loose until the drywall goes up. This method may seem a little goofy, but it requires fewer studs, and it results in an extremely stable joint. When laying out the tracks, make sure you leave a gap for the drywall to slide in.

M. LEAVE THE LAST STUD LOOSE AT T INTERSECTIONS TOO

Similar to handling inside corners, leave the last stud loose on the wall that makes up the stem of a T intersection. After the drywall is hung, that last stud on the intersecting wall will be fastened to the drywall. Once again, this method requires fewer studs and results in a rock-solid joint that's almost guaranteed not to crack the drywall mud. Leave the top and bottom tracks short to allow room for the drywall to slide behind.

PRO TIP

Stud Orientation

When installing a stud, make sure the open side is facing toward the corner where you plan to start your drywall installation. (The first stud in the corner is the exception to this rule.) Because steel studs are so stable and straight, consider installing your drywall vertically, as the pros do. Zero butt joints means that all the taped joints will be almost invisible.

Trim Nailer Know-How

Use this tool as the pros do to help make your job both quicker and easier.

Years ago, trim nailers were expensive and rare. Then, over time, prices came down and many people decided to give them a try. As expected, trim nailers made nailing faster and a lot easier on arms. As you learn to use them, you'll realize that they will also make your work faster, easier and better in lots of ways you might not expect. In the following pages, we'll show you some of the tricks and benefits that make trim nailers an essential part of a pro's daily work.

A. USE A BLOCK TO PUSH BASEBOARD

When baseboard—or the floor—isn't straight, force the trim down with a 2x4 block. The block gives you a broad surface to push against and lets you apply a lot more pressure. This trick also works with uncooperative crown molding.

B. TONGUE-AND-GROOVE PANELING THE EASY WAY

With a trim nailer, you can install tongue-and-groove paneling in a fraction of the time. Some carpenters use a finish nailer for this, but we like to use a smaller, lighter 18-gauge brad nailer, especially on ceilings. Brads don't have the holding power of 15- or 16-gauge nails, of course, but we make up for that by shooting two brads into every stud or joist.

C. USE NAILS BEFORE SCREWS

It's always difficult to keep parts aligned when screwing cabinets together. Then we discovered that a couple of shots with a finish nailer or brad nailer will keep the parts aligned while drilling pilot holes and driving screws for strong joints.

EASY ON OLD WALLS

Pros do a lot of work in old houses. And hammering nails through those old plaster walls is a recipe for cracks. A trim nailer, on the other hand, drives nails instantly, without the repeated blows that can cause cracks. We like a 15-gauge nailer best for these jobs; the nails are stout enough to push through the hard plaster and long enough to bite into the framing behind it.

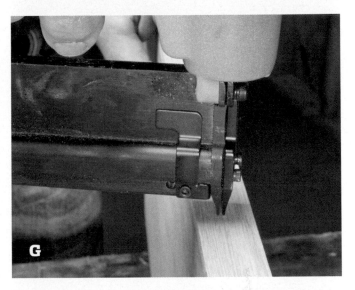

F. NAIL BEFORE YOU CLAMP

With a coat of slippery glue, parts will slide out of alignment while you're desperately trying to clamp them. Our solution is to tack the parts together with a couple of nails. That keeps the parts aligned while applying serious pressure with clamps.

G. INVISIBLE NAIL HOLES WITH A PINNER

Pins are tiny and headless, so they're hard to see even before you fill them. Afterward, nobody but you will know they're there.

D. PREFINISH PARTS

One of the best things about trim nailers is that you don't have to worry about beating up the wood, unlike with a hammer. That means you can finish parts before assembly. We especially like to finish trim before installation, which gives better results in less time. Just be sure that the soft rubber tip that came with your nailer is actually on the gun before you shoot.

E. TIGHT SPOT? USE A PINNER

The working end of our pinner is just 6-3/8 in. long and goes where none of our other nailers fit.

NAILER SAFETY
In the blink of an eye, a nailer can shoot a 2-in.-long nail into whatever is in its path. Injuries can be just as fast. Pros can tell you their own injury stories for an entire lunch hour. Always wear eye and hearing protection. And remember that nails sometimes go off course, make a U-turn and pop out where you don't expect them. So keep your hands and feet out of reach of errant nails.

H. PINNERS ARE PERFECT FOR CRAFTS

If you make a lot of gifts for friends and family, your pinner can be the go-to tool for delicate assemblies and save you the torture of gift shopping.

I. NO STUD? NO PROBLEM

Studs aren't always located where we need them. When you need to nail trim where there's no stud, dab some construction adhesive on the back of the trim and then drive nails into the drywall at 45-degree angles. That holds the trim tight against the wall while the adhesive cures. This "trap nailing" technique works fine with brad nailers and even better with finish nailers.

J. TACK TRIM FOR MARKING

To eliminate measuring errors, hold trim in place to mark the length. When a piece is too long to hold alone, tack one end to the wall with a brad nail. Then mark, yank the trim off the wall and remove the brad. Use nippers to pull the brad through the back of the trim to avoid damaging the face of the trim. That gives an accurate cutting mark and only one extra nail hole to fill later.

K. EXTEND YOUR REACH

Starting a nail with a hammer takes both hands—and that limits your reach. You can spend more time moving a ladder than driving nails when installing crown molding. A trim nailer, on the other hand, lets you reach way over to shoot a nail. And using a bench, rather than a ladder, lets you nail off even the longest runs in only two or three moves. Our aluminum bench (Werner AP-20) is available online.

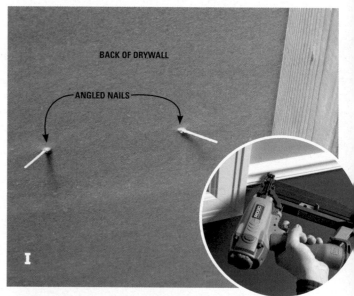

BACK OF DRYWALL

ANGLED NAILS

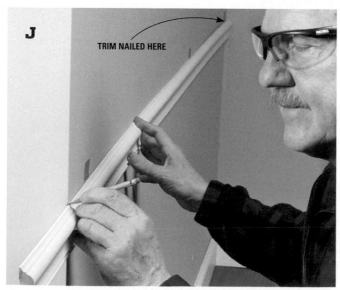

TRIM NAILED HERE

L. A PINNER MEANS NO SPLITTING

A 23-gauge pinner almost never splits wood, even on very small parts. In most situations, you can dab on a little bit of wood glue to give the joint more strength than pins alone can provide.

M. POSITION PARTS WITH A GAUGE

With a nailer in one hand and a gauge in the other, you can position parts perfectly—without measuring or marking. A combination square is a precise, adjustable gauge, but you can make a custom gauge just by tacking a couple of wood scraps together.

N. DEALING WITH STRAY NAILS

Our only gripe about trim nailers is "blowout." Careless aim is sometimes the cause, but other times the nail inexplicably takes a turn inside the wood and pops out. When this happens, grab a hammer and try to drive the nail up so you can grab the head with pliers and pull it out. This often works with 15- or 16-gauge nails, but 18-gauge brads almost always bend when you try to drive them back. In that case, our only solution is to grab the nail with pliers, bend it back and forth until it breaks off, and sink the remainder of the nail with a nail set.

WHICH NAILER DO YOU NEED?

Trim nailers are categorized by the thickness or "gauge" of the nails they shoot: The bigger the gauge number, the smaller the nail. (Seems backward, doesn't it?) Nailers that shoot the biggest trim nails—15 and 16 gauge—are usually called "finish nailers." Midsize 18-gauge nailers are called "brad nailers." The smallest nailer, the 23-gauge, is usually called a "pinner" or "micro pinner."

23-Gauge Pinner This is the nailer we use the least. Those tiny pins just don't have enough holding strength for most jobs. But don't get us wrong—there are times when pins are perfect, especially to nail small parts. Our pinner shoots pins ranging from 1/2 to 1 in. long. That's long enough for most jobs, though we occasionally wish we had a model that could handle pins up to 2 in. long, which would cost more.

18-Gauge Brad Nailer If you plan to buy only one trim nailer, this is the size to get. We use ours more than all others combined. It's perfect for standard trim, furniture making and odd jobs around the shop. Models that shoot brads up to 1-1/4-in. are common, but we strongly recommend spending a few bucks more for a gun that can handle brads up to 2 in. long.

16-Gauge Finish Nailer Like 15-gauge nailers, most 16-gauge guns shoot nails up to 2-1/2 in. long and are suitable for thick trim. The main advantage of a 16-gauge gun is that it's smaller and lighter. If you're shopping for

COMBINATION SQUARE

a finish nailer, we'd recommend the larger 15-gauge gun, simply because the fatter nails provide more holding power. But some carpenters disagree, and if you want to take their advice, get a 16-gauge nailer.

15-Gauge Finish Nailer This is the gun we usually grab for nailing large 3/4-in.-thick baseboard and trim. It's also a good choice for more demanding jobs like nailing doorjambs or stair treads. This nailer has a large piston and, because of the extra bulk, often has an angled magazine so you can get into tight spots.

Buying Interior Trim

Interior trim can add definition and refinement to a room, and wood remains a good choice for the material. To get a pleasing result with wood, you need to carefully select the individual pieces of lumber at the store, paying attention to grain and color. Today, synthetic trims can sometimes be a better option. Here are a few tips to help you, no matter which material you choose.

A. COMBINE SMALLER MOLDING TO CREATE LARGE PROFILES

You can save yourself money and hassles by buying separate pieces of trim and assembling them yourself rather than buying elaborate premilled moldings. Cutting, coping and fitting wide trim is tricky. If you mess up, you'll be wasting trim that can cost several dollars per foot. If possible, try to replicate the profile you're after by assembling the correct individual pieces yourself.

B. BUY PRIMED TRIM IF YOU'RE PAINTING

This is a no-brainer. Primed trim speeds up the finishing process. It's easier to spot defects and nail holes on primed trim, so you can fill them before the final coats of paint. It's even simpler to cope primed trim because the contrast between the raw wood and the painted surface gives you a crisp profile line to follow. So don't buy raw wood if you're going to paint.

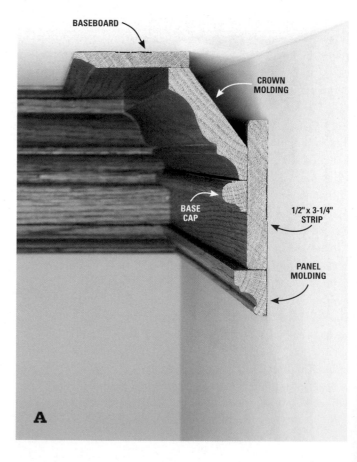

BASEBOARD

CROWN MOLDING

BASE CAP

1/2" x 3-1/4" STRIP

PANEL MOLDING

A

C. YOU CAN ORDER RARE MOLDINGS

No lumberyard or home center carries every molding profile made. Some styles are rare, especially those found in an older home. Even so, most are still made and available by special order. Take a short length of trim with you to the store and ask to see the profile chart. Any store that sells trim will have one. Match it to your sample and ask whether it can be ordered. It may be expensive, but you'll get the molding you want.

D. AVOID USING MDF TRIM IN MOIST PLACES

MDF (medium-density fiberboard) is inexpensive and makes a great material for painted trim, but only if you're installing it in a permanently dry place. Installing it near the floor or near windows where water or condensation sometimes collects is a recipe for disaster. The MDF will soak it up like a sponge, expand and shed paint in very short order. So avoid using MDF anywhere at risk of getting wet.

E. MATCH THE GRAIN

Occasionally you'll need to splice trim pieces. If you're trimming with natural wood, that splice will stick out like a sore thumb if you're not careful. If you need to splice trim on long walls, spend extra time choosing those pieces to make sure the grain patterns match and the wood tones are similar. When the pieces are joined, the splice will be nearly invisible.

GET THE LONGEST PIECES YOU CAN HANDLE

Even if you need mostly short pieces, it's wise to buy the longest trim you can fit into your vehicle. Here's why:

- You'll have fewer splices and more one-piece trim lengths, which look much better than any splice ever would.
- You'll be able to pick and choose to closely match grains so they blend together.
- You'll have plenty of short lengths left over for any smaller projects.

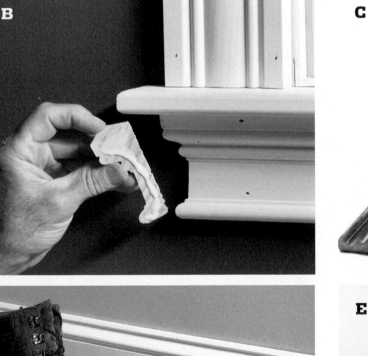

Bad

Good

Top Tools for Trim

A veteran trimming expert reveals his secret weapons to get both speed and perfection in a way few carpenters can match.

BRAD NAILER

A brad nailer is a small, lightweight tool that shoots skinny 18-gauge brad nails that are ideal for thin trim. Before you buy, check the maximum brad length. Many models shoot brads ranging from 5/8 to 2 in. long, but some max out at 1-1/4 in.

Handle Exhaust Some models exhaust through the handle, away from walls and trim.

Don't Forget the Coupling Before you leave the store, check to see if the gun comes with a coupling. Many don't. If the gun comes with a swivel coupling, buy a non-swivel version. Our pro never met a swivel coupling that didn't leak.

Easy Jam Removal Whether you're using a finish or a brad nailer, you'll occasionally hit something hard (like a drywall screw) that will cause the gun to jam. This gun lets you clear jams just by opening the magazine. Other models have a quick-release nosepiece. Without these options, you have to disassemble the nosepiece.

FINISH NAILER

For trim that's 3/4 in. thick or more, you need a 15- or 16-gauge finish nailer, which shoots fatter, longer nails (up to 2-1/2 in.). A finish nailer is also good for hanging doors and installing windows and jamb extensions. Before you buy a gun, make sure the nails it requires are widely available in your area—not just at one store at the other end of town.

Adjustable Exhaust A gun with a fixed exhaust port can leave oily stains on the wall. An adjustable port lets you aim the exhaust away from the wall.

Easy Depth Adjustment The gun should countersink nails without driving them so deep that they split the trim or blast right through. The crude way to control depth is to adjust pressure at the compressor. A better way is to get a gun with a depth dial on the nosepiece.

Angled Magazine Finish nailers come in two shapes. On some, the magazine is parallel to the handle. On others, it's angled. Angled is the way to go. It's easier to get into tight spots.

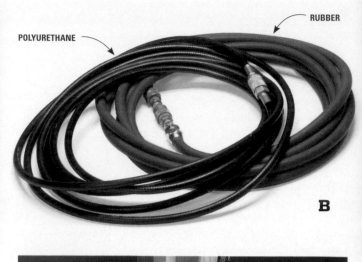

POLYURETHANE

RUBBER

B

A

C

D

A. SMALL COMPRESSORS ARE BIG ENOUGH

For most trim jobs, there's no reason to lug around a compressor that weighs 40 or 50 lbs. There are lots of options in the 20- to 25-lb. range. And that's big enough to keep up with a one-man trim crew. A little compressor can even power a big framing nailer if you give the compressor a few seconds to catch up after three to five shots.

B. ALMOST PERFECT AIR HOSE

Polyurethane air hoses are just plain better than rubber or PVC ones. They're just as tough but much lighter (especially nice when you're working from a ladder). Plus, they don't leave those nasty skid marks on walls when you yank them around a corner. The downside is that poly hoses can be gangly, tangly and hard to roll up. A 25-footer costs about $25.

C. ODD-JOB SOLUTION

You'll never know how badly you need an oscillating tool until you try one. It's handy for a litany of projects, including trim. The blade slips nicely behind trim to cut stubborn nails so you can remove trim without splitting it. It also lets you neatly trim shims—none of the slipping or cracking you sometimes get with the utility knife method. Our pro likes to hang a bunch of doors and then run around trimming them off. It's almost fun. The sanding pad is good for trim work too, especially inside corners and around balusters.

D. PRY BAR

There are a hundred kinds of pry bars out there, but this is the only one in our pro's tool pouch. With its gentle bend, you can slip the claw behind base trim from below and pry off trim without damaging the wall above the trim. This pry bar is also a favorite of painters, so look for it in the paint aisle, at paint stores or online (search for "Hyde 45600").

E. TERRIFIC TRIM LADDER

A 3-ft. ladder is perfect for trim work. That height puts you right where you need to be for crown molding and provides a perfect work surface for jobs like coping. This sturdy model (Werner TW373-30) is a whopping 30 in. wide, so it also makes a great sawhorse or a support for scaffold planks. Plus, it has steps on both sides. Find it online.

F. SPOT SANDER

Trim carpentry produces sharp edges and splinters that need to be smoothed out one way or another. Some guys like sanding sponges, but our pro prefers a 100-grit adhesive-backed sanding disc folded in half. It's tougher than regular sandpaper, doesn't eat up valuable tool pouch space and doesn't tear on sharp edges the way sponges do. It's cheap, too. You can pick up a pack at any home center.

G. NAIL SETS—IT TAKES TWO

Always carry a nail set with a small tip. It's good for setting nails with large heads and makes a good center punch to create starter holes for hinge screws. But a small nail set slips off the heads of brads, so you should also carry a larger nail set—one with a concave tip that locks onto tiny brad heads. Rubber-coated nail sets give you a better grip and, more important, the bright colors are easy to spot when you leave them lying around.

H. ODD-ANGLE CALCULATOR

The bevel gauge has been around a thousand years (give or take a millennium), and the beauty of the tool is its simplicity. It has lots of uses on trim jobs, but the most common use by far is for dealing with a corner that's way out of square. A basic bevel gauge will last a lifetime.

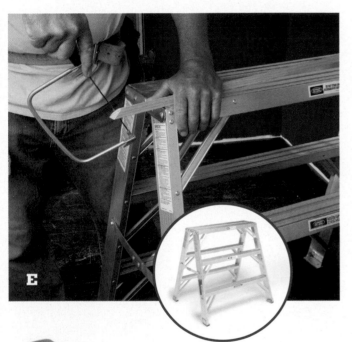

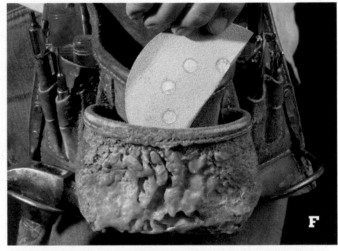

What's with the gunk? It's wood glue that has built up over the years. Our pro closes the bottle by pushing the cap against his pouch. Gross, but efficient.

CONCAVE TIP

G

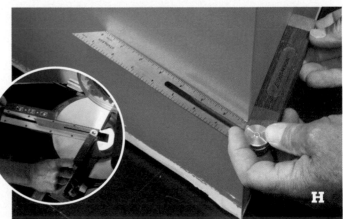

Capture the angle. Fold the bevel gauge around the corner and tighten the nut to lock in the angle. **Match the angle.** Check the angle using your miter saw. Divide that number in half and add or subtract from 45 degrees to get the perfect miter angle.

CHAPTER **SIX**

AROUND THE HOUSE

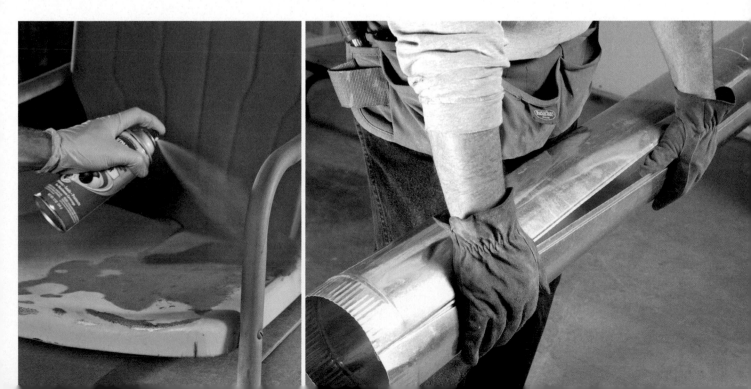

6 Silent Signs Your House Is in Trouble

Discover these points of concern before it is too late.

We don't mean to scare you…well, actually we do. Recently, we sat down with a longtime home inspector, and he told us some tales and shared some photos that were downright frightening. Much of the damage he's encountered could have been prevented if the homeowners had just heeded the silent signs that their house was in trouble.

SIGN: Bulge in Washing Machine Hose

What it means: The hose is ready to burst. A bulging washing machine hose is an emergency. It may burst next year, next week or right now. But it will fail and it won't just leak—it will gush. In just a few minutes, it can do thousands of dollars in damage.

What to do: Replace rubber hoses with braided stainless steel. Immediately turn off the valves connected to the hoses. Before your next load of laundry, you'll need to replace the hoses. New hoses will cost you around $25.

While you're at the home center picking up your new hoses, invest about another $10 in a pressure gauge that hooks onto a spigot or laundry room faucet. Your rubber hoses may have bulged because your water pressure was too high. It shouldn't be more than 80 psi. If it is, install a pressure-reducing valve (PRV) before you damage other appliances and fixtures in your house. If you already have a PRV, it may be set too high or be due for replacement.

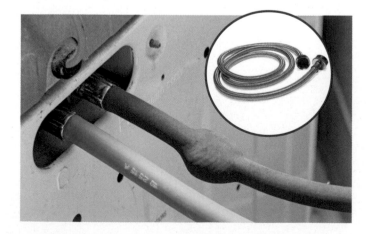

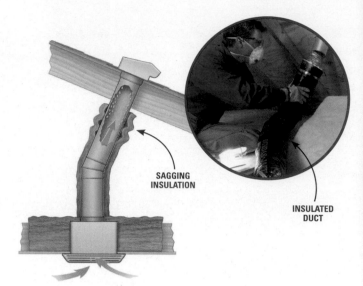

SAGGING INSULATION

INSULATED DUCT

Condensation forms in ducts. Warm air condenses on the inside of a cold duct and the water runs back down into the house. Insulate the duct. You could wrap the existing duct in insulation, but it's usually easier to replace the duct with a duct prewrapped in an insulated jacket. To see how, search at *familyhandyman.com* for "bath fan."

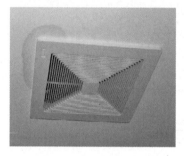

SIGN: Stains Around a Bath Fan

What it means: Condensation is forming inside the duct. The stain could be caused by a roof leak, but condensation inside the duct is the most likely cause. If you live in a cold climate, there's a good chance that the warm, moist air from the bathroom is condensing inside the duct and the water is seeping back down into the fan housing. It's soaking the drywall around the fan and may be ruining your fan motor or even the framing components in your attic.

What to do: Investigate, insulate and run the fan longer. Start by checking the damper inside the fan housing and the one on the vent outside. Vents are usually on walls or roofs, but sometimes they're in the soffits. A stuck damper can lead to heavy condensation.

A bath fan duct that's not insulated (or poorly insulated) gets really cold in the attic. A cold duct filled with warm moist air is a recipe for condensation. On exceptionally cold days, that condensed water freezes and then drips back down when the temperature rises.

Even insulated ducts get cold enough for condensation to form when the fan first starts up. If a fan is run long enough, the duct will warm up and dry out. Consider replacing the wall switch with a timer switch, which will run the fan for a set period of time.

SIGN: Efflorescence on Chimney Brick

What it means: Too much moisture inside the chimney. Efflorescence is the white material that appears on brick. It occurs when moisture moves through masonry. That moisture picks up minerals and leaves them behind in the form of tiny crystals. The minerals themselves do no harm, and a small amount of efflorescence is common. But heavy efflorescence on your chimney is a cause for concern. It's a sign of moisture inside the chimney—and when that moisture freezes, it can slowly wreck the chimney from the inside out.

Even more alarming, your flue liner could be cracked or broken, and deadly combustion gases from your furnace, fireplace or water heater may be leaking into your home.

What to do: Fix the crown or call an expert. Immediately have your chimney inspected by a licensed chimney sweep certified by the Chimney Safety Institute of America (CSIA). Search for "chimney" at *familyhandyman.com* for instructions on how to repair a crown and for additional chimney maintenance tips.

Cracks in the crown allow water in. Water that gets inside the chimney through cracks in the crown can cause efflorescence and damage the bricks.

DUCT TAPE

Seal the crown. Small cracks in the crown can be sealed with an elastomeric masonry sealer, but a crumbling crown will have to be replaced. Smear on the sealant by hand, then smooth it with a brush.

MELTED PLASTIC GROMMET

SIGN: Melted Grommets on Water Heater

What it means: Deadly gases may be entering your home. Exhaust from a gas water heater is supposed to flow through a duct and out of the house. But sometimes exhaust doesn't flow up and out. Instead, it "backdrafts," spilling deadly carbon monoxide into the air you breathe. One sign of backdrafting is damaged plastic grommets on top of the water heater, melted by the hot exhaust. This shows that your water heater has backdrafted badly on at least one occasion—and you must take action.

What to do: Get carbon monoxide alarms. Sometimes the cause of backdrafting is obvious: A vent pipe may be disconnected from a vent hood, for example, or a vent may slope downward. But even a properly installed vent might occasionally backdraft because of high winds or other unusual circumstances. The surest way to protect your family is to install carbon monoxide alarms. If you don't have CO alarms in your house, go get them today.

Install one on every level, outside sleeping areas, and within 5 ft. to 20 ft. of any sources of CO, such as water heaters, furnaces and fireplaces. If an alarm ever goes off, get out of the house immediately and call an HVAC repair service to correct the problem. The symptoms of CO poisoning are dizziness, headaches and vomiting. If anyone in the house is experiencing these symptoms, leave the house and call the fire department.

Carbon monoxide alarms save lives. Every home with an attached garage, fireplace or gas appliances should have carbon monoxide alarms. If you already have them, be sure to test and maintain them according to the manufacturer's instructions.

Bad vents cause backdrafting. Water heater vents need to slope upward at least 1/4 in. per foot. The installer responsible for this down-sloping vent apparently didn't know that hot gases rise.

INCENSE STICK

Test for proper drafting. Close all the windows and doors, and turn on all the bath and kitchen fans. That creates a worst-case scenario for backdrafting. Run some hot water and light an incense stick to see if the smoke is drawn up the vent.

Exterior damage. It's hard to properly flash a door when the deck boards are snug against it. Water can find its way behind the flashing and destroy the ledger and siding below it.

SIGN: Decking Directly Under the Door

What it means: Rot could be wrecking your house. Decks that are built right up to the bottom of a door often mean trouble. Rainwater splashes off the deck up onto the door. That much water is hard to keep out. Even if the flashing holds up, water may eventually find its way through the door components. This can ruin the siding, door and interior flooring or, worse, destroy the rim joist and other framing components both inside and outside your home.

What to do: Divert the water away. Diverting the water with gutters will help. However, the bottom line is that as long as the deck boards are up tight under the door, there's a chance of water infiltration. If you plan to build a deck, install it about 4 in. below the door threshold. And never let snow pile up against the door.

Interior damage. Splashing rainwater can work its way through the door and leak into the house, damaging the rim joist below.

Installing gutters will help. If there's an overhang above the door, install gutters to divert the water that pours off the roof. To learn how, search "install gutters" at *familyhandyman.com*.

Check the line between the meter and the house. If the main valve at the house is turned off and the meter is still spinning, you know the leak is between the meter and the house.

LOW-FLOW INDICATOR

WATER METER

MAIN WATER SHUTOFF VALVE

SIGN: The Water Meter Never Stops

What it means: You've got a leak. If all the faucets and plumbing fixtures in your house are turned off and the low-flow indicator on your water meter continues to measure running water, you're wasting water and money.

What to do: Look for the leak. Indoor leaks usually create obvious signs. Look for water stains on walls or ceilings or a puddle on the floor. Also listen to toilets—a worn-out flapper on the flush valve creates a hiss and is a common cause of slow, constant water flow.

Outdoor leaks usually seep into the ground and can go on for years without being noticed. If your water meter is outside the house (warm climates only), the first step is to check the water line between the house and the meter. Shut off the main water valve at the house and check the meter. If it's still registering water flow, you know there's a leak between the meter and the house. Fixing this problem will likely require some excavation.

A leaking water spigot may go unnoticed if a hose is attached that runs out into the yard or garden. If you find one that keeps dribbling water, a new valve seat washer is probably the solution. If the spigot leaks at the top near the handle, replace the packing nut washer. To see how, search for "faucet repair" at *familyhandyman.com*.

Irrigation systems are another cause of hidden leaks. Check for irrigation leaks by shutting off the valve in the house that feeds the irrigation system. If the meter stops spinning, you've found the problem. Narrow the search even more by looking for wet spots in the yard or areas of grass that are especially green. A malfunctioning irrigation valve is usually the cause.

Inspect the spigots. Disconnect all the hoses and make sure the spigots aren't leaking.

Check your sprinkler system. A malfunctioning irrigation valve will allow water to continue to dribble out into the yard.

Beat Bad Smells

We picked products that fight the battle against stinkiness.

Pets, sewer gas, burnt food, smoke, skunks…let's face it, sometimes life stinks. Our sense of smell is a powerful one, which explains our powerful urge to get rid of bad odors when we encounter them. We rounded up some of the most putrid, foul, stench-laden scenarios to let you know which products battle them best. With these tips in hand, you may just come out smelling like a rose.

A STINKY DRAIN
Every few months, a kitchen sink can develop a foul smell. If you use the sink every day and know a dry trap isn't the problem, whatever the cause, a cup of bleach will kill the stink…until next time.

CLEAN YOUR CAR DUCTS
Neutralize smoke and other smells in your car with an aerosol can of automotive duct cleaner. Most

products require you to spray the cleaner into the vents and the blower motor intake. One way to find your blower motor intake opening is to turn the system on defrost and hold a tissue under the dash. You can buy a can at an auto parts store for $8 to $13. One brand is Clean Air (*cleanairauto.com*).

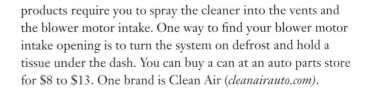

SKUNK SPRAY ANTIDOTE

Humans rarely get sprayed by skunks, but for dogs it's almost a rite of passage. If (or when) Fido gets sprayed, leave him outside for a while—the smell will subside dramatically in 24 hours and you won't stink up your whole house the way you would if you brought him in right away. It takes a lot longer than a day for the smell to disappear completely, so you'll eventually want to wash the stink out. But before you spend a bunch of money on expensive shampoos, take a tip from the Humane Society: "Mix a quart of 3% hydrogen peroxide with 1/4 cup of baking soda and a teaspoon of liquid dish soap. Bathe the dog in it and rinse." Wear gloves to avoid smelling like a skunk yourself.

SEAL IN SMOKE SMELLS

If you reclaim a property in which the renters had chain-smoked, wash down every wall and prime the walls before painting. Regular primer won't seal in the smoke smell (the yellow will bleed through, too), so get a primer designed to seal in stains and odors. It may take about 5 gallons, but you will get rid of the smoke smell!

BIG-LEAGUE STENCH STOPPER

Hockey equipment has a less than flowery reputation, so we asked Rick Bronwell, the assistant equipment manager for the Minnesota Wild hockey team, how he keeps the pros' stuff smelling good (or at least tolerable). "The most important thing is to air everything out," he said. "In addition to that, we've had success with a product called SportSense. It eliminates bacteria that cause odors but, just as important, it eliminates bacteria that can cause a skin infection."

SportSense is available in several sizes. Find it at sporting goods stores. You can use it on all kinds of sports gear.

WASH YOUR WASHING MACHINE

Do you notice a moldy smell when you open the door of your front-loading clothes washer? Front loaders, because they must be watertight, are prone to mold and mildew and must be cleaned regularly.

To get rid of the smell, once a month run the empty washer through a cycle with a mold cleaner designed for washing machines. Our appliance expert recommends a product called Affresh. Look for it at discount stores and home centers or visit *affresh.com* to find a retailer. A packet of three costs about $9. Remember to reduce mold smells by leaving the door open between loads so the interior can dry out.

REFRESH THE FRIDGE

If you've ever dealt with a fully stocked refrigerator that has lost power for several days, you truly understand the definition of "putrid." Even after a thorough cleaning/disinfecting, the stench can linger for an eternity. Try stuffing your fridge with crumpled newspapers and charcoal. The odor will be gone within several days.

DE-STINK A MICROWAVE

If you've ever used a microwave as a kiln to dry walnut coasters you were making, in addition to almost burning your house down, you probably stank up the microwave something awful. One trick that works pretty well to eradicate microwave stench is to mix 1/2 cup of vinegar with 1/2 cup of water and bring it to a boil. It may not completely remove the smell, but it makes a big difference. You can boil a little vinegar on any occasion to get rid of smells from foods like fish and bacon.

FRESHEN UP YOUR WORK BOOTS

At the end of the day, before you retire your work boots to the hall closet, fill them with cedar chips. (Actually, you can slide in an old sock that's filled with cedar chips.) We've tried several store-bought products, but cedar chips seem to work the best at absorbing moisture and eliminating odors. You can buy a bag of chips sold as animal bedding at a local pet store for $10, and it will last you for years. Change out the chips every month or so.

BAKING SODA—THE ALL-AROUND ODOR ABSORBER

The best thing we've used to make bad smells go away is baking soda. People think about it for their freezer or refrigerator, but it's good for much more than that. You can sprinkle it on carpet, work it in a bit and vacuum it up. For other items, like mattresses, cushions and clothing, dampen the fabric and gently rub it with baking soda, then wipe off the fabric and rinse it with cold water.

Defeat Rust

How to get rid of it, and how to keep it from coming back.

You're surrounded by tools and machines made out of steel. And when the coatings on those products crack, rust starts to bloom and the battle is on. You can attack rust early and nip it in the bud, or you can wait until you have a full-blown war on your hands. The choice is yours. Either way you'll need a battle plan and reliable weapons at your disposal. That's why we're going to show you the five ways to defeat rust—three methods to remove it and two steps to prevent it from coming back.

THE ELBOW GREASE METHOD

Grind, sand or scour off the rust. If you're not into chemicals and you want to remove the paint along with the rust, use a power tool like a grinder, sander, oscillating tool or drill. A grinder fitted with a stripping disc, grinding wheel, or fiber or flap disc makes quick work of heavy rust on large objects—but keep the tool moving so you don't gouge the metal. For smaller jobs, use a traditional sander. To get into small areas, use a "mouse" sander or an oscillating tool with a carbide rasp or sanding pad attachment.

Whichever tool you choose, always start with the coarsest abrasive to get rid of the rust and pockmarks. Once the rust is gone, switch to a finer grit to smooth out the swirls and grooves caused by the coarse grit. For a smooth paint job afterwards, finish with 400-grit wet/dry paper.

Match the abrasive to the shape. Use flap discs, fiber discs and sanders on large, flat areas. Switch to wire wheels for seams, corners and rounded areas.

SANDING PAD

CARBIDE RASP

STRIPPING DISC

"ROPE" WIRE WHEEL

FLAP DISC

"CUP" WIRE WHEEL

FIBER DISC

GRINDING WHEEL

STRIPPING DISC

WIRE WHEEL

"CUP" WIRE WHEEL

80-GRIT CARBIDE PAPER

THE CHEMICAL REMOVAL METHOD

Remove rust with powerful chemicals... The old standby rust remover chemicals contain either phosphoric or hydrochloric acid to dissolve the rust. They're harsh chemicals that give off some pretty intense fumes, so suit up with rubber gloves, goggles and a respirator. Find them in the paint department at any home center. You'll also need an old paintbrush, a waste tub, a 3-in. putty knife and rags.

Apply the chemicals with the old paintbrush and wait the recommended time for the chemicals to work. Then scrape off the liquefied rust. You won't get it all in a single step— count on multiple applications to completely remove heavy rust buildup. Consider a gel formula when removing rust on vertical surfaces. It'll cling better and result in less runoff.

...or with safer and gentler chemicals. Try one of the newer nontoxic and acid-free soaking solutions. We bought a gallon of Evapo-Rust at an auto parts store for about $25. These chemicals dissolve rust through the process of "selective chelation." We can tell you that it works...if you're patient.

Start by cleaning off any oil or grease. Then dunk the rusted part in a tub of solution. The product says it'll dissolve rust in either 30 minutes or overnight. Based on our experience, you'd better plan on overnight, because even this minimally rusted C-clamp (at right) took that long. Keep in mind that this is a soaking solution—you can't paint it on or spray it on. If you've got a large object, you're going to need a lot of solution, and that's going to cost a lot more.

ACID-FREE REMOVER

Buy enough solution to completely cover the rusted part. Clean off any oil or grease before soaking. Pour the solution in a plastic tub. Then drop in the rusted item and walk away.

Choose between liquid and spray converter. Rust converter comes in brushable liquid or aerosol spray. Spray provides a smoother finish but doesn't penetrate severe rust as well as brushable liquid.

THE CONVERSION METHOD

Convert it—it's the easiest method. If you can live with the look of a rough or pockmarked finish, rust converter can save you a lot of time. It kills the rust, prevents its spread and dries into a ready-to-paint primer. Buy it at any home center or auto parts store. Start by removing any flaking paint and rusty dust with a wire brush. Then either spray on the converter or apply it with a disposable paintbrush. Let it dry for the recommended time. Even though the label says you can paint after it dries into a primer coat, we recommend spraying on a real primer. Then paint. Apply a second coat of converter if you're not going to paint. Don't return leftover converter to the bottle—it will contaminate the rest. Toss it in the trash, along with the brush.

Apply converter after wire brushing. Pour a small amount of converter into a cup and work it into the rusty patches with a paintbrush. Then smooth out the brushstrokes and let it dry.

THREE WAYS TO REMOVE RUST	PROS	CONS
Grind, sand or scour off the rust	▪ No pockmarks and a smooth finish prior to painting. ▪ Complete project in a day. No waiting for chemicals to work.	▪ Dirty, dusty, hard work. ▪ Requires power tools and lots of elbow grease.
Convert the rust	▪ Easiest way to stop rust and to prime in one operation. ▪ Less expensive than chemical or mechanical methods for removing rust.	▪ Leaves a rough or pockmarked finish that'll show after you paint. ▪ It may not inhibit rust as long as traditional removal, priming and painting does.
Remove rust with chemicals	▪ Soaking removers can do all the work for you if the item is small enough. ▪ Spray removers greatly reduce the grunt work, but they require several applications and some scraping.	▪ Long wait times for the liquid removers to do their job. ▪ Makes a huge mess. ▪ Soaking removers are expensive and can be used only on small items. ▪ The surface will still be pockmarked after the rust is gone.

Pro Tip

Don't think you can spray rust-inhibiting paint onto a rusty surface and get good results. The rust will bleed right through the paint and ruin your new paint job. You have to deal with the rust with one of the methods we show here. There's just no way around it.

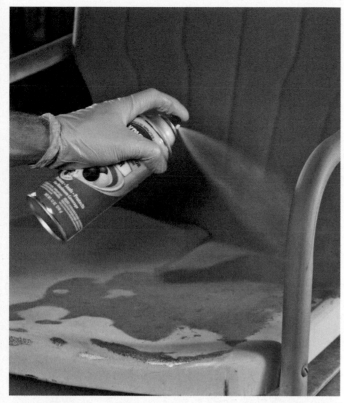

Pick your primer. Choose a regular (nonsandable) primer if the surface is completely smooth. To fill in scratches, choose a sandable primer and lightly sand when dry. Or, use a filler primer to fill in pockmarks.

PREVENT RUST: Prime First!

Prime before painting. No matter how you get the rust off, you still have to prime before painting. If the surface is smooth, simply spray on a metal primer (light gray for light-colored paints, black for darker paints). However, if the surface still has pockmarks, swirls or scratches, use a "sandable" or "filler" primer to fill in the depressions.

Surface preparation prior to priming is critical, especially if there's any old paint left on the item. Clean the surface with a tack cloth and a wax-removing solvent (buy at any auto parts store).

Prepare and prime. Clean the metal before priming. Then apply the primer over the old paint and the newly sanded metal.

Shop for rust-inhibiting paint. Several companies make rust-inhibiting paint. If you don't find the color you like, try the paint department at an auto parts store. Spray on a final topcoat of clear gloss.

PREVENT RUST: Paint & Topcoat

Pick a high-quality paint. After all the nasty prep work, why risk another bout of rust by using cheap paint? Inexpensive paint contains less pigment, fewer resin binders and no rust inhibitors. Spend a few extra bucks on a premium rust-inhibiting paint. It will contain zinc additives that provide an extra measure of protection against future rust.

Brushing usually provides a better paint bond than spraying, but it leaves brushstrokes in the finish. Spraying, however, is tricky—if you stay in one spot too long, you can wind up with paint sag marks in the finish.

Whichever painting method, seal the newly painted item with a clear topcoat. That'll add to the gloss and dramatically increase the life of the paint by reducing paint oxidation.

Apply a clear topcoat. Allow the color coat to dry completely. Then spray on a clear topcoat to extend the life of the paint.

Think Twice Before Filing an Insurance Claim

Filing an insurance claim almost always means higher premiums in the future, so it might be smart to pay for the repair out of your own pocket. Here's a general rule: If the total repair bill will be less than your deductible plus $1,000, don't file a claim. Be especially careful with water damage claims. Water damage is a red flag to insurance companies since it hints at mold abatement costs or chronic plumbing problems and future damage.

Don't Forget Surge Protection

More and more appliances now contain sensitive electronics that can be destroyed by a power surge. And the repair bill can total hundreds of dollars. So if you buy a new washer, for example, consider spending extra money on a surge suppressor. For more info, go to *familyhandyman.com* and search for "surge protection."

Silence Those Irritating Little Noises Forever

We weigh in with fixes for the most annoying of bothersome squeaks, creaks, gurgles and bangs you may hear around your home.

If you live next to railroad tracks, near an airport or have a neighbor who restores cannons for a hobby, you know all about irritating noises. But sometimes it's not the obnoxiously loud noises outside that drive us insane but those persistent little sounds in our own home. The good news is that most home noises are easy to eliminate without spending hours on repairs or a ton of money. We're sure there are at least a few tips in this story to quiet your house and ease your mind. And as for your neighbor with the cannons, maybe you should get him interested in your stamp collection.

SQUEAKY DOOR HINGE

Spray squeaky door hinges in place with a little all-purpose lube, silicone spray or dry Teflon spray. If the squeaks persist, remove the hinge pins and rub off any rust or corrosion with a steel wool pad; then coat the pins with a lubricant before replacing them. If you have teenagers in the house, you may want to hold off on fixing the entry door—that squeaking sound may be the only way you'll know when they're coming and going.

A. CLINK, CLINK, CLINK OF THE CEILING FAN CHAIN

Even if a ceiling fan is perfectly balanced, the breeze from the fan can cause the pull chain to smack up against the light fixture. Solve this problem by removing the chain and sliding a 1/4-in. plastic tube over it. You can buy 10 ft. of tubing for a few dollars at home centers.

B. RATTLING DOORS

A door will rattle when there's too much space between the door and the doorstop. The solution is to reduce or remove the gap. Here are a few different ways to do that.

FIX 1: Move the stop. Knock the doorstop flush with a hammer and a scrap piece of wood. If the stop is more than 1/16 in. out of whack, you may end up with a noticeable unfinished spot where the doorstop used to be, especially on painted doors. Add a couple of brads or finish nails to the stop if it's a door that regularly gets slammed shut by the wind or angry teenagers.

FIX 2: Bend the strike plate tang. Many strike plates have an adjustable tab or tang. Some of these tangs can be adjusted in place with a flathead screwdriver. Others need to be removed and adjusted with pliers or an adjustable wrench. The more you bend the tang toward the door, the farther the door has to travel before latching shut.

FIX 3: Fill the gap with a bumper. Another simple fix is to install a cabinet door pad/bumper on the part of the doorstop that contacts the door. Felt, cork or rubber will all work fine. Cabinet bumpers vary in thickness, so check out the size of the gap between the slab and the stop before you head to the home center. You'll find the bumpers near the cabinet hardware.

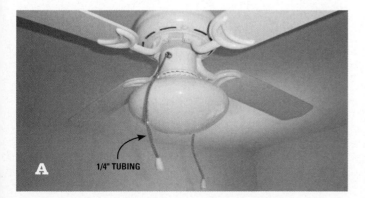

A — 1/4" TUBING

B1

B2 — DOOR-STOP

B3 — CORK DOT — DOOR-STOP

C. WATER HEATER GURGLE

Popping or gurgling coming from your water heater is a sign of excessive sediment buildup in the tank. The sound is caused by steam bubbles percolating up through the muck. On a gas water heater, the sediment creates hot spots that can damage the tank and cause premature failure. On an electric water heater, sediment buildup can cause the lower heating element to fail. Flushing offers payback in lower energy bills and extended heater life.

Start by shutting the water heater down. Turn the breaker off, and turn the thermostat to "Pilot" if you have a gas model. Shut off the water supply to the appliance and let the water cool. Then hook a hose to the drain valve at the bottom of the tank. Put the other end of the hose into a bucket and open the drain valve. Dump the bucket outside so the sediment doesn't clog your pipes. Keep draining until only clear water discharges. If the tank empties before the water turns clear, open the water valve and allow more water into the tank to further rinse it. Once you're done rinsing, close the drain valve, let the tank refill and turn the water heater back on.

D. GUTTER DRIPS

Is that dripping noise in your downspout forcing you to keep your bedroom window closed at night? Tie a synthetic rope onto one of the gutter hangers and run it into the downspout. Drops of water will cling to the rope and flow down instead of plummeting the whole length of the downspout and causing that irritating drip. Adding a rope does restrict the water flow, so this may not be the best option if your gutter is prone to overflowing or gets clogged easily.

E. SOFFIT CLATTER

Most aluminum soffits fit into a channel mounted to the wall. Sometimes the soffits fit loosely, which allows them to clatter in the wind. Set up a ladder and tap on the soffits to see which ones are loose. Next, with a plastic putty knife, insert a length of screen spline in between the soffit and the aluminum channel. The soffits may have been cut too short, so push the screen mold in far enough so it won't be seen from the ground but not in so far that it slides past the end of the soffit. A package of 25 ft. of screen spline costs around $5.

DRAIN VALVE

D

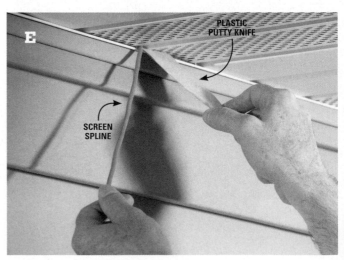

E

PLASTIC PUTTY KNIFE

SCREEN SPLINE

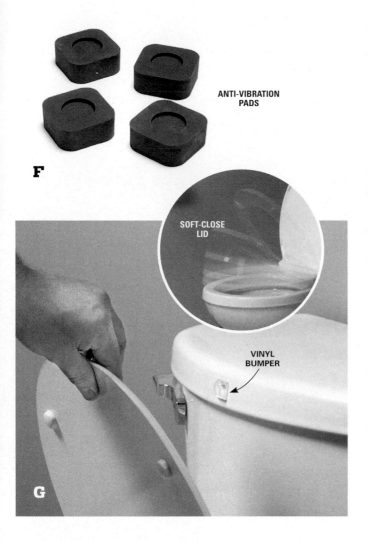

ANTI-VIBRATION PADS

F

SOFT-CLOSE LID

VINYL BUMPER

G

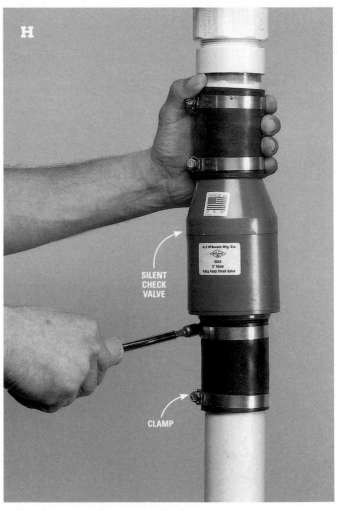

H

SILENT CHECK VALVE

CLAMP

F. APPLIANCE VIBRATION

Locating a laundry room near living areas rather than in the basement is much more convenient. But vibrations caused by washers and dryers can reverberate through floors and cause quite a racket. The noise can be eliminated or greatly diminished by the installation of anti-vibration pads under the legs of both the washer and the dryer. These pads are not a fix for appliances that are out of level; that's a different issue altogether.

G. BANG! GOES THE TOILET LID

Toilets are responsible for a whole lotta noises. Field Editor Dan Carlenzoli had this to say: "Slow-close toilet seats work great at stopping the 'clank' when lowering the toilet seat, but I was still getting woken up at night when one of my three boys opened the lid and it banged against the tank. To solve this problem, I put a vinyl bumper on the lid of the toilet tank."

A toilet seat with a slow-close lid costs about $40 at home centers, and a set of 12 vinyl bumpers is about $3.

H. SUMP PUMP THUMP

A waste line from a sewage ejector or sump pump includes a check valve to stop wastewater from flowing back into the basin. When the valve shuts, it can make a thud loud enough to be heard throughout the house. To quiet the valve, replace the old one with a "silent" check valve. Turn off the pump and loosen the clamps to remove the existing check valve. Be prepared for the water draining from above the valve. Install the new valve and you're done.

Silent check valves are available at most plumbing suppliers. If you have trouble finding one locally, search online for silent or quiet check valves.

SUMP PUMP DRIP, DRIP

Field Editor Don Wharram had a different problem with his sump pump: "The dripping noise made by water falling from the drain tile into my sump basin was extremely irritating. For sanity's sake, I tied a string to the bottom edge of the drain tile pipe and extended it right into the basin. I attached a washer on the other end of the string and made sure it wasn't so long that the pump gobbled it up. Now water follows the string, so no more dripping sound."

I

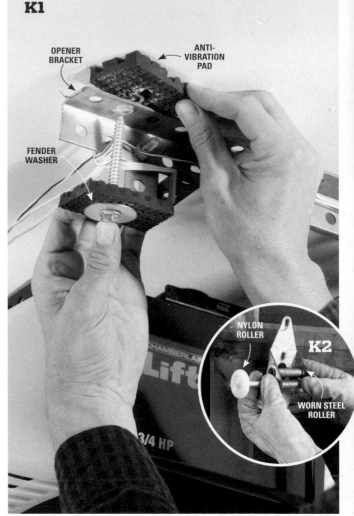

K1

OPENER BRACKET

ANTI-VIBRATION PAD

FENDER WASHER

NYLON ROLLER

K2

WORN STEEL ROLLER

J

I. JINGLING DOG TAGS

Field Editor Tabatha Bettencourt says, "The constant jingling noise from our dog's tags drove us crazy till we found the Quiet Spot Pet Tag Silencer. It's a little neoprene jacket with Velcro straps, and it even has a reflective logo. One lasts through about a year of hard farm play…we bought a stockpile of them. Now we can sleep without a jingle!"

They're available at pet stores and online for about $13.

J. WHISTLING DUCT GRILLES

If you have a grille or register that hums or whistles, all you have to do is twist the fins slightly until the noise stops. Pliers will scratch and kink the delicate fins, so use a hinge with strips of tape applied to the inside. Then grab a fin between the hinge leaves and give it a twist. Twisting all the fins so they open a little wider will give the best results.

K. GARAGE DOOR RUMBLE

A garage door in motion can produce all sorts of rumbling vibrations, which can easily migrate indoors, especially if

there's a living space above it. Here are a couple of quick and inexpensive fixes that will help reduce the rumble.

FIX 1: Install anti-vibration pads. Cushion the connection between the opener and the framing with rubber pads. Use heavy-duty rubber washers, cut pads out of an old tire or buy specially made rubber/cork anti-vibration pads. You'll be adding about an inch in thickness, so you'll need four longer lag screws and some fender washers.

FIX 2: Replace metal rollers with nylon. Nylon rollers are quieter and, unlike metal rollers, don't require periodic oiling. A 10-pack costs around $20 online or at garage door suppliers. To install them, lower the door and remove the hinges one at a time. **Beware:** On some garage doors, the bottom roller brackets (closest to the ground when the door is closed) are attached to a cable and garage door springs. In this case, you should not remove the roller or bracket without the help of a knowledgeable professional. Removing these parts with the garage door closed could result in rapid discharge of the tension in the spring and any number of safety issues.

L. POPPING DUCTS

Ducts made from sheet metal can make a popping sound when the furnace kicks on, changing the air pressure inside the ducts. One simple fix is to reinforce the sheet metal by scoring it. Simply take a straightedge and score a large "X" in the center of the sheet metal with a screwdriver. It may take a few X's in a row to stop the pop.

M. BANGING CABINET DOORS

There are two kinds of people in the world: those who shut cabinet doors, and those who slam them. If you live with a door slammer, consider installing cabinet door dampeners. The piston in the dampener slows the door down before it makes contact with the cabinet. The one shown here is adjustable and installs with one screw in less than 5 minutes. Your cabinets need to have self-closing hinges for the dampeners to work. You can buy a 10-pack at home centers and online.

N. PUT AN END TO EXHAUST VENT CHATTER

When the wind blows just right, the flapper on an electric dryer or exhaust fan vent can open and close, causing a chattering noise. One solution is to put a little weight on the flapper, enough to resist the wind but not too much or the flapper won't open when the dryer or fan runs.

Attach a few small magnets first and then run the dryer, hood vent or bath fan to make sure the flapper still opens. If the chatter is gone—great. If it persists, add another magnet. Always check that the flapper still opens when it's supposed to. Once you get the right balance, add a dab of adhesive to the magnets to keep them in place. You can get a 1/2 x 30-in. magnetic strip at home centers for a few bucks.

For noisy plastic vents, try attaching small washers with a dab of clear silicone. **Note:** These flapper-quieting tips are not for use with gas appliances.

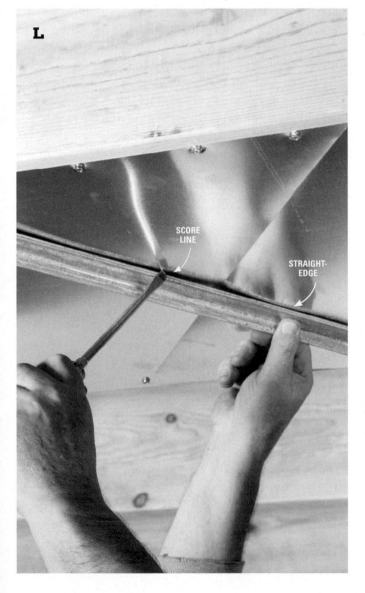

L

SCORE LINE

STRAIGHT-EDGE

M

CABINET DOOR DAMPENER

N

MAGNET

O. NOISY PIPES

Noisy pipes are a common problem with a variety of causes. Here are a few solutions to silence your unruly plumbing:

FIX 1: Cushion the pipe hangers. Pipes expand and contract when they heat up and cool down. This can cause them to tick, creak and groan as they slide by the hangers or straps holding them in place.

Minimize the irksome sound by pulling off the straps and inserting strips of felt or heavy fabric under the straps before reinstalling them. You may have to fix only the hot water supply line, because that's the one that changes temperature the most.

FIX 2: Spray foam on vibrating pipes. Supply lines can vibrate when water is running through them. Those vibrations can be amplified through the framing.

To fix the problem, isolate the pipes from wall and floor framing with expanding foam. If you can reach the offending area, spray foam between the wood and the pipes. If the area is sealed, drill a small hole and squirt in some expanding spray foam. Don't overdo it though; too much foam could literally bow out your drywall. Patch up the hole when you're done and touch it up with a little paint.

FIX 3: Replace a worn washer. An outdoor faucet with a worn-out washer can make a loud vibrating noise when it's turned on or off. You can easily replace the washer without removing the entire faucet. First, turn off the water to the faucet. Then use a wrench to remove the retaining nut.

Slide the handle and stem assembly out of the sill cock. Remove the screw at the end of the stem and remove the washer. Buy a new washer that matches the old one at any hardware store. Then reassemble the faucet. Occasionally the washer is fine, but the screw holding it is loose. If so, put a drop of thread-locking sealant (sold at hardware stores) on the threads and tighten it.

FIX 4: Install a water hammer arrester. Solenoid valves, like the ones in dishwashers, washing machines and water softeners, shut off almost instantly, which causes a ferocious *CLUNK* in your plumbing. Aside from the noise, this also puts strain on hoses and fittings. Hand-controlled faucets usually don't cause as much hammering because the shutoff is more gradual.

Install water hammer arresters, which are available at home centers for around less than $20 each. An arrester isolates the pocket of air from the water in the pipes with a rubber-gasketed piston. The closer you locate the arrester to solenoid valves, the better. The model shown is designed to mount between the spigot and the washing machine feed lines with simple hose bib connections. If necessary, add more in-line arresters in other water pipes near faucets or valves to further reduce hammering.

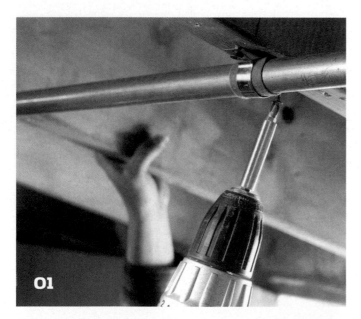

01

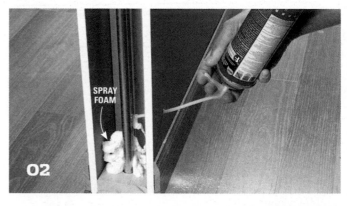

SPRAY FOAM

02

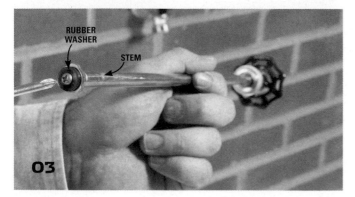

RUBBER WASHER

STEM

03

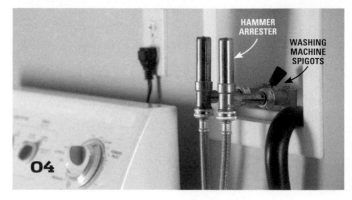

HAMMER ARRESTER

WASHING MACHINE SPIGOTS

04

Moving Furniture

Let us show you some simple techniques for moving heavy, awkward items without wrecking your back, your house or the furniture.

A

B

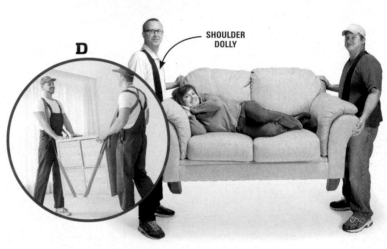

D

SHOULDER DOLLY

C

A. "HOOK" CHAIRS AROUND CORNERS

A large easy chair can be the opposite of easy to move. Follow the example of pro movers and hook large chairs around corners. Turn the chair on its side so it looks like an L and move it back-first through the doorway. Then curl it (hook it) around the door frame and slip it through.

B. CARRY TALL ITEMS HIGH AND LOW

A tall dresser, filing cabinet or shelving unit is awkward to handle. Make it a two-person job. Tip the item backward at an angle and have one person carry the top while the other carries the bottom. This centers the weight and keeps the item from swinging out of control. Transporting the item up or down stairs is easier too, since the carrying angle will roughly match the slope of the stairs.

C. STAND COUCHES ON END

If you ever have to maneuver a couch down a hallway and through a door, you may find it almost impossible to carry it horizontally and make the turn into the room. Before you enter the hallway, place the couch on its end and slide it to the doorway. You'll almost always be able to hook it (using tip A) through the door. If it's a bit taller than the door opening, start the top away from the door and gain several inches of clearance.

D. PICK UP SOME "HUMP STRAPS"

Moving and lifting straps (aka "hump straps") take the weight off your back by relying on leverage and large muscle groups. They also leave your hands free to maneuver awkward items. However, they can be tricky to use on stairs because the weight shifts completely to the downhill mover.

Look for lifting straps that can be adjusted for different-length objects as well as for different-size movers. The Forearm Forklift lifting straps shown above left are great for moving on flat surfaces. The TeamStrap Shoulder Dolly (above right) gives you better control on stairs. These and others hump straps are available for $15 to $50 at home centers and online retailers.

E. DON'T CARRY OR DRAG—SLIDE

You can buy furniture slides in many shapes and sizes at home centers and online. It's also easy to make your own sliders from plastic container covers, Frisbees, bedspreads, moving blankets, towels and carpet remnants. Use hard plastic sliders on carpeting, and soft, padded sliders on hard flooring.

F. PROTECT FURNITURE WITH BLANKETS AND PLASTIC

Moving blankets are invaluable for protecting the items you're moving, as well as your house. Sure, renting blankets is cheap, but you can buy several for just a few dollars more at home centers or *uhaul.com* and always have them on hand. (You'll use them for all kinds of other things too.) To prevent damaging the finish and fragile edges of dressers, tables and other furniture, wrap the items completely with moving blankets and then secure the blankets with stretch film.

USE A RAMP AND A ROPE

Construct a simple ramp from pieces of lumber or scaffolding planks to help maneuver big stuff up and down stairs and into your truck. If you're moving heavy items by yourself, consider securing the item with a rope tied to some sort of immovable anchor, which will allow you to lower or raise a heavy item and avoid a runaway disaster.

Field Editor Brian Gray says, "I had to move a heavy, bulky TV down the stairs by myself before the floor guys came to strip the floors. I cobbled together four 10-ft. 2x6 boards to make a ramp. I wiggled the TV onto some carpet scraps (carpet side down) at the top of the stairs. I then got a climbing rope and looped it around the TV, looped the other end around my truck axle outside and lowered the TV down the stairs that way until I reached the bottom. Beautiful!"

G. MAKE A MATTRESS SLING

Trying to wrestle a heavy, floppy mattress anywhere is tough. Many mattresses have handles, but they're not intended for carrying. They're actually made to help you position the mattress, so they're not very strong.

Here's an easier way to carry a mattress: Make a simple rope sling that will give you and your helper a lot more control. Thread the rope through the mattress handles and attach your grips as shown. Flip the mattress over so the sling is on the bottom and you're on your way.

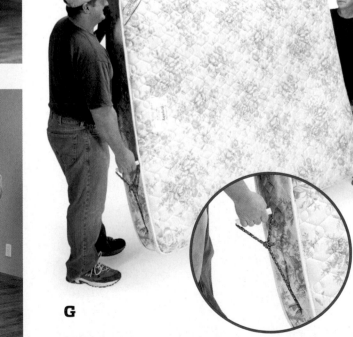

Slip a 5-in. piece of 1-in. PVC pipe over the rope ends, and then loop and tie each end to create a comfortable sling grip.

H. CUT AND FOLD A BOX SPRING

Is your box spring too big to fit in your stairway or around a tight corner? You could buy a "split" box spring designed specifically for this (and pay several hundred bucks), or you could cut your existing box spring and fold it so it fits. Sound extreme? There's actually a simple, ingenious way to cut and fold your box spring without wrecking it. See steps **1–3**.

H

1 Cut the frame. Remove the fabric covering (the most tedious part of this whole process is removing the staples), and place the box spring face down. Pull back the mattress cover along each side and cut through the frame just to the left or right of the middle crosspiece (don't cut through the crosspiece itself). Do this on each side and in the center.

2 Fold it. You can now fold the box spring like a book, as shown, and move it. Secure it with a strap to prevent it from springing open.

3 Put it back together. Screw a 1x2 along the center crosspiece cut and against the insides of the outer frame cuts to reinforce the box spring. Then staple the fabric covering in place.

I. PLAN WHERE IT LANDS

If you're moving to a new house, decide beforehand which furniture will go where. Before you move, sketch a floor plan with the correct measurements of each room, measure your furniture and create your layout. Then, as you move things in, you (or your helpers, if you're not there) can place your furniture in the correct spot and not have to touch it again. To make it easy on the movers, tape a copy of the room's plan to the wall of the room so people can tell at a glance where things go.

I

EXTEND
ARMS

PALMS
TOUCH
RUNG

LADDER
AT CORRECT
ANGLE

TOUCH TOES
TO LADDER BASE

Safe Ladder Setup

Ladder safety starts with careful setup. Sloppy setup leads to falls, even if you climb cautiously.

Setting a ladder at the correct angle is the key to stability. Too steep and it can slide sideways or tip backward. If not steep enough, the feet of the ladder may slip. To get it right, put your toes against the ladder's feet while it is standing on the ground. Stand straight up and extend your arms. Your palms should just reach the ladder's rung.

8 Most Common Electrical Code Violations

We sat down with a state chief electrical inspector as well as a seasoned field inspector to find out which electrical codes DIYers and pros mess up most often.

Many of the problems stem from the newest additions to the National Electrical Code (NEC). For example, DIYers often install GFCIs where AFCIs are required, and vice versa.

However, we also found that other common mistakes, like inadequate clearances for service panels, violate codes that have been on the books for years.

We hope the info here helps clear up the confusion that could lead to a failed electrical inspection.

1. CHOOSING THE WRONG CIRCUIT BREAKERS

To help understand which protection goes where, consider what each type of breaker was designed to do.

- **Circuit breakers** protect wiring and equipment like furnaces, air conditioners, dryers and stoves.
- **GFCIs** protect people in areas where they are likely to be using small appliances and where water is present.
- **AFCIs** prevent fires in all living areas where appliance cords are prone to be pinched or crimped, or chewed by pets.

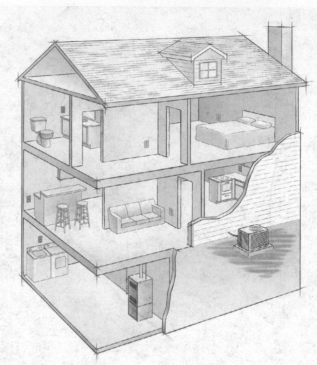

PROPER-CIRCUIT LEGEND
- ■ = Standard circuit breaker
- ■ = Ground fault circuit interrupter
- ■ = Arc fault circuit interrupter

Standard Circuit Breakers Standard circuit breakers are better at protecting wiring and equipment than preventing fires and protecting people. That's why they largely have been replaced by GFCIs and AFCIs. There are only a few places left where standard circuit breakers can be used, typically for larger appliances such as furnaces, AC condensers, dryers and stoves.

Ground Fault Circuit Interrupter GFCI breakers and outlets have been around for a while, and most people know they're required in bathrooms, kitchens and outdoors, but our experts are still finding violations, especially in these areas: garages, crawl spaces, storage/work areas in unfinished basements, wet bars (within 6 ft. of a sink) and sump pumps. And don't forget that GFCIs need to be readily accessible in order to be reset. This means they shouldn't be installed on the ceiling or buried under a hydro massage tub without an access panel.

Arc Fault Circuit Interrupter AFCIs are the new kid on the block. They used to be required only on bedroom

circuits, but the NEC now requires AFCI protection in all living areas. AFCIs were designed with fire protection in mind. They're equipped with sophisticated electronics that can detect an arcing condition (like in a frayed lamp cord), which may not be detected by a standard circuit breaker until after a fire has started. AFCI protection is not just required for new construction; it's now also required where branch-circuit wiring is modified, replaced or extended into existing homes.

Common Violations
- ■ No GFCI protection in wet bars.
- ■ GFCI installed in inaccessible spots such as on ceilings.
- ■ No AFCI protection on basement finish or remodeling projects.

2. FORGETTING THE TAMPER-RESISTANT RECEPTACLES

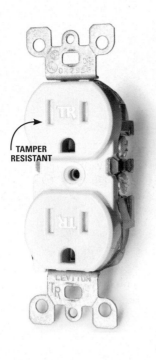

TAMPER RESISTANT

Tamper-resistant receptacles are designed to stop a kid from inserting an object, such as a paper clip. They're required for all locations, indoors and out. Tamper-resistant receptacles are a great invention, so use them—it's code.

Common Violation

Replacing an existing receptacle with a conventional one. When an existing receptacle is replaced, the NEC requires the installation of a tamper-resistant receptacle.

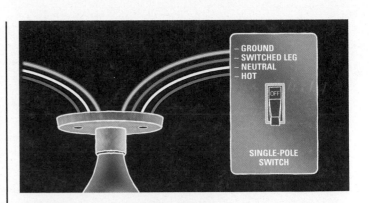

GROUND
SWITCHED LEG
NEUTRAL
HOT

OFF

SINGLE-POLE SWITCH

3. WIRING SWITCHES WITHOUT A NEUTRAL

All switch locations now need a neutral wire. This code was mainly implemented to accommodate potential future uses. Electronic switches require a small amount of constant electricity and therefore need a neutral wire run to them. There are exceptions to this code, but if the walls are currently open anyway, don't make the next guy fish in a wire. Do it right and make sure there's a neutral wire in the box.

Common Violation

One common occurrence of a missing neutral wire is a dead-end single-pole switch loop. One way to solve this problem is to run a three-wire cable with ground to the last switch on the run.

4. USING A GROUND ROD ELECTRODE WHEN A BETTER SYSTEM IS AVAILABLE

For a long time, metal underground water piping was considered the best grounding electrode available, but virtually all underground water piping today is plastic. And it turns out that rebar in concrete footings or in the foundation of a house is actually a more effective grounding system than the ground rods we've been using for decades. So if there's rebar in the new footings, that rebar needs to be used as the primary grounding electrode. This new provision in the NEC requires a lot of coordination between the trades and project managers. Electricians usually show up long after the concrete guys have moved on, but good communication is much easier work than busting up concrete.

The Bottom Line

If a new home has footings with at least 20 ft. of 1/2-in. rebar, the rebar embedded in those footings needs to be used as the primary grounding electrode.

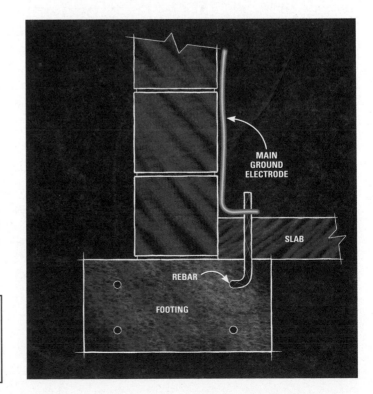

MAIN GROUND ELECTRODE

SLAB

REBAR

FOOTING

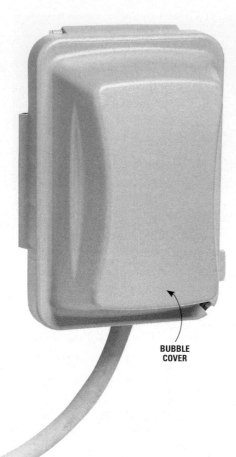

BUBBLE COVER

5. INSTALLING A FLAT WEATHER-RESISTANT COVER ON AN OUTDOOR RECEPTACLE

Flat covers provide protection only when a receptacle isn't in use, but it's not uncommon for extension cords to be plugged in for extended periods of time—for holiday lights, for example. In-use or "bubble covers" provide protection at all times. The NEC defines a "wet location" as an area that is subject to saturation with water or other liquids and unprotected locations exposed to the weather. The NEC has another definition for "damp locations" that is more subjective, but if you think the receptacle is going to get wet, use an in-use cover. And don't forget the weather-resistant receptacle. The NEC requires that all 15- and 20-amp receptacles be rated as weather-resistant and tamper-resistant when installed in both wet and damp locations.

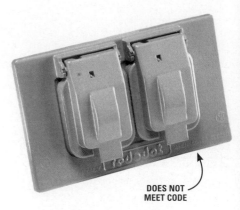

DOES NOT MEET CODE

Common Violation

Often it's assumed that an exterior outlet sheltered by a roof overhang can be covered with one of the older, flap-style outlet covers, but that decision is up to the inspector, so it's better to play it safe and install a bubble cover.

REFRIGERATOR FOOTPRINT

6. CROWDING A SERVICE PANEL

A service panel requires a working clearance that's 30 in. wide, 3 ft. deep and 6 ft. 8 in. high. Here's a good rule of thumb: If you can't park a refrigerator in front of the panel, you don't have enough working space. These clearances are designed to protect the person working on the panel. It's difficult to work safely when your arms are pinned to your sides. Also, the panel needs to be readily accessible, meaning the area should not be used as storage space or require a ladder for access.

Common Violations

- Panels in closets, crawl spaces and bathrooms.
- Panels encroached upon by laundry tubs, a sump basket, ducting and pipes.

7. NOT ENOUGH RECEPTACLES IN THE FOYER AREA

The purpose of this code is to reduce the use of extension cords. From any point along a wall line, a receptacle outlet needs to be within reach of a 6-ft. appliance cord, and that 6 ft. cannot be measured across a passageway. The bottom line is that extension cords start fires and create tripping hazards—the fewer there are, the better.

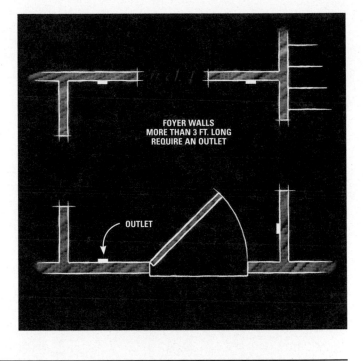

FOYER WALLS
MORE THAN 3 FT. LONG
REQUIRE AN OUTLET

OUTLET

Common Violation
Failure to install receptacles in walls that are 3 ft. long or longer.

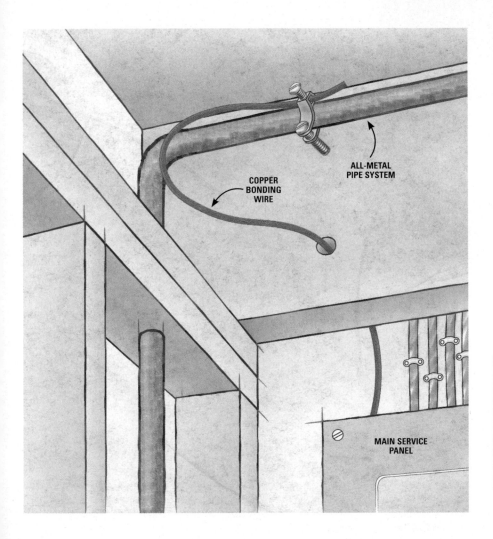

COPPER
BONDING
WIRE

ALL-METAL
PIPE SYSTEM

MAIN SERVICE
PANEL

8. INSUFFICIENT BONDING

Grounding is not bonding. Plumbing, phone lines, coaxial cable and gas piping systems need to be not only grounded but also bonded to one another. Bonding equalizes the voltage potential between conductive systems. This greatly reduces the risk of a person becoming the path for current flow between two conductive systems if one of the systems becomes energized. Also, in the case of a lightning strike, equalized voltage potential minimizes the risk of a very high current jumping (arcing) between two systems and causing a fire.

Common Violations
■ Replacing an old fuse box and assuming the system is bonded.
■ Unbonded satellite and cable installations.

Repair Charred Wiring

So you're finally getting around to replacing the ceiling light fixture when you discover that the wiring insulation has turned to charcoal and cracked off. The usual reason insulation gets ruined is that the bulbs in the fixture exceeded the fixture's wattage rating. That extra heat literally baked the insulation. Usually the insulation outside of the ceiling box is OK, but you'll have to repair the damaged insulation inside the box. No, you can't just wrap the bare wires with electrical tape. That's not an acceptable long-term fix. Here's the right way to fix the problem.

Since the wiring in a ceiling fixture is usually 14-gauge, you can fix it with insulation stripped from a 12-gauge wire. Pick up a short length of 12-2 nonmetallic cable and a package of heat shrinkable tubing. Strip insulation off the 12-gauge wires (**Photo 1**). Next, slide the new insulation onto the old wires (**Photo 2**). Then secure the new insulation with heat shrinkable tubing (**Photo 3**). When you're done, you can connect the new fixture without worrying about the old wires shorting out. Just be sure to follow the wattage maximum of the fixture when you select bulbs.

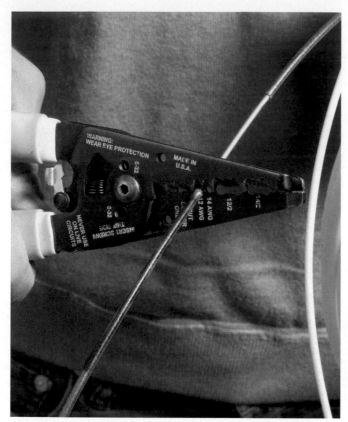

1 **Get new insulation.** Peel off the outer jacket of 12-2 nonmetallic cable. Then strip off about 8 in. of insulation from the black and white wires.

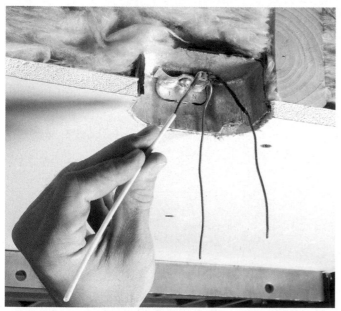

2 **Reinsulate the old wires.** Remove as much old insulation as possible. Then straighten out the old bare wire. Slide on new insulation (white goes on the neutral, black on the "hot"). Hold the insulation in place and slide on a short piece of heat shrinkable tubing.

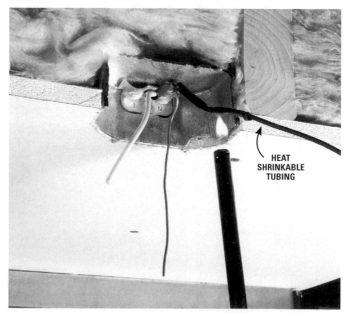

HEAT SHRINKABLE TUBING

3 **Shrink the tubing.** Wave the flame from a lighter under the heat shrinkable tubing. Keep the flame moving so the heat does all the work and the tubing doesn't burn.

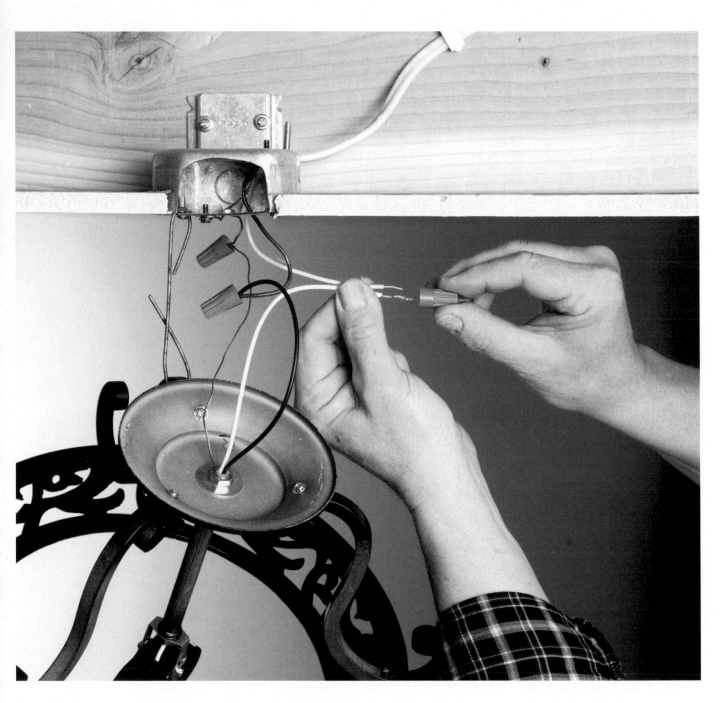

Tips for Replacing a Light Fixture

When you want to do it yourself, we can help make it easier.

Swapping out a light fixture is one of those DIY jobs that's theoretically quick and simple, but it often becomes a 3-hour series of problems. So we talked with two of our master electricians. They have seen—and solved—all of the common frustrations and offered these tips to help DIYers through the job quicker and safer. We won't cover the basic steps in replacing a light fixture, but you can find a complete step-by-step guide at *familyhandyman.com* by searching for "ceiling fixture."

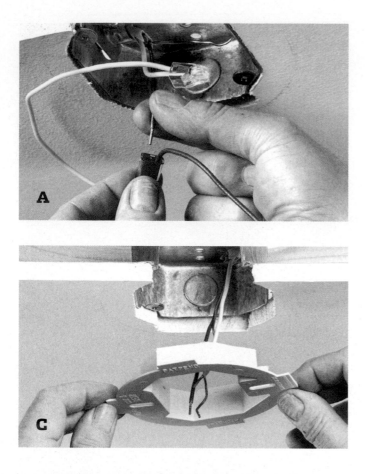

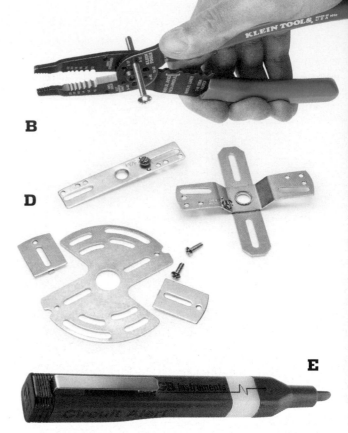

A. SHORT WIRES, NO PROBLEM

When the wires in the box are too short, making connections is aggravating. You'll want to hunt down whoever installed them and throttle that person. But instead, just go to a home center and pick up a few stab-in connectors. In tight spaces, they're much easier to use than twist-on nuts. Push a "pigtail" (a new piece of wire) into the connector, then push the connector onto the old wire. Presto! You've got plenty of length to connect to the fixture's wires. Make sure the wire you use for the pigtail is the same gauge as the existing wire.

B. SLICK SOLUTION FOR LONG SCREWS

If the fixture mounting screws are too long to fit in the box, you'll need to cut them. A hacksaw works but makes a mess of the threads. A wire stripper with built-in bolt cutters is the way to go. Thread the screw into the correct size threaded hole until it is the length you need, and squeeze the handle. As you remove the screw, the tool cleans up the threads at the cut end. Get this tool at a local home center.

> ### CAUTIONARY INSTRUCTIONS
> If you have aluminum wiring, don't work on it yourself. The connections require special techniques. Call in a licensed pro who's certified to work with it. For more information, go to *cpsc.gov* and search for "aluminum wiring."

C. EXTEND THE BOX

If the junction box is recessed more than 1/4 in. from the surface of the wall or ceiling, you've got a code violation. This is common when a layer of drywall or wood was installed over the original ceiling. To correct it, add a box extender. If you can't find one for round or octagonal boxes at home centers, search online.

D. BUY EXTRA HARDWARE

The mounting brackets supplied with your fixture may not work with your junction box. So when you buy your new fixture, also pick up a few other styles of mounting brackets. Better to spend an extra five bucks than to make a trip to the hardware store in the middle of the job.

E. FLIPPING THE BREAKER ISN'T ENOUGH

Even after you turn off the breaker that controls the light's circuit, you can still get shocked. How? Some junction boxes contain wiring from multiple circuits. So even if you cut the power to the light fixture, there may still be live wires in the junction box. To be safe, check all the wires in the box with a noncontact voltage detector before you disconnect any wires. Just touch each wire's insulation with the tester. If the light glows, the wire is live.

F. PROBE FOR THE SCREW HOLE

Many fixtures have a canopy that's held in place by two screws. Aligning the first screw is easy enough because you can tilt the canopy a little and aim for the screw hole above it. To align the second screw, stick a skinny screwdriver or a nail into the canopy hole and rotate the canopy until you find the screw hole.

G. THIRD HAND

Connecting a fixture takes three hands: one to hold the fixture and two to make the connections. If you don't have a third hand, hang the fixture from a scrap of wire or a coat hanger while you make the connections.

H. MAKE A STRONG CONNECTION

Light fixtures almost always require a connection between solid wire and stranded. That's frustrating because the connector twists and pushes the stranded wire but doesn't grab it. Here's the solution: First, cut off the old exposed solid wire and then strip off 1/2 in. of the insulation. On the stranded wire, strip off 5/8 in. Hold the wires together so the stranded wire extends about 1/8 in. beyond the solid wire and twist on the connector. The end of the stranded wire will bunch up inside the tip of the connector, locked in place for a secure connection.

I. BUY BETTER CONNECTORS

The twist-on connectors supplied with most fixtures are all plastic—with no metal threads inside. The plastic doesn't grip the wires for an easy, secure connection. So when you buy the fixture, spend an extra few bucks on a pack of assorted small connectors with metal threads.

Check Your Wiring Before You Buy

If your home was built before 1985, beware: Many new light fixtures can't be connected to pre-1985 wiring because the insulation on the wiring can't withstand the heat generated by the fixture. These fixtures carry a warning on the label: "Use wire rated for at least 90 degrees C."

If you know your wiring was installed before 1985, you'll have to choose a fixture that doesn't carry this warning. Hanging fixtures, for example, usually don't require newer wiring because they don't heat the wiring as much as fixtures that mount directly against the ceiling. The alternative is to replace the wiring, which may be a small job, or huge, depending on the situation.

If you don't know the age of your wiring, look at the fine print. If you have plastic sheathed cable (Romex is one common brand) and can see the outer sheathing, look for "NM-B" or "UF-B." Or look for "THHN" or "THWN-2" on the insulation of individual wires. If you see any of these, the wiring can handle the heat.

F

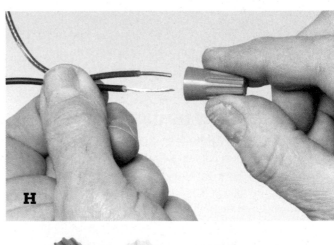

H

G

I

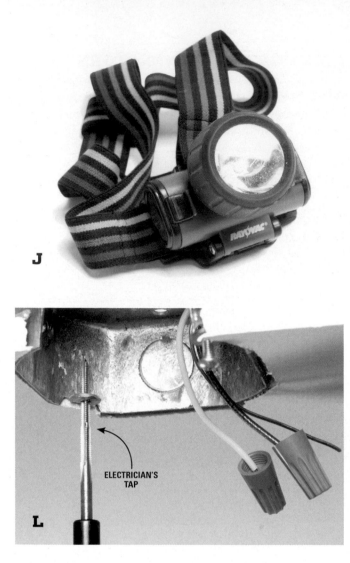

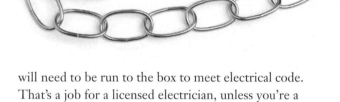

ELECTRICIAN'S
TAP

WARNING:
LIVE WIRE

M

J. WHY WORK IN THE DARK?

If the light fixture and outlets in the room are on different circuits, plug in a couple of lamps before you shut off the power to the fixture. Otherwise, strap on a camping headlamp. You'll find them everywhere, some for less than $10.

K. CHECK FOR GROUND

Your new light fixture will have a ground wire (green coated or bare copper). But if you have an older metal box, there may not be a ground wire inside the box to connect to. Adding a ground wire to the box isn't difficult; just connect a 6-in. section of bare copper wire to the box by driving a No. 10-32 ground screw (available at home centers) into a threaded hole in the box. But before you do that, you have to make sure the box itself is grounded.

Here's how: Turn on the power and make sure the light switch is turned on. Find the hot wire (typically black or red) using your noncontact voltage tester. Next, you'll need a circuit tester. Touch one of the tester's probes to the bare end of the hot wire and the other to the box. If the light glows, the box is grounded. If not, a ground wire

will need to be run to the box to meet electrical code. That's a job for a licensed electrician, unless you're a very knowledgeable DIYer.

L. STRIPPED-HOLE FIX

The built-in screw holes on a metal box are easy to strip. And if that happens, your first impulse might be to use a drywall screw. Bad idea—the sharp tip can poke through wire insulation. Instead, use an electrician's tap to cut new threads in the hole. This will enlarge the hole from a No. 8-32 screw size to a No. 10-32, so you may need a couple of new screws, too.

M. CHANDELIER CHAIN TOO LONG? THERE'S A TOOL FOR THAT!

Raising a chandelier is as easy as removing a few chain links. But opening and closing links without scratching or misshaping them can be a pain. That's why some whiz kid invented chain pliers. This tool bends links open and closed gently and neatly. Search online for "Westinghouse 70099" (around $20). Sure, it's a splurge, but don't you want a tool your buddies have never seen before?

Run Wires Under a Sidewalk

If you want to get power to a pond or just want an outlet in the back 40, you may have to run wires under a sidewalk. Here's how to do it. The idea is to drive a length of 1/2-in. rigid electrical conduit under the walk. You'll need to cap off both ends of the conduit: one end to keep the dirt out, the other so you can pound on it without damage. We recommend a 1/2-in. coupling and plug on both ends. Lift the conduit up off the bottom of your trench with some blocks, and bang away.

New Dimmer? Check the Rating

If you're installing a dimmer switch, keep in mind that each switch is rated to handle a maximum wattage. If you're trying to dim six 100-watt lightbulbs, use a switch rated for at least 600 watts. Newer models are fairly generous with their allowances (usually about 600 watts), but that won't cut it if you're trying to dim seven 100-watt bulbs.

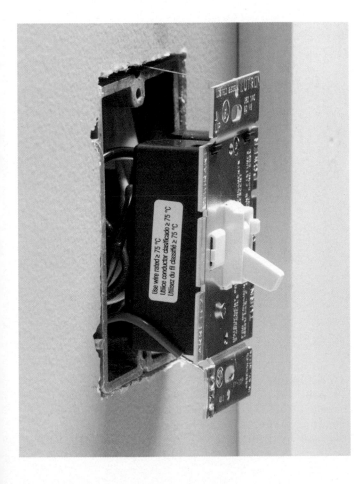

Check the rating. Make sure the wattage rating on your new dimmer is at least as high as the old one.

Pro Wiring Advice

You can wire faster, better and neater.

Even if you have years of wiring experience under your belt, there are always a few tricks you may not know. And a good way to discover them is to watch another veteran at work. That's what we did. And it didn't take long to discover some real gems.

We gleaned tips, tricks and techniques from two master electricians with decades of experience between them. From straightening cable to labeling wires, here are tips to help you wire better and faster.

UNCOIL WITHOUT KINKS

Pulling plastic-sheathed cable through holes in the framing is a lot easier if you straighten the cable out first. If you simply pull the cable from the center of the coil, it'll kink as you pull it through the studs. The trick is to lift a handful of coils from the center of the roll **(Photo 1)** and toss them across the floor as if you're throwing a coiled rope. Next, walk along the length of cable, straightening it as you go **(Photo 2)**. The electricians we talked to prefer this method because they can keep the cable contained in the plastic wrapper for easier handling and neater storage.

1 **Avoid kinks.** Don't just pull cable from the roll. Instead, lift a few loops from the center of the roll. Four loops will reach about 12 ft.

STRAIGHTENED CABLE

2 **Straighten before pulling.** Toss the coil across the floor. Then straighten it by hand before pulling it through the framing.

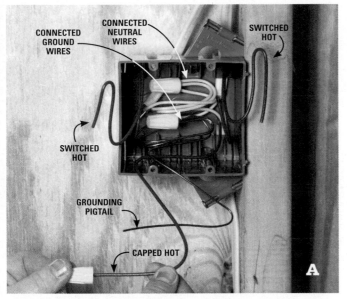

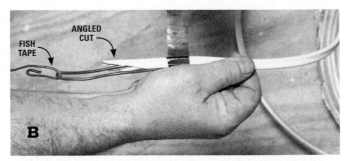

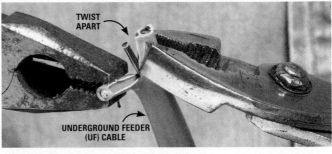

Connect it securely. Bend one wire back to form a big loop and wrap the whole works with electrical tape.

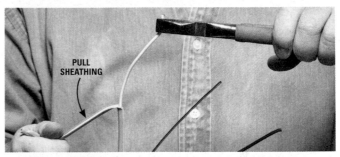

3 Separate the end. Twist the end of the UF with two pairs of pliers to separate the wires.

4 Strip off the sheathing. Peel the sheathing from the wires and cut it off.

Fold the wires. Neatly packed wires save space and eliminate confusion.

A. PACK BOXES NEATLY

If you've done much wiring, you've surely had times when you could barely push the switch or outlet into the box because there were so many wires. The solution is to arrange the wires neatly and then fold them carefully into the box. Here's how to keep wires neat and compact: First, gather all the bare ground wires along with a long pigtail and connect them. Fold them into the back of the box, leaving the pigtail extended. Next, do the same for the neutral wires. If you're connecting switches (as is shown here), you don't need a neutral pigtail. Leave the hot wire extra long and fold it back and forth across the bottom of the box. (See "Multiple Switches, One Hot Wire" on p. 237 for how to connect switches to this wire.) Put a wire connector cap on the hot wire to identify it. Such a neatly packed box will make it easy to identify the wires and leave you plenty of room for the switches.

B. NO-SNAG FISH TAPE CONNECTIONS

After going to all the trouble of working your fish tape to its destination, the last thing you want is to lose the cable or get your tape stuck on something inside the wall as you pull it back. Here's how to avoid both problems: Start by stripping an 8-in. length of cable. Using side cutters, cut off all but one wire. Cut at a steep angle to avoid a "shoulder" that could catch on something. Then bend the single wire around the loop on the end of the fish tape and wrap the whole works with electrical tape to form a smooth bundle **(Photo B)**. Now you can pull the wire without worrying that it might fall off, and the smooth lump won't get snagged by or stuck on obstructions.

PEEL UF LIKE A BANANA

Underground feeder (UF) cable has a tough plastic sheathing that allows you to bury it directly in the ground without running it through a conduit (of course, it has to be buried deep enough to satisfy the electrical code). But that tough sheathing is also difficult to remove—unless you know this trick. Start by separating the black and white wires from the bare copper by grabbing each with pliers and twisting **(Photo 3)**. They're easy to tear apart once you get them started. Pull them apart until you have about a foot of separated wires. Next, remove the sheathing from the insulated wires by grabbing the end of the wire with one pliers and the sheathing with another pliers and working them apart. After you get the sheathing separated from the insulated wire at the top, just peel it off **(Photo 4)**. Repeat the process to remove the sheathing from the black wire. Finally, cut off the loose sheathing with scissors or a knife.

C. TEST BEFORE TOUCHING

When you've done a lot of wiring, it's easy to get complacent about whether the power is off. But don't. Use a noncontact voltage detector to check every wire in the box or area you're working. Always check the tester on a wire or cord you know is live to make sure it's working before you rely on it. Noncontact voltage detectors are available at home centers, hardware stores and online. The Klein NCVT-1 tool shown here (available at *amazon.com*) has a green light that indicates it's turned on and working—a nice feature that's well worth the extra money.

IDENTIFY ROUGHED-IN WIRES

Save yourself a lot of headaches by identifying the wires as you install them. It's a lot harder to figure out which wires go where when they're covered with drywall. The electricians we talked to use a code for marking wires, and so can you. **Photo 5** shows one example. Another method is to use a label **(Photo 6)**, but by the time you get back to connect switches and outlets, you may find that drywallers, tapers and painters have covered the label or knocked it off. That's why it's best to use nonlabel coding whenever possible. Develop a system and write it down. You'll never have to guess which are the "line" and "load" and which wires are the travelers for your three-way switch.

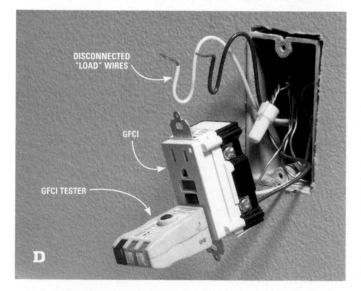

D. TROUBLESHOOTING GFCIS

We asked our electrical pros what problems they run into with GFCIs and how to solve them. For starters, we found that most complaints occur when several outlets are protected by one GFCI. There are several possible causes, ranging from a light or appliance with a ground fault that's plugged into a downstream outlet to a defective GFCI or even a circuit with too much cable. To determine whether the problem is with the GFCI itself or downstream, turn off the power to the GFCI and disconnect the wires from the "load" terminals. Push the reset button (if it doesn't click, you'll have to reset it after the power is back on) and plug a GFCI tester into the GFCI outlet before you turn the power back on. If the GFCI trips after you turn the power on, replace it. If it holds, then the problem is with one of the downstream outlets. To avoid the time-consuming process of troubleshooting the "load" outlets, the easiest and best solution is to replace each of them with a new, tamper-resistant GFCI.

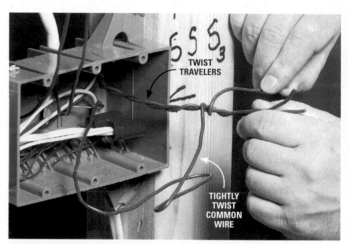

5 Code your wires. Here's one example: Wrap three-way switch "travelers" loosely, and wrap the common wire tightly around them for easy identification later.

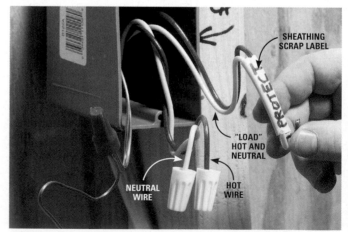

6 Label wires. You can also use scraps of plastic sheathing to label the wires. Here we labeled the wires that will be GFCI protected.

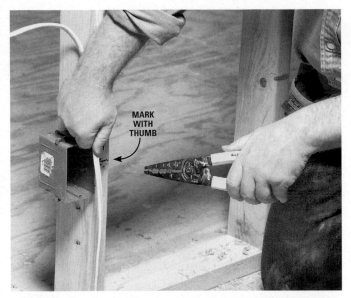

7 **Mark the spot.** Hold the cable near the box and mark with your thumb where it extends slightly past the box.

MARK WITH THUMB

SCORE HERE

REMOVE SHEATHING

8 **Strip the sheathing.** Score the sheathing at the thumb mark and slide it off. Then feed the wires into the box.

STRIP SHEATHING FIRST

It's tempting to push your roughed-in cable through the knockouts in the box and worry about how to strip the sheathing later. But that's the hard way. It's much easier to remove the sheathing before you push the wires into the box. The only trick is to make sure you have the cable in about the right spot before marking it **(Photo 7)** and removing the sheathing **(Photo 8)**. As long as you don't have the cable stretched tight, there will be enough "play" to make final adjustments after you've inserted the conductors into the box. Remember, the electrical code requires that at least 1/4 in. of sheathing be visible inside the box.

MULTIPLE SWITCHES, ONE HOT WIRE

A box with three switches is crowded enough without adding extra wire connectors and pigtails. Here's a wiring method that eliminates extra connections and creates a neater installation. Instead of running a separate pigtail from the hot wire to each switch, just leave the hot wire extra long. To connect the switches, simply score the wire with your wire stripper and push the insulation to expose about 3/4 in. of bare wire **(Photo 9)**. Wrap this bare section at least three-quarters of the way around the screw terminal of the first switch. Repeat the process for the remaining intermediate switches **(Photo 10)**. Connect the last switch in the usual manner, looping the wire around the screw in a clockwise direction.

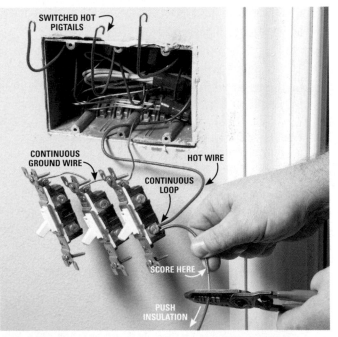

SWITCHED HOT PIGTAILS

CONTINUOUS GROUND WIRE

HOT WIRE

CONTINUOUS LOOP

SCORE HERE

PUSH INSULATION

9 **Save box space.** Run a continuous hot wire from switch to switch. Score the insulation and push it to expose bare wire.

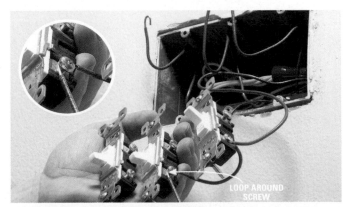

LOOP AROUND SCREW

10 **Go from switch to switch.** Wrap the exposed section of wire around the screw and run it to the next switch.

Convert Propane Gas Grill to Natural Gas

Convert a propane gas grill to natural gas and never look back. Your decision may not be based on cost but that you never want to run out of fuel in the middle of a barbecue. If that's your winning strategy, check to see if you can convert yours.

First, contact the grill manufacturer to see if it offers a conversion kit for your model (some companies refuse to sell conversion kits). The conversion kit includes new gas jets, a flexible gas hose, quick-disconnect gas fittings and gas valve limiter stops. If you can get a conversion kit for yours, great. If not, you're out of luck. Do NOT follow the "jet-drilling" instructions on the internet. It's just plain dangerous.

Next, check with your local plumbing inspector to see if you'll be allowed to use flexible gas hoses. Some inspectors require a more permanent installation.

If you're good to go, run a gas line to the grill and install a shutoff valve at the end of the run. Secure the valve to either the building or your deck, according to local code. Then install the quick-disconnect fitting that comes with the conversion kit. Remove the grates and burner assemblies, and change out the jets **(Photo 1)**. Install the limiter stop **(Photo 2)**. Finally, remove the propane pressure regulator and hose and then install the new hose.

PRO TIP

Hire a licensed plumber/gas fitter to install the gas supply line to where the new flexible gas hose will connect, and have it pressure-tested and inspected. The pro will also determine the proper gas size, pressure and key components required for your new grill based on its location. It is also recommended to secure the grill with a stainless steel tether or cable.

Buy a conversion kit. You'll save money by buying a complete conversion kit rather than buying the parts separately.

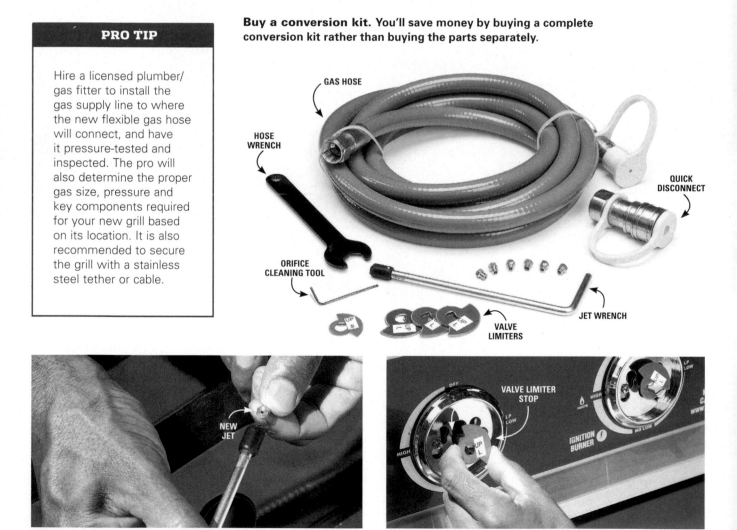

1 **Swap the jets.** To remove the old jets, use the jet wrench that comes with the conversion kit (or a socket on an extension bar). Then install the proper jets for your grill model.

2 **Limit the valve flow.** Remove the valve knob by pulling it straight off. Then slide on the limiter stop. Reinstall the knob by pressing it on.

Les Talks Plastic Pipes

We asked Les Zell, a master plumber, to tell us some of his tips on working with plastic plumbing. Not surprisingly, he had plenty to share. Here are a few of his best pointers.

LES IS AN ABS GUY

"I pretty much use only ABS black pipe and rarely use the white PVC stuff. It's all about the glue. Gluing ABS is a one-step process, which makes it faster to work with than PVC. Purple PVC primer is messy, emits noxious fumes, and it's just ugly."

ABS cement lasts longer in the can and dries clear, making it more forgiving if you get a drip or two on the floor. ABS cement also dries faster, which reduces the risk of connections pushing apart before they set up. Les believes the labor saved by using ABS more than makes up for the extra money spent on pipes and fittings. ABS is also lighter and more flexible, which Les says makes it easier to flex for bending into tight spaces.

"It's not only me. None of my plumber buddies use PVC either." The only downside—retailers don't always carry ABS.

LES ON PLUMBING WISDOM

Les believes that new plumbers will learn 75% of what they need to know during the first year on the job. But he also says that it takes 20 years to learn the next 24% and the rest is unknowable.

A. DON'T GLUE YOURSELF INTO A CORNER

In many assemblies, there are pipes that move and pipes that don't. If you start gluing fittings together willy-nilly, you may end up in a situation where you're unable to attach the last fitting because one or both of the pipes don't move enough to slide the fitting on.

"The last fitting to be glued should be the one on a pipe that has a little wiggle room," says Les. That's usually where a vertical run meets a horizontal one so you can snug on an elbow or a tee from two directions.

B. YOU CAN REUSE A LANDLOCKED FITTING

If you have to replace some piping but it's tough to replace the fitting, it's possible to ream out the old fitting and reuse it. This happens a lot. Let's say there's a tee coming out of the back of a cabinet with a broken pipe leading to it. Or the fitting is so buried up in the floor joists that you can't get at it. Les just cuts off the pipe near the knuckle, then uses a Socket Saver to ream out the pipe to expose the inside of the fitting. (Note: A Socket Saver can damage a fitting as well, so use care.) Then he can cement a new pipe into the old fitting and reuse it. "It's a lot simpler than ripping out cabinets, drywall or concrete to replace the fitting."

C. USE DULL BLADES FOR BIGGER OR TIGHTER CUTS

When Les cuts larger pipe or has trouble getting the tubing cutter (I) into tight spaces, he uses a recip saw fitted with an older, dull wood blade. "A new wood blade with aggressive teeth tends to grab on to the pipe and rattle the whole works, and a metal blade melts the plastic rather than cutting it."

D. DEBURR FOR LEAK-FREE CONNECTIONS

Leftover burrs on the end of a pipe will create channels in the cement when you push the fitting onto the pipe—and then will stay there like little canals. That's when you'll get leaks or flunk a pressure test. Les always scrapes away burrs with a utility knife before joining the pipes.

E. AVOID CALLBACKS—USE STRAPS

Changes in temperature can cause changes in the lengths of plastic pipes. When hanging pipe from plastic J-hooks, you'll hear a tick when the pipe slips past the J-hook. Les says he gets tons of service calls from panicky customers believing these ticks to be water drips from a leaky pipe. To prevent that ticking noise, it's best not to have the pipe touching any wood substrate or framing member. Les generally uses plastic straps and never gets false alarm calls on his plumbing.

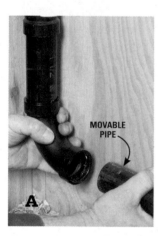

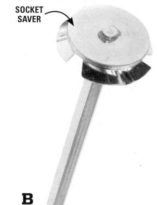

SOCKET SAVER

MOVABLE PIPE

DULL BLADE

PLASTIC STRAP

LONG SWEEP

SHORT SWEEP

F

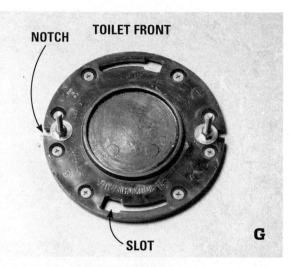

NOTCH   **TOILET FRONT**

SLOT

G

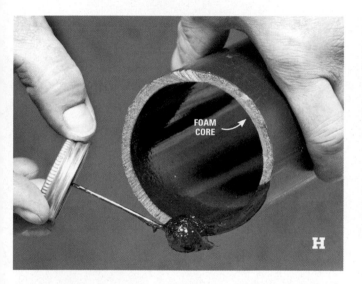

FOAM CORE

H

I

F. LEARN LES'S ELBOW RULE

For pipes under 3 in., there are two basic types of 90-degree elbows used: short sweep and long sweep.

Les has a good system to remember when to use the two types of elbows: "If water is speeding up as it turns the corner (usually going from horizontal to vertical), use a short sweep. If water is slowing down (usually from vertical to horizontal), use a long sweep."

G. SKIP THOSE CLOSET FLANGE SLOTS

Les has serviced dozens of toilets with broken closet flanges. Toilets are top-heavy, which stresses the closet bolts that hold a toilet to the closet flange. The plastic on the sides of the adjustable slots that receive the bolts is thin and prone to cracking. Les always turns the flange 90 degrees and anchors the toilet using the notches instead. He makes sure the notches are parallel to the wall behind the toilet. "One more thing: Don't use flanges with metal collars; metal rusts." Also of note: There are stainless steel collars that will not rust.

H. SEAL THE ENDS!

Most ABS pipes have either a cellular or a foam core that air will actually pass right through. "If you don't believe it, wrap your lips around the pipe wall and blow through it." If you don't seal pipe ends with cement, air will escape into the porous center core and find its way out of the plumbing system, and you'll fail a pressure test every time. "Can you even imagine that disaster? You'd have to replumb everything!"

I. LES LOVES TUBING CUTTERS

For pipes up to 2 in., Les prefers a tubing cutter (a giant version of the type used for copper tubing). "It makes a perfectly straight cut with no burrs or shavings to clean up. But, best of all, it doesn't take up much room in the tool bucket."

Regular pumping removes sludge and scum from the tank.

Septic Smarts

**Save big money by understanding how a septic system works—
and what can go wrong.**

A well-designed, properly installed septic system can last for decades—or fail in just a few years. It's up to you.

Maintaining a healthy septic system isn't all that expensive, but you could easily spend tens of thousands to dig up and replace a septic system that has totally failed. As the old saying goes, an ounce of prevention is worth a pound of cure.

Good maintenance starts with understanding how a septic system works and how it can fail. Let's take a look underground and see what's supposed to happen in a well-functioning septic system. After that, we'll show you why things go wrong and give you some pointers for keeping your system in top shape.

HOW IT WORKS

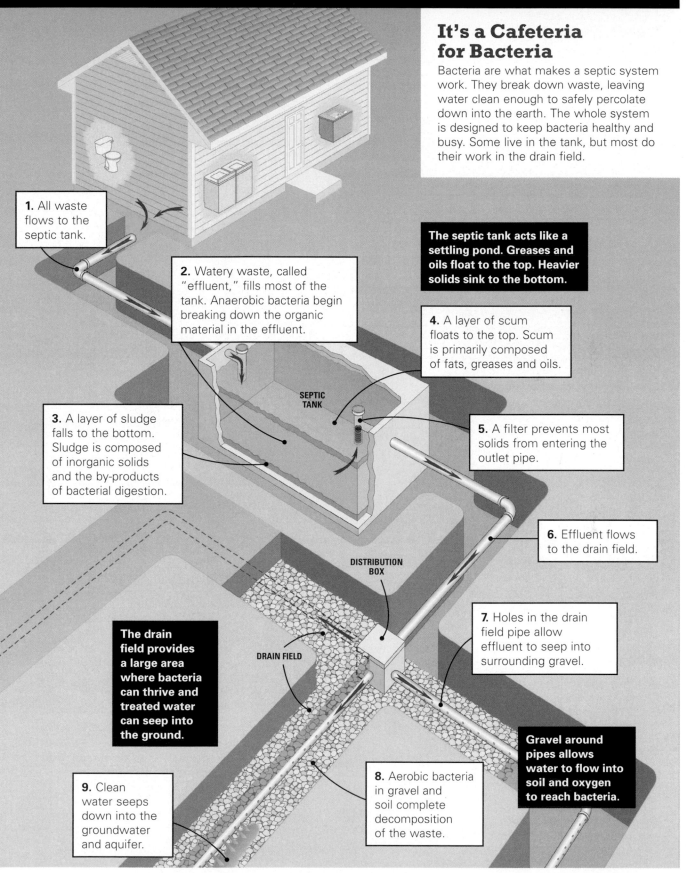

It's a Cafeteria for Bacteria

Bacteria are what makes a septic system work. They break down waste, leaving water clean enough to safely percolate down into the earth. The whole system is designed to keep bacteria healthy and busy. Some live in the tank, but most do their work in the drain field.

1. All waste flows to the septic tank.

2. Watery waste, called "effluent," fills most of the tank. Anaerobic bacteria begin breaking down the organic material in the effluent.

3. A layer of sludge falls to the bottom. Sludge is composed of inorganic solids and the by-products of bacterial digestion.

SEPTIC TANK

The septic tank acts like a settling pond. Greases and oils float to the top. Heavier solids sink to the bottom.

4. A layer of scum floats to the top. Scum is primarily composed of fats, greases and oils.

5. A filter prevents most solids from entering the outlet pipe.

6. Effluent flows to the drain field.

DISTRIBUTION BOX

The drain field provides a large area where bacteria can thrive and treated water can seep into the ground.

DRAIN FIELD

7. Holes in the drain field pipe allow effluent to seep into surrounding gravel.

Gravel around pipes allows water to flow into soil and oxygen to reach bacteria.

9. Clean water seeps down into the groundwater and aquifer.

8. Aerobic bacteria in gravel and soil complete decomposition of the waste.

Don't Abuse the System

A septic system that was properly designed and installed needs only occasional pumping to remove the sludge and scum from the tank. But without knowing it, you can do things that harm—or destroy—the system.

Waste that decomposes slowly (or not at all) gets flushed down drains. Cigarette butts, diapers and coffee grounds often cause problems.

If used heavily, garbage disposals can send too much solid waste into the system. It's best not to put food down the drain.

Lint from synthetic fibers flows from washing machines. Bacteria in the tank and drain field can't break it down.

Household chemicals like disinfecting cleaners and antibacterial soaps kill bacteria. Most systems can handle light use of these products, but the less you use them, the better.

Too much wastewater over a short period of time flushes out the tank too rapidly.

Too much sludge reduces bacteria's ability to break down waste. Excess sludge can also overflow into the drain field.

Sludge or scum plugs holes in the pipe.

Compacted soil and gravel block seepage of effluent and deprive bacteria of oxygen. This is often caused by cars driving or parking on the drain field.

Roots from trees and shrubs can clog and damage a drain field.

SEPTIC SOLUTIONS

A. Get your tank pumped… Your tank must be pumped out regularly by a pro. Pumping removes the buildup of sludge and scum, which slows down bacterial action in the tank. Your tank may need pumping each year, but it's possible to go two or three years between pumpings, depending on the size of your tank and the amount of waste you run through the system. Ask your inspector to make a rough recommendation for how often your tank should be pumped.

…but don't hire a pumper until you need it. Regular inspections and pumping are critical. But if you're not squeamish, you can check the sludge level yourself with a device called the Sludge Judge. It is widely available online. Once you've determined that your tank is one-third full of sludge, call a contractor to come pump it out.

B. Protect your drain field from lint. Install a filter on your washing machine's drain. This device prevents lint, particularly the synthetic fibers that bacteria can't digest, from entering the system.

C. Install an effluent filter. Ask your contractor to install an effluent filter on the outflow pipe of your tank. (It will probably cost $50 to $100, plus labor.) This device helps prevent solids from entering the drain field and will need to be cleaned out on occasion by a contractor.

Get an inspection. A thorough initial inspection by a pro will cost a few hundred dollars depending on the size of the system and where it is located; after that, regular inspections cost less. Your pro will be able to tell you how often your system should be inspected.

Simple as a septic system may seem, evaluating its health really requires an expert. There are plenty of contractors who will gladly pump the sludge out of your tank, but many don't fully understand how a septic system works or how it should be maintained. We highly recommend looking for a contractor who has received some formal training in the science of septic systems. Some states have adopted certification programs for septic contractors—check with your secretary of state's office to see if yours is among them.

A complete inspection will determine whether your system is up to code (many are not) and the condition of the tank and drain field. A good inspector will also be able to tell you whether your tank is large enough for your household and the maximum volume of water you can pass through the tank in a day.

You may be able to improve the performance of your system by adding bacteria with a product such as RID-X. Your pro should be able to tell you if your system would benefit from this treatment.

Alternatives to a new drain field. If an inspection or sewage backup reveals that your drain field is in trouble, the ultimate solution is to replace it. The cost can be huge,

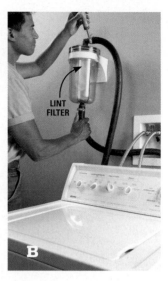

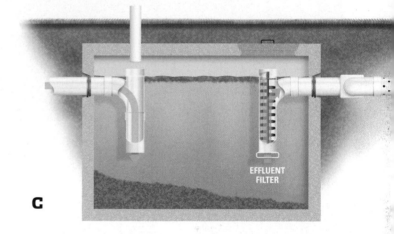

however, so it's worth discussing possible other options with a contractor.

- **Clean the pipes.** A contractor can clear out the drain field pipes with a rotary pressure washer.
- **Treat the system with chemicals.** Ask your contractor about treating your system with a commercial product (not a homemade one) that increases the amount of oxygen in the drain field. One option is Septic-Scrub (*arcan.com*).
- **Loosen the soil.** In states where it's legal, some contractors can fracture compacted soil around the pipes by injecting high-pressure air in numerous locations around the drain field. This process is called terra-lifting.

Don't overload the system. Limit your water use. Reducing the amount of water that runs into your tank, particularly over a short period of time, will prevent the flushing of untreated waste into your drain field. You can replace old toilets with low-flow models, install reduced-flow showerheads and, simplest of all, wash laundry throughout the week rather than just on Saturday morning.

Using PEX Piping

Got questions about this plumbing option? We'll answer them here.

If you haven't discovered PEX yet, you're missing the biggest revolution in plumbing since the flush toilet. PEX is flexible plastic tubing that you can use for everything from plumbing repairs to installing water lines in an entire house. You'll find PEX tubing, fittings and tools at home centers, hardware stores and online. Let us answer the most common questions about PEX for you, give you some tips for working with it and provide sources for more information.

"PRO" CRIMP RING

CINCH CLAMP

COPPER CRIMP RING

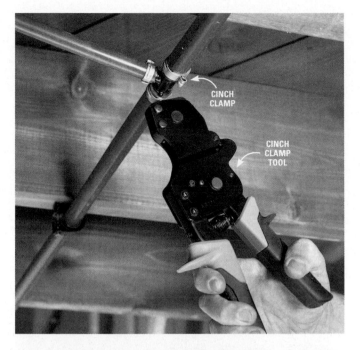

CINCH CLAMP

CINCH CLAMP TOOL

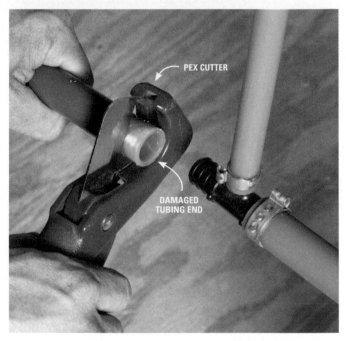

PEX CUTTER

DAMAGED TUBING END

WHICH IS BETTER— PEX OR COPPER?

PEX (cross-linked polyethylene) has several advantages over copper:

- **PEX is cheaper than copper.** Half-inch PEX tubing costs about 50¢ per foot (depending on the brand name) compared with about $2 per foot for copper. Some of the savings will be offset by the need for a special tool to install the fittings, but if you're doing a medium to large plumbing job, you'll usually save by using PEX instead of copper.
- **PEX is faster to install than copper.** If you use a manifold and home-run system (shown in the top right photo on p. 248), it's like running a garden hose to each fixture—super fast and easy. But even if you install PEX in a conventional main line and branch system, the connections are quicker to make than soldering copper.
- **PEX won't corrode like copper.** If you live in an area with acidic water, copper can corrode over time. PEX is unaffected by acidic water and is therefore a better choice in these areas.

DO I NEED SPECIAL TOOLS?

No. You can use stab-in or compression fittings to make the connections. But they're too expensive to be practical on large projects. For most jobs, you'll want to invest in a special tool to make connections. There are several PEX connection methods, but only two are affordable enough to be practical for DIYers: crimp rings and cinch clamps (photo above).

Crimp rings are a band of metal, usually copper, that you slip over the fitting and compress with a crimp ring tool. The main drawback to the crimp ring method is that you'll need either separate crimping tools for 1/2-in. and 3/4-in. fittings or a universal tool with a swappable insert (not shown). This adds a little up-front cost to this method. A combo kit with interchangeable crimp jaws can be found online.

Cinch clamps work more like the traditional band clamps you're probably familiar with. You slip the cinch clamp tool over the protruding tab and squeeze to tighten the cinch clamp. The same tool works for all sizes of cinch clamps. We like the one-handed version shown in the top right

photo because you can hold the ring in place with one hand while tightening it with the other.

The only other special tool you'll need is a scissors-like cutter for the tubing (bottom photo).

HOW DO I SPLICE PEX INTO MY EXISTING PIPE?

There are several methods. The easiest is to cut out a section of pipe and slip in a stab-in tee (top left photo on page 248). SharkBite is one common brand of stab-in fitting. This method doesn't require soldering, which can be a big time-saver. But check with your plumbing inspector if you're

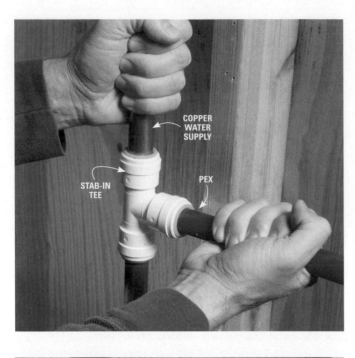

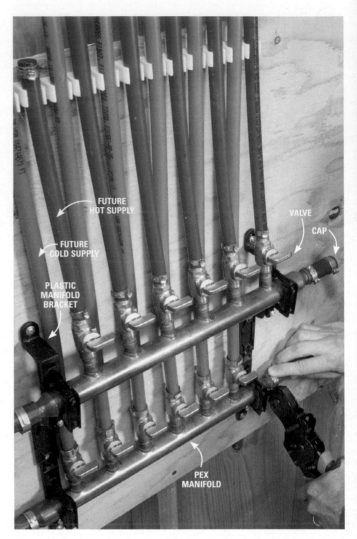

planning to bury this connection in a wall or ceiling. Some areas don't allow stab-in fittings to be concealed. Another method is to solder in a tee and a PEX adapter. Then slip the PEX tubing over the adapter and attach it with your chosen connection method (bottom photo).

DO I HAVE TO USE MANIFOLDS WITH PEX?

No. You can install PEX just as you would other pipe, with main lines and branches to each fixture. But you lose a lot of the benefits of PEX with that system since it requires so many fittings. With the home-run system, you install a manifold in the utility room or some area that's close to the

main water line and water heater and then run a separate PEX tube to each fixture as shown above. This system uses more tubing but is fast and requires only two connections: one at the manifold and another at the fixture end. You can also use a hybrid system where you run 3/4-in. hot and cold lines to a set of fixtures—for example, a bathroom—and install a smaller manifold behind an access panel. Then you just make short runs of 1/2-in. PEX tubing to each fixture.

DO I HAVE TO USE RED FOR HOT AND BLUE FOR COLD?

No. The colors are just to help you keep track of the hot and cold lines. You can use white PEX for everything if you prefer.

PRO TIP
PEX will need a dechlorinating system for areas with high chlorine. High chlorine concentration can cause pinholes in PEX.

COPPER
STUB-OUT

DROP-EAR
BEND
SUPPORT

HOT
WATER
SUPPLY

COLD
WATER
SUPPLY

DOES IT MEET CODE?

There is no unified national plumbing code. Before starting your plumbing job, check with your local inspector for specific local requirements.

IS PEX RELIABLE?

PEX has been used for decades in other countries, where there are thousands of homes with 30-year-old, leak-free PEX. Most of the problems with PEX systems (in the United States and elsewhere) have been caused by sloppy installation or faulty fittings rather than the tubing itself.

CAN I CONNECT PEX TO MY WATER HEATER?

No. First extend a pipe 18 in. from your water heater and then connect the PEX to that pipe.

WHICH TUBING SHOULD I USE FOR INTERIOR WATER LINES?

For water lines, there are three grades: PEX-A, PEX-B and PEX-C. They're manufactured differently, with PEX-A being slightly more flexible. If you're ordering online, go ahead and spend a bit extra for PEX-A. But don't go running around town looking for it; the difference isn't that big. The plumbers we talked to would be willing to use any of the three types in their own homes. Visit *supplyhouse.com* for PEX tubing, fittings, tools and information. PEX is also popular for in-floor radiant heating systems, for which you need PEX tubing with an oxygen barrier.

HOW DO I CONNECT PEX TO MY PLUMBING FIXTURES?

There are several methods. If the connection will be visible, like under a wall-hung sink, and you would prefer the look of a copper tube coming out of the wall, use a copper stub-out (top photo). You can connect a compression-type shutoff valve to the 1/2-in. copper stub-out and then connect your fixture. In areas that are concealed, like under a kitchen sink or vanity cabinet, you can eliminate a joint by running PEX directly to the shutoff valve. Use a drop-ear bend support to hold the tubing in a tight bend (bottom photo). There are several types of shutoff valves that connect directly to PEX.

If you're using a manifold system with valves, you may not need to install a shutoff valve at the fixture. Ask your plumbing inspector. We recommend adding one, though. It doesn't raise the cost much and is more convenient than running downstairs to shut off the water when a repair is needed.

EXPANSION/
CONTRACTION LOOP

WHAT ABOUT EXPANSION?

PEX expands and contracts more than copper, so don't stretch it tight. Let it droop a little between fasteners. On long runs, it's a good idea to install a loop (top photo) to allow for contraction. Another advantage of the loop is that if you mess up and need a little extra tubing, you can steal it from the loop. Also, since PEX moves as it expands and contracts, make sure to drill oversize holes through studs or joists so it can slide easily, and don't use metal straps to attach it. Use plastic straps instead.

WILL PEX BREAK OR SPLIT IF IT FREEZES?

Probably not. Manufacturers are reluctant to say, but reports from the field suggest PEX can withstand freezing. You should still protect tubing from freezing, but since PEX can expand and contract, it's less likely to break than rigid piping.

WHAT IF I GOOF? CAN I TAKE IT APART?

Sure—there's a special tool for cutting off crimp rings, and you can use side cutters to remove cinch clamps. But a rotary tool (Dremel is one brand) fitted with a cutoff blade works great for cutting either type of connector (bottom photo). After you remove the crimp ring or cinch clamp and pull the PEX from the fitting, cut off the end of the tubing to get a fresh section for the new connection. If you damage the fitting with the rotary tool, replace the fitting rather than risk a leak.

MISPLACED
CINCH CLAMP

CUTOFF
WHEEL

CINCH
CLAMP

ROTARY
TOOL

4 Tricks to Get Out of Plumbing Jams

Most faucet repairs are pretty easy—if everything goes well. But when faucet repairs go badly, they can quickly turn into a nightmare. Most of the problems happen during disassembly. We asked plumbers to tell us how to handle the biggest headaches. But you have to know when to say when. There may come a point when you have to say, "Forget it. I'm buying a new faucet!"

1. CUT AND REPLACE

If a cap doesn't twist free and the cap is metal, not plastic, heat the cap with a heat gun and grip it with the bare teeth of a slip-joint pliers.

If heating doesn't work, or your faucet is plastic, cut the cap with a rotary tool and a cutting wheel. Then jam in a flat-blade screwdriver and widen the opening until the cap unscrews. Buy a replacement cap at the home center for about $10. Coat the new cap threads with plumber's grease to prevent it from sticking again.

2. GET AGGRESSIVE WITH SETSCREWS

If the hex wrench that comes with your repair kit won't loosen the setscrew on the faucet, don't force it—you'll just ruin the head. Spend a few bucks for a 3/8-in.-drive hex socket kit. Buy a tube of valve grinding compound (like Permatex No. 80037) at an auto parts store and apply a dollop to the hex tip to reduce the likelihood of stripping the setscrew. Then use a ratchet to break the screw free. If it still won't budge (and the handle is metal and not plastic), try heating it with a heat gun. As a last resort, drill out the center of the setscrew and use a screw extractor to remove the rest of it. Buy a new setscrew and coat it with anti-seize compound before reinserting it.

1 Cut and wedge. Slice down the side of the cap with a rotary tool and a cutting wheel. Don't worry about cutting the plastic seal (you'll be replacing that), but avoid cutting into the brass threads.

2 Get a grip and loosen with leverage. Squeeze the hex socket deep into the setscrew with one hand and pull the ratchet handle with the other. Then loosen the setscrew with a quick yanking motion.

HEX SOCKET

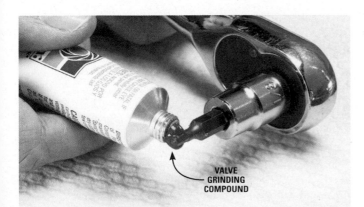

VALVE GRINDING COMPOUND

3. SPECIAL TOOLS ARE WORTH IT

Replacement cartridges usually come with a plastic loosening tool. If the cartridge is really stuck, the loosening tool can actually break off the cartridge ears and turn the job into a real nightmare. Even if you get the cartridge to rotate, you may still have to yank hard to get it out. Save yourself a lot of time (and sweat) by forking over some cash for a Danco No. 86712 cartridge puller from *amazon.com* or a home center. Install it and pull the cartridge in minutes.

4. KNOW WHEN TO THROW IN THE TOWEL

It makes sense that a pivoting kitchen spout will leak if the O-rings are worn. But brass wears too. So if you've replaced the spout O-rings and the leak reappears in a few months (or weeks), check the inside of the spout. You may need to replace the faucet.

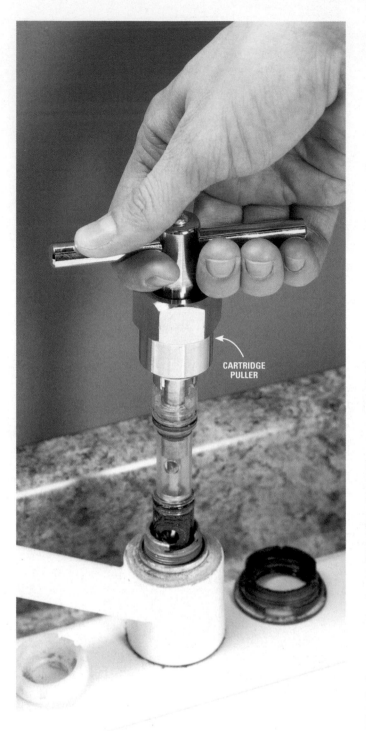

CARTRIDGE PULLER

3 **Twist, pull, done.** Line up the prongs on the tool with the ears on the cartridge and tighten the screw at the top of the T-bar. Then turn the large nut with an adjustable wrench and twist the T-handle as you turn. The cartridge will pull right out.

SPOUT

O-RINGS

WEAR GROOVES

4 **Don't fight it; replace it.** If you feel a groove where the O-rings mate to the spout, the faucet is toast. Don't waste any more time and energy on O-ring repairs—you'll never get a long-lasting seal. Replace the faucet.

Working with Round Duct Pipe

Never handled a ducting project? We've got you covered.

Whether you're adding new heat runs in a basement or changing the layout of an existing HVAC system, you'll probably be working with round metal duct pipe. We invited Bob Schmahl to give us a few pointers. Bob's been a tin bender for decades. He insists he still doesn't know everything about ductwork, but we aren't convinced. These tips should help make your next job run much smoother.

A. DON'T PEEL OFF OLD TAPE

If you have to disassemble existing fittings, there's no need to peel off the old foil tape first. Instead, just score the tape at the seam with a utility knife and remove the screws right through the tape. When it comes time to retape, just clean off the dust and apply new tape right over the old.

B. INSTALL DAMPERS AT THE REGISTERS

Adding heat runs in a basement may change the airflow in the rooms above. Each register should have its own damper that can be accessed for adjustment. If those dampers can't be accessed from below, you'll want to install them close enough to the register so that you can reach them through the register opening. Bob likes 4 x 10-in. boots (not shown)—you can easily fit your hand in them to adjust the dampers and there are more grate cover options for that size.

C. ASSEMBLE THE PIPE LIKE A ZIPPER

When assembling pipe, start at one end and work the seam together like a zipper. Use one hand to keep the two edges close and the other to apply downward pressure. Use your leg, a workbench or the ground to support the back side of the pipe. If you make a mistake and have to dismantle a pipe, slam it down flat on the ground, seam side up. It should pop right apart.

D. BOB'S NOT A FAN OF FLEXIBLE DUCT

There's no question that flexible duct is easier to install than metal pipe, but consider this: Flexible duct can degrade over time. It collects dust and is almost impossible to clean. Flexible duct needs to be larger than pipes to allow the same amount of airflow. The most common problem Bob has seen: "People get careless and turn corners too sharp, which creates kinks that severely restrict airflow."

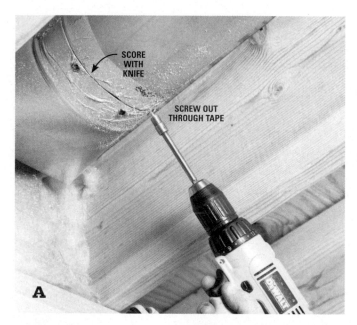

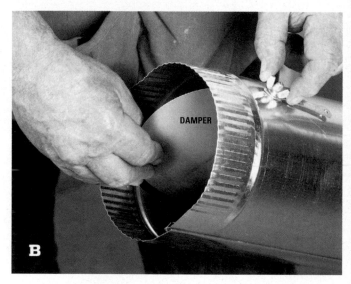

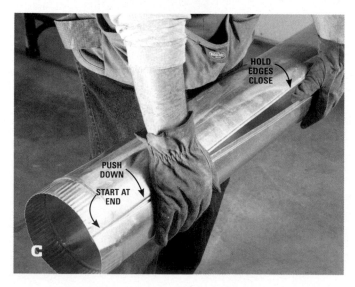

E

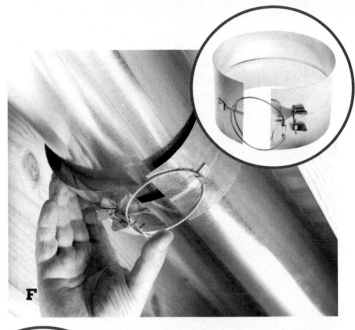

F

BACKING

TAPE

G

ANGLE
DRILL

H

E. CAULK THE TAKE-OFFS

Caulk (don't tape) the connection between the trunk line and a take-off (elbow) before you connect pipes to it. That way, you'll be able to turn the take-off out of the way to caulk above it. Regular silicone is fine.

F. OVERLAP BUTT JOINTS WITH DRAW BAND CONNECTORS

When you're installing a pipe between two fixed parts, it's impossible to slip in the piece using the crimped ends and still get the required 1-1/2-in. overlaps at both ends. Overlap one side as you normally would and create a butt joint on the other. Use a draw band connector to complete the butt joint. If your supplier doesn't carry them, make your own by cutting a piece of pipe to overlap the ends, and then screw and tape the band into place. If you're working with 6-in. pipe, you'll need to use 7-in. pipe for the bands.

G. LEAVE BACKING ON THE TAPE

If the ducts are going to be concealed, all seams need to be taped or caulked. Here's Bob's trick for taping a seam on a pipe that's installed close to the subfloor: Cut a piece of tape to length. Peel off part of the backing. Slide the tape up and over the pipe. Finally, pull down on the backing, which will pull the tape along with it. Inspectors will want to know you've used an approved tape, so buy the stuff with writing on it, or keep the roll on-site until inspection.

H. A HOLE CUTTER WORKS GREAT IN TIGHT SPOTS

Aviator snips work fine to cut holes in a trunk line, but only if there's enough space. If you're dealing with close quarters and you own a right-angle drill or attachment, you may want to invest in a sheet metal hole cutter. Otherwise, you might have to take down the trunk line. You can buy a hole cutter online for around $70. Malco is one manufacturer.

I. MAKE TWO MARKS FOR CUTTING

When cutting pipe, Bob likes to mark the size he needs on each side of the open seam with a marker. Flat metal is easier to cut than curved, so he uses his knee to support and flatten the pipe while he opens it up. Then you just sight on the far mark while you make the cut. It'll be straight and perfect every time. Bob prefers snips made by Malco, around $35 at *amazon.com*. And unless you enjoy trips to the ER, wear gloves when cutting pipe—the stuff is razor sharp.

J. MOVE ONE RING AT A TIME

Figuring out the right combination of turns to get an elbow to point in the right direction can be perplexing. Bob recommends moving one "gore" (elbow ring) at a time, starting with the connected side. And don't make 90-degree turns if you don't have to. A 90-degree elbow creates the same resistance as adding 5 ft. of pipe.

K. USE SUPPORT BRACKETS AND THREE SCREWS

Each pipe needs support. You can use just about any support you want, but adjustable steel support brackets are quick and easy. And don't forget to screw the pipe to the joist hanger so the pipes won't rattle when someone stomps across the floor above. Every connection needs three screws. They don't have to be evenly spaced. Use 1-in. galvanized zip screws designed for sheet metal.

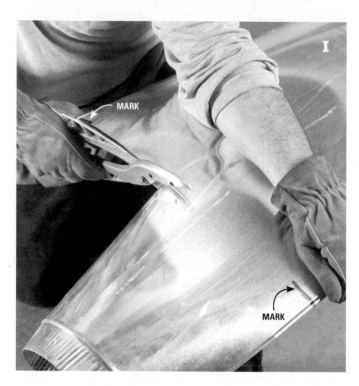

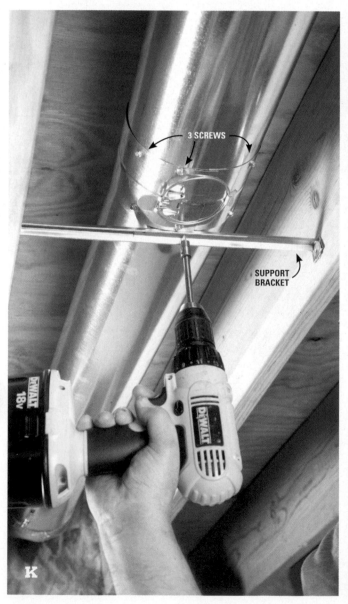

Furnace Repair

The most common repairs are easy—and you can save hundreds of dollars in 15 minutes.

High-efficiency (92% and higher) condensing gas furnaces are complex. They have multiple sensors and safety systems, all run by a computer. Some of the components are complex in themselves, and special equipment is required to diagnose and repair them. But other parts are pretty straightforward and easy to replace.

We talked to the experts at Superior Heating, Air Conditioning & Electric in Anoka, MN, to get the lowdown on which furnace problems generate the most service calls, which of those repairs can be performed by a DIYer and which ones are "pro only." It turns out that most of the problems they encounter are simply caused by a clogged furnace filter or any of three easy-to-fix

furnace parts: the igniter, the flame sensor and the high-limit switch.

If you're willing to risk spending money upfront to buy all three parts ahead of time, you may be able to fix your own furnace in less than an hour and save money on a service call. If the parts don't fix the problem, at least you've replaced the most likely suspects before calling the pros.

We'll show you what the parts look like and where they are installed on a typical furnace. But every furnace brand is different. Your best bet is to find a service manual for your particular furnace online. We think these repairs are relatively easy for a DIYer, but if you feel uncomfortable with any of the steps we show here, call a pro.

FLAME SENSOR

SEALED COMBUSTION CHAMBER

GAS VALVE

IGNITER

POWER SWITCH

PRESSURE SWITCH TUBING

HIGH-LIMIT SWITCH (BEHIND)

SHUT OFF THE POWER
All furnaces have a power cutoff switch inside the blower compartment that disconnects power to the furnace controls when the front panel is removed. But there's still power coming into the furnace, so always turn off the furnace power at the switch on the side of the furnace and at the circuit breaker panel before disconnecting any wires or testing/replacing any parts. And never run the furnace with the front panel off.

WHERE THE PARTS ARE

High-efficiency furnaces are jam-packed with valves, sensors, motors and flue pipes. We've removed many of those larger components from this furnace (above) so you can see what the parts look like and where they're located. They won't be as easy to see in your furnace. Here are some tips to help you find the igniter, flame sensor, high-limit switch and pressure switch tubing.

The igniter and flame sensor are located inside a sealed combustion chamber and aren't usually visible. But they can be replaced without removing the combustion chamber cover. If you don't have a service manual showing their location, consult the furnace-wiring diagram on the furnace to identify the wire colors for the igniter and flame sensor. To locate the sealed combustion chamber, follow the gas piping from the gas valve to a box with a cover and an inspection window. Then look for the wires going to the igniter and flame sensor. The high-limit switch is usually located below the sealed combustion chamber. The pressure switch will always have flexible tubing running to it.

BEFORE YOU START

The igniter and the flame sensor are like tires on your car—they wear out every four to five years. So it makes sense to keep spares on hand. Igniters and flame sensors cost about $50 each at appliance parts stores and furnace dealers. Or you can find them for less online. But first you'll need the make, model number and serial number of your furnace. Find all that information on the manufacturer's label **(Photo 1)**.

Then contact an authorized furnace dealer or visit a local appliance parts store and buy the parts. Some furnace dealers won't give out parts numbers or sell parts to DIYers. And appliance parts stores don't always stock parts for every brand. In that case, search the internet for "furnace parts" and enter your furnace brand and model number to find the right parts (*theignitorstore.com* is one source).

CHECK THE POWER, THEN THE FILTER

Repair experts tell us that they often show up at a residence only to find that the unit isn't getting power because of a tripped breaker or a flipped switch. So check that first. Flip the switch on the side of your furnace, and flip the breaker off and on again before you even think about replacing any parts.

Next, check the filter. A clogged air filter restricts airflow through the heat exchanger, causing the furnace to overheat. The high-limit switch detects the dangerous overheating and signals the computer to shut off the burners and run the blower fan to cool off the heat exchanger. Once the furnace cools, the computer tries to fire up again. But if the filter remains clogged and the furnace overheats four or more times (the actual number varies by manufacturer), the computer will shut down the furnace until it's repaired.

If the filter is filthy, you've most likely discovered the cause of the shutdown. Replace it with a new one. Then reset the furnace **(Photo 2)**. If the furnace won't restart, repeated overheating may have damaged the high-limit switch. Consult the wiring diagram inside the furnace door or service manual to find the switch's location. Then test it **(Photo 3)**. If the switch is bad, remove the retaining screws and pull it out of the heat exchanger, noting the position of the sensor. Install the new switch with the sensor facing as it was.

LABEL SHOWING THE MODEL AND SERIAL NUMBERS

1 **Find model and serial numbers.** Yank off the furnace cover and inspect the side panels in the burner area to find the manufacturer's label. Write down (or take a cell phone photo of) the model number, serial number and date of manufacture.

2 **Perform a furnace reset.** Flip the furnace power switch to off and wait for at least five minutes. Then turn on the power and let the furnace restart.

HIGH-LIMIT SWITCH

3 **Test the high-limit switch.** Disconnect the wires going to the high-limit switch and connect a continuity tester to the switch terminals. If the test light doesn't glow, the switch is bad.

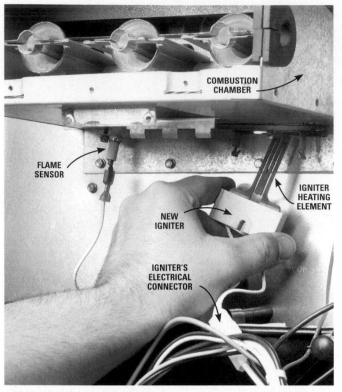

REPLACING THE IGNITER AND FLAME SENSOR

Most high-efficiency furnaces use a "hot surface" igniter that heats up to 1,800 degrees F to light the burners. Once lit, the burners then heat a flame sensor. The furnace's computer uses the signal from the flame sensor to confirm a successful ignition and turn off the igniter. However, over time, the constant heat/cool cycles cause the igniter to crack and fail, and the flame sensor can develop surface corrosion, causing it to send an incorrect signal to the computer. Or one can simply wear out.

The igniter can be held in place either by screws or by a snap-clip arrangement. Use a lighted flexible mirror to discover the method used on your furnace. Then remove the screws or unsnap the retainer and remove the old igniter. Use care when you install the new igniter—it's brittle and can crack or shatter easily **(Photo 4)**.

Next, remove the flame sensor. If the sensor element is covered with corrosion and you don't mind replacing the sensor later, you can try cleaning it **(Photo 5)**. Otherwise, just replace it.

ONE LAST PREVENTIVE MEASURE

Condensing gas furnaces attain their efficiency by extracting water from the exhaust gases. Sometimes condensation from that exhaust can form in the pressure switch tubing. This silicone tubing runs between the flue and the heat exchanger and safety pressure switch. Experts tell us they usually remove those tubes and blow them out with compressed air as a preventive measure **(Photo 6)**.

4 **Install the new igniter.** Slide the new igniter into position, avoiding contact with skin and hard surfaces. Then secure the part with a screw or snap connectors. Plug the igniter's electrical connector into the furnace wiring harness.

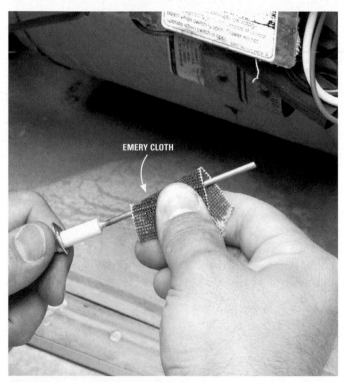

5 **Clean off the crud.** Apply light pressure and scrub off any buildup or corrosion from the sensor with emery cloth or No. 0000 steel wool.

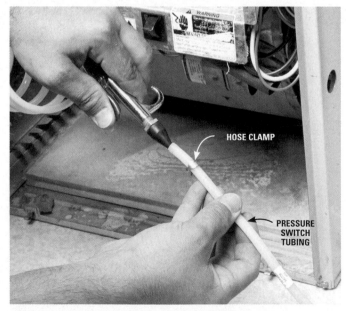

6 **Clear the pressure switch tubing.** Connect a compressed air gun to one end of the tubing and aim the other end toward the floor. Blow out each tube and reinstall.

Not as good: Completely enclosing a compressor with a cover, even a purchased one like shown at right, can trap moisture, which leads to corrosion. It also creates a perfect nesting place for mice. The simple cover, above, is actually much better.

Looks Funny, Works Great

This air conditioner compressor covered with a plastic sandbox lid may look funny. But this is actually a good way to protect your compressor in the off-season. Covering the top keeps out debris and protects the compressor from falling branches or ice during the winter in cold climates. And the open sides allow air to circulate. The only downside of the "turtle shell" system is that it will surely blow off and should be strapped down in some way.

SPECIAL SECTION

REMODELING

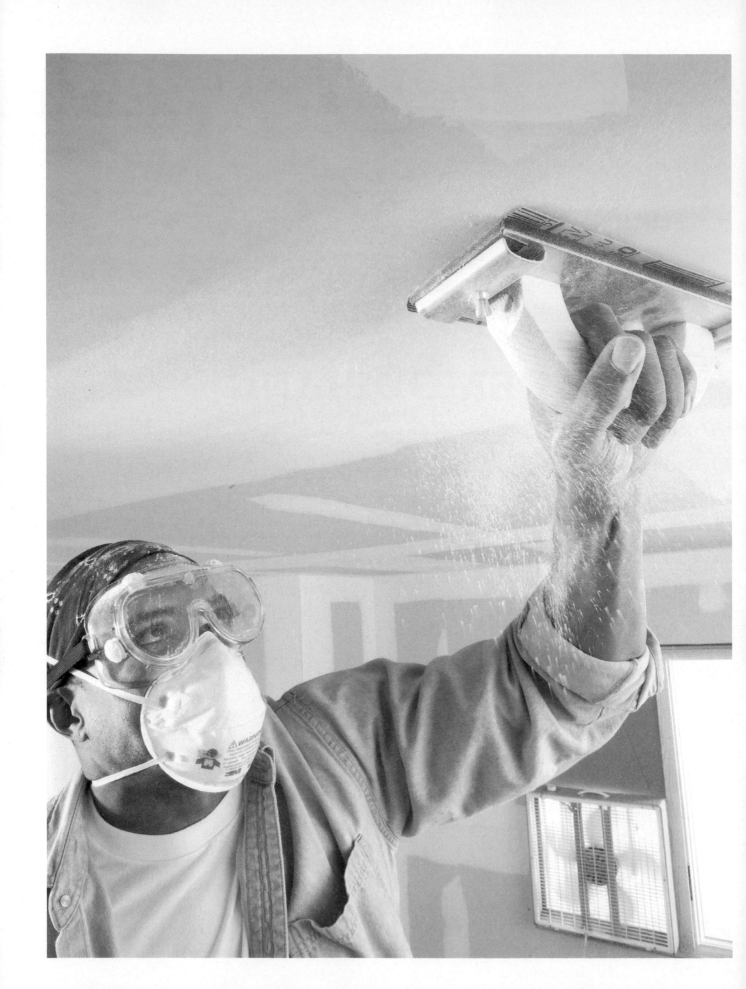

Smart Altering

The key to a smart remodeling project is efficiency. And in order to be efficient, you need to work fast, safe and clean.

When remodeling, you have to contain the mess in the areas where you're working and protect those areas where you're not. You also need to think ahead and organize the job materials, both the new and the old. These tips will help your next project run smoother, save you time and money, and prove to your customer that you're a true pro.

A. BLOW THE DUST OUTSIDE

Set a box fan in a window and blow the dust out of your work area. Wedge the fan into place with scrap pieces of foam and a few rags. For the best results, open windows beyond the dusty area or on the opposite side of the room to help keep the air moving in the right direction.

B. SEPARATE YOUR LUMBER

When you unload lumber at a job site, set the studs, top plates and bottom plates in different piles. That way, every time you start a new wall section, you won't have to move 20 studs to grab the top plate buried at the bottom of the pile. Also, moving lumber from one side of the room to the other is not an efficient use of time, so make sure your pile is located in a close but out-of-the-way location.

C. PROTECT FINISHED FLOORING WITH HARDBOARD

Rosin paper, cardboard and drop cloths are all legit ways to protect a floor—that is, until you knock your trim gun off the top of a 6-ft. ladder. If you really want to ensure that a floor stays dent and scratch free, cover it with 1/8-in. hardboard. It's pretty cheap and, as the name suggests, it's pretty hard. Cut the sheets with a circular saw or jigsaw, and to prevent scratches, make sure both the floor and the hardboard are perfectly clean before you lay the hardboard down. Tape the seams with masking tape to keep the dirt and debris from slipping through the cracks. When the job is done, pull up the sheets and save them for the next job.

D. FASTER CONCRETE FASTENING

A concrete screw installation tool allows you to use one tool without having to switch between a masonry bit and a screw-driving bit. Just drill the hole, slip the driver shaft over the masonry bit and then sink the screw. If you have a bunch of concrete fasteners to install, the tool is definitely worth the money. The Tapcon version shown here is one of several brands.

E. PULL THOSE NAILS

A good rule of thumb: "Never let a chunk of lumber leave your hand until you've dealt with the nails." If you're going to reuse lumber from a demo job, make sure you pull the nails right away. If you aren't going to reuse the wood, just bend the nails over. Stepping on a nail is a bad way to remember that it's been 10 years since your last tetanus shot.

F. MAKE A PLASTIC PASSAGE

Hanging a sheet of plastic from the ceiling is a good way to isolate a room that's being remodeled. But instead of hanging one continuous sheet to keep the dust in, hang two and overlap them 4 ft. or so. That way you'll have a handy door to walk through, which beats having to duck under the plastic every time you come and go. Lay a scrap piece of lumber on the bottom of the plastic to keep it in place.

G. COVER THE RETURN AIR VENTS

A furnace is extremely efficient in spreading dust from a room under construction to all the other rooms in the house. Sure, an expensive furnace filter may catch most of the dust, but it'll also get clogged in hours instead of weeks, and running a furnace with a clogged filter could result in costly furnace repairs.

Avoid these problems by covering the return air vents in, or near, the area where you're working. If you're kicking up a dust storm, shut the furnace down until that phase of the job is done. Replace the furnace filter once the whole job is done.

CLEAN UP EVERY DAY

It's tempting to leave the mess at the end of the day, knowing you're just going to mess up the site again tomorrow, but a true professional leaves a job site clean. You may be the best at what you do, but your customers won't be able to recognize your craftsmanship through all that filth, especially if it gets tracked around the house while you're gone. Also, showing up at a pigsty is not a positive way to start your workday.

H. BE A SMART PACKER

Renting a trash bin isn't cheap, so take advantage of every square inch by strategically placing debris in the container instead of tossing it in willy-nilly. Long boards should always run the length of the container. Set in large, hollow items like bathtubs or sinks open side up so you can fill them instead of creating a void.

Use small pieces as fill around larger ones. Think of the debris as puzzle pieces, each with its own proper spot. If your trash bin has a door, don't park the bin so close to the house that you can't open it. Walking in heavy items is a lot easier than lifting them over the side. Also, make sure you order the proper size. If you explain your project to the sanitation company, the staff should be able to suggest a bin size that's right for your project.

I. USE OLD PAINT AS PRIMER

If you have a bunch of cans of old paint that you're confident you'll never use again, mix the paints and use the result as a drywall primer. When you mix several different colors, the result always seems to be a dark brownish/mauvy color, so you may want to skip this tip if your final wall color is going to be really light. Mixing different sheens doesn't matter, but don't mix latex with oil.

J. MAKE BIG PIECES

Tearing out drywall can be frustrating because it always seems to crumble into little pieces, and it takes a long time to demo a wall one handful at a time. Take a little extra time to find the seams between the sheets, and cut them open with a utility knife. Then bust out a couple of holes for your hands to fit through. Instead of pulling super hard right away, tug and wiggle the drywall away from the studs until the screw heads break through.

K. KNOCK IT OFF FROM THE BACK SIDE

Who says you have to pull drywall from the wall? If the drywall on one side of a wall has already been removed, pound off the other side from the back with a sledgehammer. You should be able to remove several large chunks at a time if you keep the blows close to studs and don't pound too hard.

KNOW WHEN TO HAVE IT DELIVERED

Before you load those 80 sheets of drywall onto your trailer and shear an axle on the freeway, ask about your delivery options. Most suppliers charge a fee, but you need to weigh that fee against your time, your gas and your back. Maneuvering 8-ft. sheets of drywall up a narrow stairway doesn't make sense if a crane truck can deliver 12-ft. sheets right up to a second-story window. And lifting 60 bundles of shingles up a ladder is just plain silly when you can have them hoisted right onto the roof.

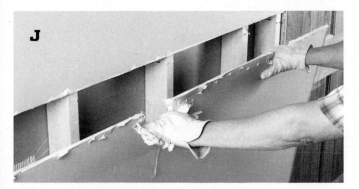

Demolition Shortcuts

Get to your new look sooner with this professional advice.

Most remodeling jobs start with some kind of demolition. Knocking down walls and tearing up floors are not the easiest jobs, nor are they the cleanest. But there is something cathartic about bashing a perfectly sound (or perfectly wretched) structure into bits. We've gathered some tips to make your next demo project more efficient, less of a mess and safer. We've even thrown in a few back-saving ideas.

A. CUT THE JAMB AND PULL

You can knock a doorjamb sideways out of its opening, but the nails or screws holding it in place will put up strong resistance to the shear force you apply.

An easier way is to cut one of the sides in half with a reciprocating saw and then pull the rest away straight from the framing. You can easily pull away any nails or screws holding the doorjamb in place by using the leverage of the jamb itself. Make your cut at an angle so the two cut sections don't wedge against each other and prevent you from pulling them apart. This same technique works for pulling out windows.

B. CUT FIBERGLASS SURROUND INTO PIECES

Some bathrooms are built around a shower or tub surround. This means that even if you manage to remove all the fasteners holding the surround in place, odds are you're not getting it out the door in one piece. You're going to have to dice it up. Make the long cuts with a circular saw, and finish the curved areas with a recip saw. Wear eye protection because fiberglass throws a bunch of chips when it's cut. And a dust mask is a must—fiberglass dust is not something you want to breathe in. Most important, thoroughly investigate the areas where you'll be making your cuts to avoid severing any electrical wires or plumbing pipes.

C. CUT AROUND THE WINDOW WITH A RECIP SAW

Spray foam insulation does an excellent job of insulating around a window—and a surprisingly good job of keeping the window or door in place. Even if you remove all the fasteners holding in a window, you won't be able to pull the window out until you deal with the spray foam.

Don't bother pulling the nails or screws out of an old window. Just run a recip saw between the window and the framing to cut the fasteners and the foam at the same time. You may want a buddy on the other side of the window to keep it from falling out when you're done cutting around it. With a long enough blade, you can even slice through the nailing flange at the same time. That's important if you're trying to save the siding around the opening.

D. PULL NAILS WITH A NIPPER

If you're replacing windows, doors or flooring and you want to salvage the trim, end-nipper pliers are a handy tool to pull out brad and finish nails. The rounded end provides plenty of leverage, and if the nail breaks, you can always cut it down flush. Don't squeeze too hard when gripping the nail or you may nip it off prematurely.

ANGLE-CUT JAMB

A

CUT WITH A CIRCULAR SAW

RECIPROCATING SAW

CIRCULAR SAW

B

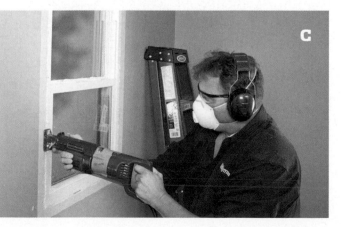

C

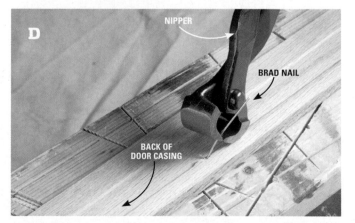

NIPPER

BRAD NAIL

BACK OF DOOR CASING

D

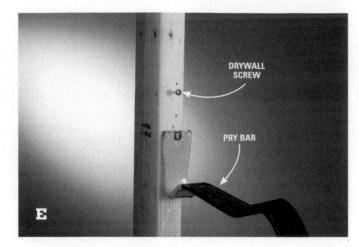

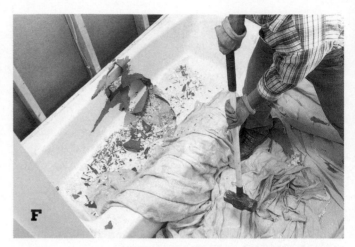

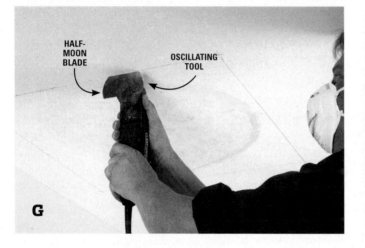

E. PULL DRYWALL SCREWS

When you pull drywall from a wall, the screws usually stay in the studs. Unscrewing them with a drill is not the most efficient way to remove them because the screw heads are usually deteriorated or full of drywall mud. Use a pry bar or your hammer claw to pull them out, just as you would with nails. Drywall screws are brittle, so if some joker used 3-in. screws to install the drywall, snap them off with your hammer.

F. BUST UP CAST-IRON TUBS (AND OTHER STUFF)

Cast-iron tubs are ridiculously heavy, so unless it's a priceless collector's item, you don't want to have any part of moving one. Your best bet is to bust it up in place. It can be tough to get the cracking started, so begin hitting the tub at the edge. Once it does start breaking, pound your way along the smashed edges.

Throw a tarp or thick sheet of plastic over the top to cut down on flying shards of iron. And wear your safety gear, especially hearing protection—busting up a cast-iron tub is like having a front row seat at a church bell convention. This tip works on just about anything brittle: old toilets, radiators, concrete laundry tubs, etc.

G. SLICE UP DRYWALL WITH A MULTITOOL

There seems to be no end to the odd jobs that can be done with an oscillating tool, and here's an example: If you have to remove a section of damaged drywall, cut it out with a multitool equipped with a half-moon blade. The tool will cut almost as fast as you can pull it. And because the oscillations on the blade are so short and the teeth are so fine, the tool creates half the dust that a reciprocating or keyhole saw would. Plus, the recess you cut will be much straighter and cleaner, making the patching work much easier.

H. CUT IT UP WITH A CIRCULAR SAW

Sledgehammers, pry bars and reciprocating saws aren't the only demo heroes on the job site—your circular saw can be used for a heck of a lot more than cutting studs and sheets of plywood. Fitted with the right blade, your circular saw can cut up roofing, tin, concrete, rebar, steel doors and fiber cement. With a demo blade, you can even cut up nail-embedded debris all day long.

I. RENT A WALK-BEHIND FLOOR SCRAPER

Some old vinyl sheet or tile floors are super easy to pull up. Others are so thoroughly glued down that you're lucky to remove quarter-size chunks with every whack of your handheld floor scraper. If a shovel and hand scraper are not getting the job done, rent a walk-behind scraper. You can save yourself a bunch of time and prevent a whole lot of wear and tear on your back and wrists. Many floor scrapers have an attachment for busting up ceramic tiles as well.

J. KNOCK OUT STUDS SIDEWAYS

A sledgehammer works great for busting up studs, but don't take a whack at the middle of a stud—it'll just wobble back and forth and probably bounce the head of the sledge right back in your direction. Hit a stud as close to the bottom plate as you can but not so hard that you pull out the nails on the top plate—that's a good way to catch a falling stud in the noggin. Hit the bottom of each stud just enough to dislodge it from the nails that were holding it. Then grab hold of it and pull it off the top plate.

K. CUT OFF THE NAILS ON THE PLATES

After you've bashed the studs out of place, use a reciprocating saw to slice off the nails that held them on the plates. Even if you're not planning to reuse the plates, this is a good way to avoid stepping on a nail. Make sure you use a bimetal saw blade; it'll slice right through the nails.

L. SUCK OUT INSULATION

Tearing down a drywall ceiling is not a super pleasant experience, but tearing down a ceiling that has 14 in. of blown-in insulation above it is a complete nightmare. Avoid that gigantic mess by sucking out all the insulation in the attic before pulling down any drywall.

If your local rental center doesn't carry the huge vacuum required for the job, call an insulation contractor in your area. Many blow-in insulation installers also have the equipment to suck out the insulation. But this service isn't cheap: Expect to pay about $1 to $2 per sq. ft. You might be able to get a deal if you use the same company to blow in new insulation. Make sure your insulation is fiberglass or cellulose. If you even suspect there's vermiculite insulation in the attic, get an expert opinion before touching the stuff—it could contain asbestos.

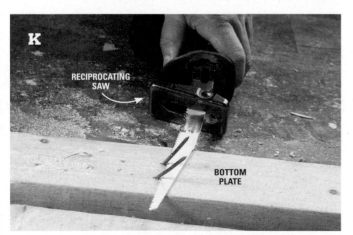

Before You Redo Your Kitchen

Ordering a lot of pizza while your kitchen is out of commission might blow your remodeling budget. Instead, set up a kitchen in your laundry room. You already have a sink there, so all you really need are a few small appliances: a microwave, a coffee maker, and maybe a hot plate and a "dorm room" fridge. Add some shelving and a towel bar, and you'll have a functional place to prepare those budget-friendly mac-and-cheese dinners.

Model First, Then Remodel

A quick, crude model of a kitchen island, cabinetry or even furniture is the best way to determine if it's too big or too small. Leave it in place and live with it for a few days before you decide whether it's a convenience or a curse. OSB makes a great modeling material because it's inexpensive. But for ease of building, you can't beat 1-in.-thick foam insulation. You can carry a 4 x 8-ft. sheet with one hand, cut it with a utility knife and strap parts together with masking tape. You can even mock up walls and doors.

BEER HELPS TOO →

FOAM INSULATION

OSB